WITHDRAWN
UTSA Libraries
D0387280

papers in QUANTITATIVE ECONOMICS

2

Edited by Arvid M. Zarley

THE UNIVERSITY PRESS OF KANSAS
Lawrence/Manhattan/Wichita

© Copyright 1971 by the University Press of Kansas
Standard Book Number 7006-0079-5
Library of Congress Catalog Card Number 68-25878
Printed in the United States of America

PREFACE

The papers contained in this second volume constitute a small selection of papers presented at the meetings of the Kansas-Missouri joint seminars in theoretical and applied economics which were held during the academic year 1968-69. The meetings that year were held at the campuses of Washington University, The University of Kansas, The University of Colorado, and The State University of Iowa. The support for the programs was the result of an award from the National Science Foundation for the three year period 1968 through 1971.

I wish to thank Mrs. Lois Clark and Mrs. Kathy Ward for their help in preparing the manuscript. In addition, several people have contributed editorially to this volume among which James P. Quirk, Peter W. Frevert, James C. Moore, and Trout Rader deserve special mention.

Arvid M. Zarley

CONTENTS

The Compensation Principle in Welfare Economics — 1
John S. Chipman and James C. Moore

Interrelated Consumer Preference and Voluntary Exchange — 79
Theodore C. Bergstrom

Pareto Optimality and Competitive Equilibrium in a General Equilibrium Model of Economic Growth — 95
Mohamed Ali El-Hodiri

Spatial Price Equilibrium, Location Arbitrage and Linear Programming — 105
S. A. Johnson

Investment Decision, Uncertainty and the Incorporated Entrepreneur — 121
Vernon L. Smith

The Abstract Transportation Problem — 147
Arnold M. Faden

International Trade and Development in a Small Country, II — 177
Trout Rader

THE COMPENSATION PRINCIPLE IN WELFARE ECONOMICS

by

John S. Chipman and James C. Moore*
University of Minnesota and Purdue University

1. Introduction

Few topics in theoretical economics have received more attention over the past thirty years than has the Compensation Principle. Given its first explicit statements by Pareto [28, 29] and Barone [7], and later by Viner [36] and Hotelling [19], it was adopted by Hicks [17] and Kaldor [21] as the basis of a "New Welfare Economics." It was subsequently criticized both on the basis of its implicit value judgments (e.g., Little [24]) and on the efficacy of its use in evaluating social alternatives (e.g., Baumol [8] and Scitovsky [34]). It is the contention of the authors, however, that the ordering of social alternatives induced by the Compensation Principle has never been subjected to a thorough and systematic analysis; and the principal intent of this article is to provide such an analysis.

We shall be concerned here only with the logic and the historical development of the Compensation Principle. There will be no attempt to justify (or refute) the value judgments upon which the Compensation Principle is based. The model to be used in our analysis is presented in the next section, and the most basic portion of the analysis itself is presented in Section 3. The principal result of this section suggests that, in the absence of knowledge of the exact form of each consumer's preference ordering, the ordering induced by the Compensation Principle does not effectively extend the Pareto ordering very much. In fact, our analysis suggests that, in the absence of such complete knowledge, the ordering induced by the Compensation Principle is perhaps best viewed as the Pareto ordering with a new domain of definition: aggregate production bundles rather than distributions of aggregate bundles.

In Section 4 we present an analysis of a concept which has been quite important in recent discussions of the Compensation Principle and upon which we rely quite heavily in Section 5: the notion of a utility possibility set introduced by Samuelson ([31] and, especially, [32]).

The characterization of the contract curve in the general case (m consumers and n commodities) and the application of the Compensation Principle to a particular, and important, topic in normative economics--the evaluation of real national income--are the topics taken up in Section 5. We find, perhaps not too surprisingly, that under the kinds of assumptions made about preference orderings in the usual Edgeworth box analysis, the contract curve in the general (m x n) case satisfies the same kinds of properties satisfied in the 2 x 2 case. Our findings with regard to the evaluation of real national income are somewhat more complicated. In general, one cannot use the Compensation Principle to say that an economy is "better off" if its national income has increased; but our analysis suggests that it may be possible to determine a fairly general class of preference orderings for which this statement can be made (in fact, we note a particular class of preference orderings for which the statement can be made).

The literature on the Compensation Principle, discussed only in passing here, is surveyed in [12].

2. Basic Concepts

Let E_n denote n-dimensional Euclidean Space, and E_n^+ the non-negative orthant:

$$E_n^+ = \{x \in E_n \mid x \geqq 0\};^1$$

where, as is usual, we define the vector inequalities $\geqq$, $\geq$, $>$, for $x, y \in E_n$ by:

$$x \geqq y \text{ iff } x_i \geqq y_i \text{ for } i = 1, \ldots, n,$$

$$x \geq y \text{ iff } x \geqq y \text{ and } x \neq y,$$

$$x > y \text{ iff } x_i > y_i \text{ for } i = 1, \ldots, n;$$

and where we shall use the symbol "0" to denote both the scalar "zero" and the origin in E_n. In line with this notation, we shall denote the real numbers by E_1, and the non-negative real numbers by E_1^+.

Suppose we have m consumers and n commodities, and that we adopt the generic notation X to denote points in E_{mn}, which we shall think of as m x n matrices. The entry x_{ij} will be taken to denote quantity of the jth commodity available for consumption (per period of time) by the ith individual; the row vector (sub-vector) x^i standing for the commodity bundle available for consumption (per period of time) by the ith consumer. We shall assume throughout this paper that the ith consumer's consumption set (cf. Debreu [13], pp. 50-52) is the non-negative orthant in E_n. Accordingly, we introduce the following:

Definition 1: A point (or matrix) $X \varepsilon E^+_{mn}$ will be called an allocation (or distribution).

We shall also assume throughout the sequel that each consumer has a preference ordering defined over allocations. More formally:

Definition 2: We shall say that the binary relation R_i defined on E^+_{mn} is a preference ordering if R_i is a complete preordering[2] of E^+_{mn}; that is, R_i satisfies:

a) completeness[3]: $(X, \overline{X} \varepsilon E^+_{mn})$: $X R_i \overline{X}$ or $\overline{X} R_i X$ (or both),[4]

b) reflexivity: $(X \varepsilon E^+_{mn})$: $X R_i X$,

c) transitivity: $(X, X', X'' \varepsilon E^+_{mn})$: $X R_i X'$ and $X' R_i X'' \Rightarrow X R_i X''$.

Given a preference ordering R_i we will, as is usual, define the relations P_i (strict preference) and I_i (indifference) on E^+_{mn} by:

$X P_i \overline{X}$ iff $X R_i \overline{X}$ and not $\overline{X} R_i X$,

$X I_i \overline{X}$ iff $X R_i \overline{X}$ and $\overline{X} R_i X$,

respectively. Where we say that R is an m-tuple of preference orderings, we shall mean that $R = (R_1, \ldots, R_m)$, where R_i is a preference ordering (as defined in Definition 2) for $i = 1, \ldots, m$.

If X is an allocation, the function $\sigma(X)$ defined by:

$$(1) \quad \sigma(X) = \sum_{i=1}^{m} x^i$$

expresses the vector of total quantities of the commodities available. If X is an allocation (i.e., $X \varepsilon E^+_{mn}$), $\sigma(X) \varepsilon E^+_n$. Hence a vector $y \varepsilon E^+_n$ will be called an aggregate commodity bundle; and a matrix $X \varepsilon E^+_{mn}$ will be said to be an allocation of y if $\sigma(X) = y$.

Definition 3: A set $Y \subset E^+_n$ will be called a situation.

A situation Y will be called disposable if:

$$(y, \bar{y} \in E_n^+): y \in Y \text{ and } 0 \leqq \bar{y} \leqq y \Rightarrow \bar{y} \in Y.$$

Given a situation Y, the attainable set (of allocations) for Y, A(Y), is defined by:

$$A(Y) = \{X \in E_{mn}^+ \mid \sigma(X) \in Y\}.$$

Definition 4: We shall say that E is an economy (cf. Debreu [13], p. 75) iff E is an ordered pair of the form:

(2) $E = (R, Y)$

where $R = (R_1, \ldots, R_m)$ is an m-tuple of preference orderings, and Y is a situation (i.e., $Y \subset E_n^+$).

Before proceeding further with our development, we should note that, while an economy of the form (2) looks very much like a pure exchange economy (at least in the case in which Y is an n-dimensional rectangle); we may interpret such a formalization in rather a different way. First of all, our analysis can be taken to apply to a fairly general class of economies involving variable factors of production and a finite number, ℓ, of producers. On this point see Appendix 1 of this paper. Secondly, the set Y in (2) may be taken to represent the set of all aggregate vectors y attainable as the net result of production and trade with the rest of the world.[5] Our terminology ("situation") is, of course, intended to emphasize this latter interpretation.

In most of the work to follow, we shall (explicitly) assume that the consumer preference orderings (R_i) satisfy various properties in addition to being a preordering. While these properties will generally be quite familiar to the reader already, we shall nonetheless provide formal definitions of these properties, and a brief discussion of some of them here.

Definition 5: The preference ordering R_i will be said to be individualistic[6] if:

$$(\bar{X}, \hat{X}, \tilde{X}, X \in E_{mn}^+): X \, R_i \, \bar{X}, \; \hat{x}^i = x^i, \text{ and } \tilde{x}^i = \bar{x}^i$$

together imply $\hat{X} \, R_i \, \tilde{X}$.

If each preference ordering is individualistic, each consumer pays attention only to the bundles available to him in determining his preferences. As a consequence, the allocations X may be partitioned into equivalence classes; each class having the same i^{th} row x^i; the symbol x^i may also be taken to represent such an equivalence class, and the symbol $\dot{R}_i$ may be used to denote the so-called "quotient ordering" among equivalence classes. Thus we may write:

$$X \; R_i \; \overline{X} \text{ iff } x^i \; \dot{R}_i \; \overline{x}^i.$$

In cases where we assume that each R_i is individualistic, however, we shall frequently not distinguish between R_i and $\dot{R}_i$ if it does not appear that this will cause undue confusion.

Definition 6: The preference ordering R_i will be said to be monotonic if:

$$(X, \overline{X} \in E^+_{mn}) \colon X \geqq \overline{X} \Rightarrow X \; R_i \; \overline{X} \text{ and } X > \overline{X} \Rightarrow X \; P_i \; \overline{X}.$$

It should be noted that if R_i is individualistic, then R_i is monotonic if and only if:

$$(x^i, \overline{x}^i \in E^+_n) \colon x^i \geqq \overline{x}^i \Rightarrow x^i \; \dot{R}_i \; \overline{x}^i \text{ and}$$

$$x^i > \overline{x}^i \Rightarrow x^i \; \dot{P}_i \; \overline{x}^i.$$

Our next definition will apply only in the case where R_i is individualistic.

Definition 7: Suppose R_i is an individualistic preference ordering, and let $\dot{R}_i$ denote the quotient ordering derived from R_i. Then we shall say that R_i is strictly monotonic if:

$$(x^i, \overline{x}^i \in E^+_n) \colon x^i \geq \overline{x}^i \Rightarrow x^i \; \dot{P}_i \; \overline{x}^i.$$

Definition 8: The preference ordering R_i will be said to be continuous iff:

$$(X \in E^+_{mn}) \colon R_i \, X \equiv \{\overline{X} \in E^+_{mn} \mid \overline{X} \; R_i \; X\} \text{ and}$$

$$X \, R_i \equiv \{\overline{X} \in E^+_{mn} \mid X \; R_i \; \overline{X}\} \text{ are both closed sets.}$$

The reader will easily be able to verify the fact that if R_i is individualistic then R_i is continuous if and only if:

$$(x^i \in E_n^+): \dot{R}_i x^i \equiv \{\bar{x}^i \in E_n^+ \mid \bar{x}^i \dot{R}_i x^i\},$$

$$x^i \dot{R}_i \equiv \{\bar{x}^i \in E_n^+ \mid x^i \dot{R}_i \bar{x}^i\}$$

are both closed.

Definition 9: The preference ordering R_i will be said to be:

a) weakly convex if

$$(\bar{X}, X \in E_{mn}^+) (\lambda \in [0, 1]): XR_i\bar{X} \Rightarrow [\lambda X + (1-\lambda)\bar{X}] R_i\bar{X}.$$

b) convex if R_i is weakly convex and

$$(X, \bar{X} \in E_{mn}^+) (\lambda \in]0, 1[): XP_i\bar{X} \Rightarrow [\lambda X + (1-\lambda)\bar{X}]P_i\bar{X}.$$ [7]

Once again the reader can easily verify the fact that if R_i is individualistic, R_i is, e.g., weakly convex if and only if $\dot{R}_i$ satisfies:

$$(x^i, \bar{x}^i \in E_n^+) (\lambda \in [0, 1]): x^i\dot{R}_i\bar{x}^i \Rightarrow [\lambda x^i + (1-\lambda)\bar{x}^i]\dot{R}_i\bar{x}^i.$$

Definition 10: Let R_i be an individualistic preference ordering, and let $\dot{R}_i$ denote the quotient ordering derived from R_i. Then R_i will be said to be strictly convex if:

$$(x^i, \bar{x}^i \in E_n^+) (\lambda \in]0, 1[): x^i\dot{R}_i\bar{x}^i \quad \text{and}$$

$$x^i \neq \bar{x}^i \Rightarrow [\lambda x^i + (1-\lambda)\bar{x}^i] \dot{P}_i\bar{x}^i.$$

Definition 11: The preference ordering R_i will be said to be homogeneous if:

$$(X, \bar{X} \in E_{mn}^+) (\lambda \in [0, +\infty[): XR_i\bar{X} \Rightarrow (\lambda X) R_i (\lambda\bar{X}).$$

Analogously to our previous cases, we see that if R_i is individualistic, then R_i is homogeneous iff:

$$(x^i, \bar{x}^i \in E_n^+) (\lambda \in [0,+\infty[): x^i\dot{R}_i\bar{x}^i \Rightarrow (\lambda x^i) \dot{R}_i(\lambda\bar{x}^i).$$

Definition 12: Let $R = (R_1, \ldots, R_m)$ be an m-tuple of preference orderings. Then we define the Pareto ordering induced by $(R_1, \ldots, R_m)$ (which we shall also denote by R)[8] on E^+_{mn} by:

$$X \; R \; \overline{X} \text{ iff } X \; R_i \; \overline{X} \text{ for } i = 1, \ldots, m.$$

(We then write $X \; I \; \overline{X}$ if both $X \; R \; \overline{X}$ and $\overline{X} \; R \; X$; and $X \; P \; \overline{X}$ iff $X \; R \; \overline{X}$ and not $\overline{X} \; R \; X$.) As usual, we shall say that $X \in E^+_{mn}$ is Pareto optimal for an economy $E = (R, Y)$ if X is an R-maximal element of A(Y) (see Definition 3); that is:

a) $X \in A(Y)$, and

b) $\overline{X} \; P \; X$ for no $\overline{X} \in A(Y)$.

It is well known, and can easily be proved, that R is a preordering of allocations (it is not, in general, complete, however).

3. The Kaldor-Hicks-Samuelson Ordering

The Compensation Principle, as we shall deal with it here, amounts to accepting the following preordering[9] as a criterion for social choice among situations.[10]

Definition 1: Let R be an m-tuple of preference orderings. We define the Kaldor-Hicks-Samuelson Ordering, $>$ (abbreviated KHS ordering), induced by R on the power set of E^+_n by:

$$Y_2 > Y_1 \text{ iff } (X \in A(Y_1)) \; (\exists \overline{X} \in A(Y_2)):$$

$$\overline{X} \; R \; X, \text{ for } Y_1, Y_2 \subset E^+_n.$$

It is worth emphasizing the order of the quantifiers in the above definition. It does not say that $Y_2 > Y_1$ means that there exists an allocation $\overline{X} \in A(Y_2)$ such that $\overline{X} \; R \; X$ for all $X \in A(Y_1)$ (this would certainly be too strong). Nor does it say that there exists $X \in A(Y_1)$ such that $\overline{X} \; R \; X$ for some $\overline{X} \in A(Y_2)$ (this would be too weak). It simply asserts that any allocation of an aggregate bundle in Y_1 can be bettered (or at least equaled) by an allocation of some aggregate bundle in Y_2.

We first note the following fact, the proof of which is obvious.

Lemma 1. If R is an m-tuple of preference orderings, and > is the KHS ordering induced by R, then:

$$(Y_1, Y_2 \subset E_n^+): Y_2 \supset Y_1 \Rightarrow Y_2 > Y_1.$$

Theorem 1. If R is an m-tuple of preference orderings and > is the KHS ordering induced by R, then > is a preordering of situations.

Proof: The reflexivity of > is an immediate consequence of Lemma 1. To prove transitivity, suppose $Y_1, Y_2, Y_3 \subset E_n^+$ and that $Y_3 > Y_2$ and $Y_2 > Y_1$. Let $\hat{X} \varepsilon A(Y_1)$. Then since $Y_2 > Y_1$, there exists $\overline{X} \varepsilon A(Y_2)$ such that $\overline{X}\ R\ \hat{X}$. Moreover, since $Y_3 > Y_2$, $(\exists X \varepsilon A(Y_3)): X\ R\ \overline{X}$. Hence $X\ R\ \hat{X}$ (since R is obviously transitive), and we conclude that $Y_3 > Y_1$.

Q.E.D.

Suppose we consider Lemma 1 for a moment. We obtain from it the intuitively very obvious conclusion that $Y_2 > Y_1$ if $Y_1 \subset Y_2$. However, since it happens infrequently that $Y_1 \subset Y_2$ for two situations occurring as a result of two real alternative policy measures;[11] Lemma 1 cannot always provide a very useful decision rule for policy makers. On the other hand, if one actually knew the exact form of each R_i, then one might be able to formulate a policy rule which would apply to the comparison of much more diverse situations. Thus, consider the following example.

Suppose R_i is defined on E_{mn}^+ by:

$$X\ R_i\ \overline{X} \text{ iff } x_{i1} \geqq \overline{x}_{i1} \text{ for } i = 1, \ldots, m.$$

Then we clearly have $Y_2 > Y_1$ iff $(y \varepsilon Y_1)\ (\exists \overline{y} \varepsilon Y_2): \overline{y}_1 \geqq y_1$. In particular, > is a complete preordering (of the power set of E_n^+) in this case.

This example can be generalized to a somewhat more interesting special case, which actually incorporates the example just given. In order to develop this extension, we first state the following result, a proof of which is provided in Appendix 2.

Theorem 2. Let R_i be a preference ordering of E_{mn}^+ which is monotonic, continuous, weakly convex, and homogeneous.

Then there exists a continuous real-valued utility function $\bar{f}^i$ representing R_i on E^+_{mn}, and satisfying:

i) $\bar{f}^i$: $E^+_{mn} \to E^+_1$, $\bar{f}^i(0) = 0$,

ii) $\bar{f}^i$ is positively homogeneous of degree one on E^+_{mn},

iii) $\bar{f}^i$ is concave on E^+_{mn}.

Theorem 2 has the following obvious consequence.

Corollary: Suppose R is an m-tuple of identical preference orderings (i.e., $R_i \equiv R_k$ for i,k = 1, ..., m), each of which is individualistic, monotonic, continuous, weakly convex, and homogeneous. Then there exists a continuous real-valued utility function, $g(x^i)$, such that g represents[12] $\dot{R}_i$ on E^+_n for i = 1, ..., m, and g is concave and positively homogeneous of degree one on E^+_n.[13]

Theorem 3.[14] Suppose R is an m-tuple of identical preference orderings, each of which is individualistic, monotonic, continuous, weakly convex, and homogeneous. Then, letting g be as in the above corollary, we have:

$$\hat{Y} > Y \text{ iff } (y \in Y)\,(\exists \hat{y} \in \hat{Y})\text{: } g(\hat{y}) \geqq g(y) \text{ for } \hat{Y},\ Y \subset E^+_n.$$

In proving Theorem 3 it will be convenient to make use of the following two lemmas.[15]

Lemma 2. If g: $E^+_n \to E_1$, and g is concave and homogeneous of degree one on E^+_n; then for any positive integer ℓ, and any $\{x^1, \ldots, x^h, \ldots, x^\ell\} \subset E^+_n$, we have: $g(\sum_{h=1}^{\ell} x^h) \geqq \sum_{h=1}^{\ell} g(x^h)$.

Proof: If $\{x^1, \ldots, x^h, \ldots, x^\ell\} \subset E^+_n$, then using the concavity and homogeneity of g in turn, we have:

$$g(\sum_{h=1}^{\ell} x^h) = g[\sum_{h=1}^{\ell} (1/\ell)(\ell x^h)] \geqq \sum_{h=1}^{\ell} (1/\ell)\, g(\ell x^h) = \sum_{h=1}^{\ell} g(x^h).$$

Lemma 3. Under the hypotheses of Theorem 3, if $\bar{y} \in E^+_n$ and $\bar{\mathbf{X}} \in A(\{\bar{y}\})$; then there exist non-negative real numbers w_i (i = 1, ..., m) such that:

i) $\sum_{i=1}^{m} w_i = 1$ (and hence the allocation $\hat{X}$ defined by $\hat{x}^i = w_i\bar{y}$ for i = 1, ..., m is a member of $A(\{\bar{y}\})$),

ii) $(w_i\bar{y})R_i\bar{x}^i$ for i = 1, ..., m,

iii) if, taking g as in the corollary to Theorem 2, we have $\sum_{i=1}^{m} g(\bar{x}^i) > 0$; then we may let $w_i = \dfrac{g(\bar{x}^i)}{\sum_{k=1}^{m} g(\bar{x}^k)}$ for i = 1, ..., m.

<u>Proof</u>: We distinguish two cases:

a) $\sum_{i=1}^{m} g(\bar{x}^i) = 0$. Since $g(x^i) \geqq g(0) = 0$ for each i, it is clear that we must have $g(\bar{x}^i) = 0$ for i = 1, ..., m, in this case. Hence we may let $w_i = 1/m$ for i = 1, ..., m to obtain conclusions (i) and (ii).

b) $\sum_{i=1}^{m} g(\bar{x}^i) > 0$. In this case it is clear that, defining $w_i = [g(\bar{x}^i)/\sum_{k=1}^{m} g(\bar{x}^k)]$ for i = 1, ..., m, we have $0 \leqq w_i \leqq 1$ for each i, and $\sum_{i=1}^{m} w_i = 1$. Moreover, $g(w_i\bar{y}) =$

$$w_i g(\bar{y}) = \left[\frac{g(\bar{y})}{\sum_{k=1}^{m} g(\bar{x}^k)}\right] g(\bar{x}^i) \geqq g(\bar{x}^i) \text{ for } i = 1, \ldots, m;$$

where the last inequality is by Lemma 2. Q.E.D.

It is easy to see that, under the conditions of Lemma 3, a distribution $X \in A(\{\bar{y}\})$ is Pareto optimal for $E = (R, \{\bar{y}\})$ whenever there exist $w_i \geqq 0$ (i = 1, ..., m) such that

$$(1) \quad \sum_{i=1}^{m} w_i = 1, \; \bar{x}^i = w_i\bar{y} \text{ for } i = 1, \ldots, m.$$

Moreover, if each R_i is also strictly convex, $\bar{X}$ will be Pareto optimal for E only if (1) is satisfied. If in this latter situation m = n = 2, this reduces to the well-known condition that the set of Pareto optima is the diagonal of the Edgeworth box.

Proof of Theorem 3: Suppose $Y, \hat{Y} \subset E_n^+$, and that:

i) $\hat{Y} > Y$. Let $y \in Y$, and define X by $x^i = (1/m)y$ for $i = 1, \ldots, m$. Since $\hat{Y} > Y$, $(\exists \hat{X} \in A(\hat{Y}))$: $\hat{X}\ R_i\ X$ for $i = 1, \ldots, m$. Hence, if we define $\hat{y} = \sigma(\hat{X}) = \sum_{i=1}^{m} \hat{x}^i$, we have:

$$g(y) = \sum_{i=1}^{m} (1/m)\ g(y) = \sum_{i=1}^{m} g(x^i) \leqq \sum_{i=1}^{m} g(\hat{x}^i) \leqq g(\hat{y}),$$

where the last inequality is by Lemma 2.

ii) $(y \in Y)\ (\exists \hat{y} \in \hat{Y})$: $g(\hat{y}) \geqq g(y)$. If $Y = \emptyset$, it follows at once from Lemma 1 that $\hat{Y} > Y$. Suppose $Y \neq \emptyset$, and let $X \in A(Y)$. If $\sum_{i=1}^{m} g(x^i) = 0$, we have $g(x^i) = 0$ for $i = 1, \ldots, m$; and hence for any $\hat{y} \in \hat{Y}$ (note that our assumption here implies $\hat{Y} \neq \emptyset$ if $Y \neq \emptyset$), the distribution $\hat{X}$ defined by:

$$\hat{x}^i = (1/m)\ \hat{y} \quad \text{for } i = 1, \ldots, m,$$

is such that $\hat{X}\ R\ X$. Suppose, then, that $\sum_{i=1}^{m} g(x^i) > 0$.

By (ii) and (iii) of Lemma 3,

(2) $g(\bar{x}^i) \geqq g(x^i)$ for $i = 1, \ldots, m$,

where

$$\bar{x}^i = w_i y, \text{ and } w_i = [g(x^i)/\sum_{k=1}^{m} g(x^k)], \text{ for } i = 1, \ldots, m.$$

By assumption $(\exists \hat{y} \in \hat{Y})$: $g(\hat{y}) \geqq g(y)$. Define the allocation of $\hat{X}$ by:

$$\hat{x}^i = w_i\ \hat{y} \quad \text{for } i = 1, \ldots, m.$$

We then have $\sigma(\hat{X}) = \hat{y}$ (and hence $\hat{X} \in A(\hat{Y})$), and:

$$g(\hat{x}^i) = w_i\ g(\hat{y}) \geqq w_i\ g(y) = g(\bar{x}^i) \geqq g(x^i)$$

for $i = 1, \ldots, m$; where the last inequality is by (2).

Hence it follows that $\hat{X}$ R $\hat{X}$, and since X ε A(Y) was arbitrary, we conclude that $\hat{Y} > Y$.

Q.E.D.

It is clear that, under the conditions of Theorem 3, the KHS ordering is a complete preordering of situations. Thus, at least under the very stringent hypotheses of Theorem 3, the Compensation Principle can provide a very useful criterion for the comparison of situations. In contrast, Lemma 1 makes only a very weak requirement on the consumer preference orderings, but at the cost of obtaining a much weaker ordering of situations. The question we would now like to pursue can be stated, roughly,as follows: "Is it possible to obtain a stronger ordering of situations than the inclusion ordering obtained in Lemma 1, but with weaker requirements on consumer preference orderings than those assumed in Theorem 3?" Suppose we begin by attempting to formulate the question more exactly.

Let $\mathcal{R}_o$ denote the set of all m-tuples of preference orderings (i.e., if $\mathcal{R}$ denotes the set of all complete preorderings of E^+_{mn}, let $\mathcal{R}_o = \mathcal{R} \times \mathcal{R} \times \ldots \times \mathcal{R}$ [m times]). Suppose we now re-define the Kaldor-Hicks- Samuelson ordering as follows.

<u>Definition 2</u>: Let $\mathcal{R}_1 \subset \mathcal{R}_o$. We define $>_{\mathcal{R}_1}$ on the power set of E^+_n in the following way:

$$\hat{Y} >_{\mathcal{R}_1} Y \text{ iff } (R \in \mathcal{R}_1)\ (X \in A(Y))\ (\exists \hat{X} \in A(\hat{Y})): \hat{X}\ R\ X.$$

(Note: if $\mathcal{R}_1$ is of the form $\mathcal{R}_1 = \{R\}$ for some R ε $\mathcal{R}_o$, we shall denote $>_{\mathcal{R}_1}$ by "$>_R$".)

Notice that if $\mathcal{R}_2 \subset \mathcal{R}_1 \subset \mathcal{R}_o$, and $\hat{Y} >_{\mathcal{R}_1} Y$, then $\hat{Y} >_{\mathcal{R}_2} Y$. We note also that, using this definition, Lemma 1 can be restated as follows:

<u>Lemma 1'</u>. $Y \subset \hat{Y} \Rightarrow \hat{Y} >_{\mathcal{R}_o} Y$.[16]

If we believe the true m-tuple of preference orderings, R, to lie in some subset of $\mathcal{R}_o$, say $\mathcal{R}_a$ (which we shall call the <u>admissible set</u>), then the relevant preordering of situations for policy-making purposes is $>_{\mathcal{R}_a}$ (given that we have accepted the Compensation Principle as a criterion for social choice). Lemma 1 tells us that if we take $\mathcal{R}_a = \mathcal{R}_o$, we can say that $Y_2 >_{\mathcal{R}_a} Y_1$ if $Y_1 \subset Y_2$. However, in this case we are proceeding as if we have essentially no knowledge of consumer preference orderings. If we believe we can safely assume that each consumer preference ordering is, say, continuous and monotonic, then we can take the admissible set R_a to consist only of those m-tuples of preference orderings R such that R_i is continuous and monotonic for i = 1, ..., m. The admissible set, R_a, then becomes a proper subset of R_o. As we add further restrictions, the admissible set R_a will shrink still further, and the result in Theorem 3 suggests the possibility that, by following this procedure, we may be able to obtain a strengthened preordering of situations. Our next result tells us, however, that restrictions on R_a of a purely qualitative kind (more exactly, if we require only that each preference ordering satisfies Definitions 5 - 11 of the previous section) do not get us very far.

Theorem 4. Let $R_1 \subset R_o$ represent the set of all m-tuples of preference orderings R satisfying:

R_i is individualistic, strictly monotonic, continuous, strictly convex, and homogeneous for i = 1, ..., m; and let R_2 denote that (proper) subset of R_1 satisfying:

$R_1 \equiv \ldots \equiv R_m$ for each R ε R_2. Then if Y_1 and Y_2 are situations which are disposable and bounded, we have:

$$Y_2 >_{R_2} Y_1 \text{ implies } \overline{Y}_2 \supset Y_1.$$ [17]

Proof: If $Y_1 = \emptyset$ our conclusion is trivial, and if $Y_2 = \emptyset$, it is obvious that we must have $Y_1 = \emptyset$ if $Y_2 >_{R_2} Y_1$. Consequently, suppose Y_1 and Y_2 are non-empty, disposable and bounded situations satisfying $Y_1 \not\subset \overline{Y}_2$. Then (see Figure 1)

(3) $(\exists\, \overline{y} \geq 0): \overline{y} \in Y_1 \setminus \overline{Y}_2.$

Consider the set

$$L \equiv \{\lambda \geqq 0 \mid \lambda \overline{y} \in \overline{Y}_2\}.$$

We note that, since Y_2 is disposable and $\overline{y} \notin \overline{Y}_2$, 0 ε L and L is bounded above by 1. Therefore, defining $\overline{\lambda} = \sup L$, we have, since $\overline{Y}_2$ is compact and $\overline{y} \notin \overline{Y}_2$:

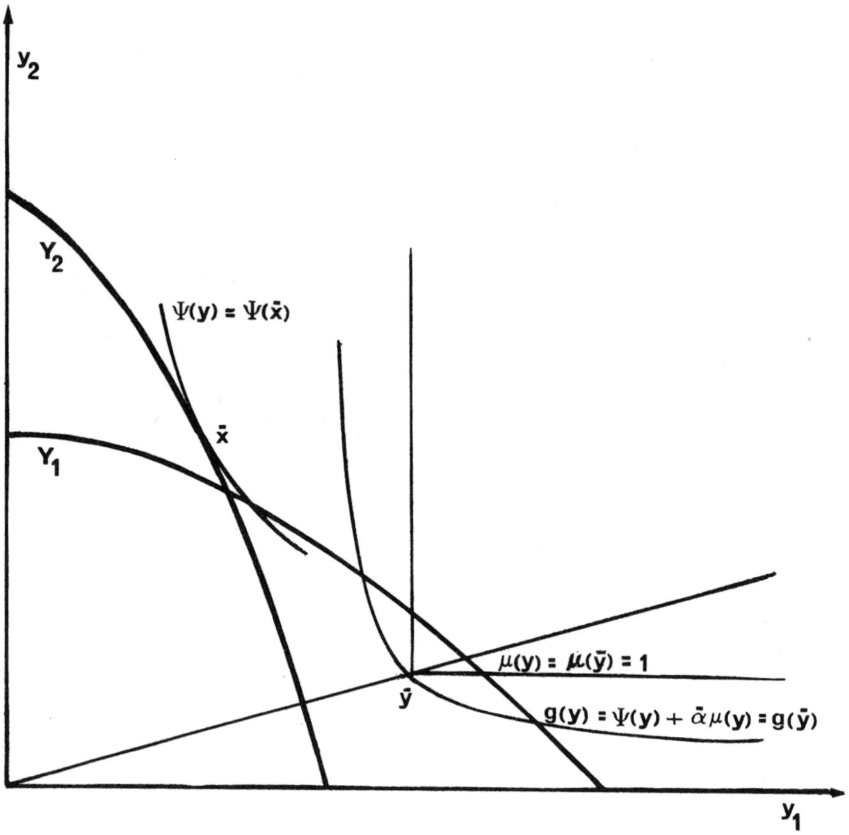

Figure 1

(4) $\bar{\lambda}\,\bar{y} \in \bar{Y}_2$,

(5) $0 \leqq \bar{\lambda} < 1$.

Define the function Ψ, where Ψ: $E_n^+ \to E_1^+$, by:

(6) $\Psi(x) = (\sum_{j=1}^{n} (x_j)^{\frac{1}{2}})^2$ for $x \in E_n^+$.

Clearly Ψ is continuous on E_n^+, and consequently, since $\bar{Y}_2$ is compact, Ψ attains a maximum on $\bar{Y}_2$ at, say, $\bar{x} \in \bar{Y}_2$. Choose $\bar{\alpha} > 0$ so that:

(7) $\bar{\alpha} > \dfrac{\Psi(\bar{x}) - \Psi(\bar{y})}{1-\bar{\lambda}}$;

noting that it is clear from (5) that such a choice is always possible.

Next define $J = \{j \in \{1, \ldots, n\} \mid \bar{y}_j > 0\}$, and define the function μ, where $\mu\colon E_n^+ \to E_1^+$, by

(8) $\mu(x) = \underset{j \in J}{\mathrm{Min}}\,(x_j/\bar{y}_j)$ for $x \in E_n^+$.

We note that, since Y_2 is disposable, we have by (4) and (5):

(9) $(y \in Y_2)\colon \mu(y) \leqq \bar{\lambda}$

while, obviously,

(10) $\mu(\bar{y}) = 1$.

We now define the function g on E_n^+ by:

(11) $g(y) = \Psi(y) + \bar{\alpha} \cdot \mu(y)$.

Clearly $g\colon E_n^+ \to E_1^+$, and we prove in Appendix 3 that g is strictly increasing, positively homogeneous of degree one, continuous, strictly quasi-concave, and concave on E_n^+. Hence it is clear that, defining $\bar{R}_i$ on E_{mn}^+ by

$X\,\bar{R}_i\,\bar{X}$ iff $g(x^i) \geqq g(\bar{x}^i)$ for $i = 1, \ldots, m$,

we have $\bar{R} \in \mathcal{R}_2$. However, if $y \in Y_2$, we have from (9) and the definition of $\bar{x}$:

(12) $g(y) = \Psi(y) + \bar{\alpha}\,\mu(y) \leqq \Psi(\bar{x}) + \alpha\bar{\lambda}$.

On the other hand, from (10):

(13) $g(\bar{y}) = \Psi(\bar{y}) + \bar{\alpha}$.

Consequently, from (7), (12), and (13), we have:

$$(y \in Y_2)\colon g(\bar{y}) - g(y) \geqq \Psi(\bar{y}) - \Psi(\bar{x}) + \bar{\alpha}(1 - \bar{\lambda})$$

$$> \Psi(\bar{y}) - \Psi(\bar{x}) + \left[\frac{\Psi(\bar{x}) - \Psi(\bar{y})}{1 - \bar{\lambda}}\right](1 - \bar{\lambda}) = 0;$$

that is:

$$(y \in Y_2): g(y) < g(\bar{y}).$$

It then follows from Theorem 2 that $Y_2 \not>_{\bar{R}} Y_1$; and hence, since $\bar{R} \in \mathcal{R}_2$, we have $Y_2 \not>_{\mathcal{R}_2} Y_1$. Q.E.D.

Notice that Theorem 4 tells us that even given the very stringent conditions of Theorem 3, the Compensation Principle is not much help, in general, in making a social choice among situations unless the function g is known.[18] Further qualitative restrictions on the preference orderings R_i would, of course, result in an admissible set of preference orderings $\mathcal{R}_a$ different from the set $\mathcal{R}_1$ used in Theorem 4; and, as long as such a set did not contain the class $\mathcal{R}_2$ defined in Theorem 4, might result in a preordering $>_{\mathcal{R}_a}$ of situations stronger than the inclusion ordering of Lemma 1. Moreover, in practice it might be feasible to obtain an estimate, $\bar{R}$, of the true m-tuple of preference orderings; and to then take $\mathcal{R}_a$ to be the set of all m-tuples satisfying appropriate qualitative restrictions and lying within some pre-assigned distance (using a suitable metric) of $\bar{R}$. In view of Theorem 3, such a procedure at least holds some promise, albeit being a difficult one to handle from a purely theoretical point of view.

Our discussion to this point may have tended to suggest that the source of the difficulty leading to the impossibility result of Theorem 4 stems from the fact that we can't in practice take $\mathcal{R}_a$ to be a singleton set. To a certain extent this is the difficulty, at least in the sense that qualitative restrictions which turn out to be sufficient to give a strong ordering of situations when $\mathcal{R}_a$ is a singleton turn out to be insufficient to effectively extend the inclusion ordering when $\mathcal{R}_a$ is taken to be the whole class of preference orderings satisfying the same qualitative restrictions (as witness the fact that the class $\mathcal{R}_2$ used in the proof of Theorem 4 is exactly the same class from which we were taking a single element in Theorem 3). On the other hand, the mere fact that $\mathcal{R}_a$ is a singleton is not by any means sufficient to ensure that a stronger preordering of situations will be obtained. To see this we need only consider a slight modification of the example suggested, in a different context, by Koopmans (see [23], pp. 83-85).

Suppose $m \geqq n$ (i.e., the number of consumers is at least equal to the number of commodities), and let the consumers be partitioned into n non-empty and non-overlapping groups, with R_i being defined for each consumer in the j_o^{th} group by:

$$\bar{x}^i R_i x^i \text{ iff } \bar{x}_{ij_o} \geqq x_{ij_o}.$$

(In other words, the consumers in the j_o^{th} group care only about the j_o^{th} commodity, and their preference orderings are strictly monotonic in that commodity.) In this case it is clear that if Y_2 and Y_1 are closed disposable situations we have $Y_2 >_{\mathcal{R}} Y_1$ iff $Y_1 \subset Y_2$.

To consider the other side of the coin for a moment, let n = 2, and let $C_i \subset E_2^+$ be a non-empty closed convex cone containing at least one non-degenerate half-ray for i = 1, ..., m. We then define for each i(i = 1, ..., m) the class of preference orderings $\mathcal{R}_i$ as follows:

$R_i \varepsilon \mathcal{R}_i$ iff R_i is individualistic and such that:

a) R_i is strictly monotonic in C_i,

b) if $x^i \varepsilon E_2^+$ is above C_i, then $x^i I_i \hat{x}^i$, where $\hat{x}^i = (x_{i1}, \alpha)$ with $\alpha = \text{Max } \{\hat{x}_{i2} \varepsilon E_1^+ \mid (x_{i1}, \hat{x}_{i2}) \varepsilon C_i\}$,

c) if $x^i \varepsilon E_2^+$ is below (to the right of) C_i, then $x^i I_i \tilde{x}^i$, where $\tilde{x}^i = (\beta, x_{i2})$ with $\beta = \text{Max } \{\tilde{x}_{i1} \varepsilon E_1^+ \mid (\tilde{x}_{i1}, x_{i2}) \varepsilon C_i\}$;

and $\mathcal{R}_a$ by $R \varepsilon \mathcal{R}_a$ iff $R_i \varepsilon \mathcal{R}_i$ for i = 1, ..., m. If we then define $C = \sum_{i=1}^{m} C_i$, it is clear that for closed disposable situations Y_1 and Y_2,

$$Y_2 >_{\mathcal{R}_a} Y_1 \text{ iff } (Y_1 \cap C) \subset (Y_2 \cap C).$$

Clearly if C is a proper subset of E_2^+, this results in a significant strengthening of the inclusion ordering obtained in Lemma 1, even though $\mathcal{R}_a$ is not a singleton.

The preceding two examples at least suggest that, given suitable qualitative restrictions on all preference orderings, the question of whether we can then obtain a preordering of situations which is significantly stronger than the inclusion ordering is more a question of relative similarity (as between individuals) of the individual preference orderings than of whether we can take R_a to be a singleton.[19]

We note next that, taking $R_a = R_1$, as defined in Theorem 4, the condition $\overline{Y}_2 \supset Y_1$ is not sufficient for $Y_2 >_{R_a} Y_1$. To see this, we need only let Y_1 be a compact convex set having an interior point, and let Y_2 be its interior. Then we have $\overline{Y}_2 \supset Y_1$, but clearly $Y_2 \not>_{R_1} Y_1$. The following two examples, with which we conclude this section, essentially show that we cannot dispense with the conditions on situations used in Theorem 4.

We first note that if $\overline{R}$ denotes the subset of R_o consisting of all $R \in R_o$ satisfying:

R_i is monotonic for $i = 1, \ldots, m$,

then the condition

$$(14) \quad (y \in Y_1)(\exists\, \overline{y} \in Y_2) \colon \overline{y} \geqq y,$$

implies $Y_2 >_{\overline{R}} Y_1$. If Y_2 does not satisfy disposability, then obviously (14) can hold without Y_1 being a subset of Y_2.

Secondly, note that we cannot replace "$\overline{Y}_2 \supset Y_1$" with "$Y_2 \supset Y_1$" in the conclusion of Theorem 4. To see this, let $n = 2$ and define (see Figure 2):

$$Y_1 = \{y \in E_2^+ \mid 0 \leqq y_1 \leqq 1,\ 0 \leqq y_2 \leqq 1\}$$

$$Y_2 = \{y \in E_2^+ \mid 0 \leqq y_1 \leqq 2,\ 0 \leqq y_2 < 1\}.$$

Suppose R is an m-tuple of preference orderings each of which is individualistic, strictly monotonic, and continuous. Let $X \in A(Y_1)$. If $\sum_{i=1}^{m} x_{i2} < 1$, we can let $\overline{X} = X$ to obtain $\overline{X} \in A(Y_2)$ such that $\overline{X}\ R\ X$. Suppose, then that $\sum_{i=1}^{m} x_{i2} = 1$,

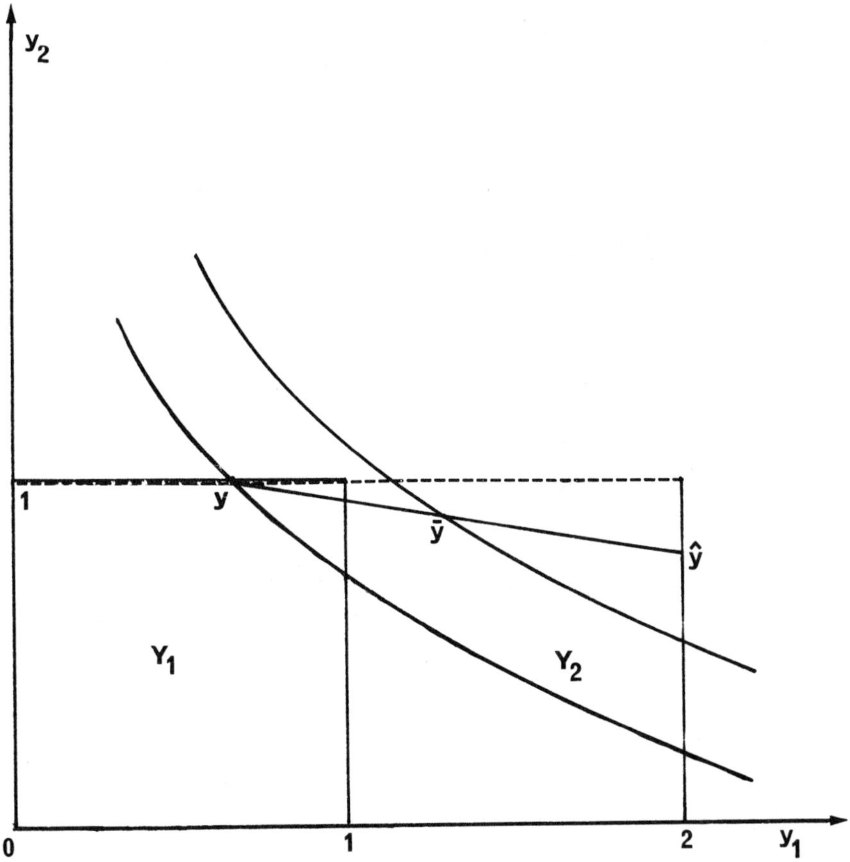

Figure 2

define $y = \sigma(X)$, and let $i_o \in \{1, \ldots, m\}$ be such that $x_{i_o 2} \geqq x_{i2}$ for $i = 1, \ldots, m$. Then we note that

(15) $x_{i_o 2} > 0$.

Now, since R_{i_o} is strictly monotonic,

$$(x^{i_o} + \tfrac{1}{2}[(2,1) - y]) \; P_{i_o} \; x^{i_o}.$$

Hence by the continuity of R_{i_o} and (15), there exists $\hat{y}_2 < 1$ such that, defining $\hat{y} = (2, \hat{y}_2)$, we have:

$$(x^{i_o} + \tfrac{1}{2}[\hat{y} - y]) \; P_{i_o} \; x^{i_o}.$$

Define the allocation $\overline{X}$ by:

$$\overline{x}^i = \begin{cases} x^i \text{ for } i \neq i_o, \\ x^{i_o} + \tfrac{1}{2}[\hat{y} - y] \text{ for } i = i_o. \end{cases}$$

Then $\overline{X}$ P X, and

$$\sum_{i=1}^{m} \overline{x}^i = y + \tfrac{1}{2}[\hat{y} - y] = \tfrac{1}{2}[y + \hat{y}] \in Y_2.$$

Hence we see that

$$Y_2 >_{\mathcal{R}_3} Y_1$$

(where $\mathcal{R}_3$ is defined as the set of all $R \in \mathcal{R}_o$ such that each R_i is individualistic, strictly monotonic, and continuous), even though $Y_1 \not\subset Y_2$.

4. The Utility Possibility Set

In this section we shall be concerned with the notion of a utility possibility set, a concept due fundamentally to Professor Samuelson.[20] The analysis of the next section will depend quite heavily on the results obtained here.

Since nearly all of the results of this and the following section require that each R_i be individualistic,[21] we shall throughout the remainder of this paper always assume that this condition holds. Under these conditions there is no point in distinguishing between R_i and $\dot{R}_i$; hence <u>throughout this and the following section, when we say that R_i is a preference ordering, we shall mean that R_i is a complete preordering of E_n^+ (rather than E_{mn}^+)</u>.

Let us begin by recalling that, if R_i is a continuous preference ordering, then there exists a continuous function f^i, which we can assume is such that $f^i\colon E_n^+ \to E_1^+$, representing R_i on E_n^+.[22] Throughout the sequel, it will be convenient to adhere to the following definition.

Definition 1: When we say that f^i is a utility function representing a preference ordering R_i, we shall mean that:

a) $f^i: E_n^+ \to E_1^+$,

b) $f^i(x^i) \geqq f^i(\bar{x}^i)$ iff $x^i \; R_i \; \bar{x}^i$,

c) $\inf_{x^i \varepsilon E_n^+} f^i(x^i) = 0.$

Clearly if R_i is a continuous preference ordering, there are an infinite number of utility functions representing R_i. Because of this, we shall adopt the following additional bit of notation.

Definition 2: Let R be an m-tuple of continuous preference orderings. We define the space of utility functions associated with R, F(R), by:

F(R) = the set of all m-tuples $f = (f^1, \ldots, f^i, \ldots, f^m)$ of continuous real-valued functions such that f^i is a utility function representing R_i for $i = 1, \ldots, m$.

Given an m-tuple $f \; \varepsilon \; F(R)$, we define a vector-valued function having domain E_{mn}^+ and range E_m^+, which we also denote by f,[23] by:

(1) $f(X) = (f^1(x^1), f^2(x^2), \ldots, f^m(x^m))$ for $X \; \varepsilon \; E_{mn}^+$.

We now define the utility possibility set as follows.

Definition 3: Let E = (R, Y) be an economy in which R_i is continuous for $i = 1, \ldots, m$; and let $f \; \varepsilon \; F(R)$. We define the utility possibility set associated with E and f, $U(E; f)$, by:

$$U(E; f) = f[A(Y)] = \{u \; \varepsilon \; E_m^+ \mid (\exists X \; \varepsilon \; A(Y)): u = f(X)\} \subset E_m^+.$$

[Note: we shall sometimes wish to fix an m-tuple of preference orderings R, and an $f \; \varepsilon \; F(R)$ and consider a sequence of economies of the form $E_h = (R, Y_h)$ for $h = 1, \ldots, q$. In such a case, and where it appears not to be confusing, we shall denote $U(E_h; f)$ by $U(Y_h; f)$ for $h = 1, \ldots, q$.]

Let R be an m-tuple of continuous preference orderings, and let $Y_1, Y_2 \subset E_n^+$. Clearly the following is simply a restatement of our definition of the KHS ordering for this case:

(2) $Y_2 >_R Y_1$ iff for every $f \in F(R)$ we have:

$$(u \in U(Y_1; f)) (\exists \bar{u} \in U(Y_2; f)): \bar{u} \geqq u.$$

Turning now to the properties of the utility possibility set, we note that the first of the following remarks is fairly obvious from the definition of A(Y). The second remark is then an immediate consequence of the first, given the continuity of each f^i.

Remark 1. If $Y \subset E_n^+$ is compact, then A(Y) is compact.

Remark 2. Let $E = (R, Y)$ be an economy, let Y be compact, and suppose R_i is continuous for $i = 1, \ldots, m$. Then

$$(f \in F(R)): U(E; f) \text{ is compact.}$$ [24]

Remark 3. If R_i is a continuous and monotonic preference ordering and f^i is a utility function representing R_i, then:

$$f^i(0) = \inf_{x^i \in E_n^+} f^i(x^i) = 0.$$

Definition 4: Let $E = (R, Y)$ be an economy in which R_i is continuous for $i = 1, \ldots, m$; and let $f \in F(R)$. Then we define:

$$\hat{U}(E; f) = \{u \in E_m^+ \mid (\exists X \in A(Y)): u \leqq f(X)\}, \text{ and}$$

$B(E; f) = \{u \in E_m^+ \mid u$ is on the relative boundary (relative to E_m^+)[25] of $\hat{U}(E; f)\}$.

Lemma 4. Let $E = (R, Y)$ be an economy satisfying:

1) R_i is continuous and monotonic for $i = 1, \ldots, m$,

2) Y is disposable.

Then

$$(f \in F(R)): U(E; f) = \hat{U}(E; f);$$

that is, <u>U(E; f) is disposable</u>.

<u>Proof</u>: Let $f \in F(R)$.

Clearly $U(E; f) \subset \hat{U}(E; f)$. To show the converse, we note that if $0 \leqq \bar{u} \leqq f(\hat{X})$ for some $\hat{X} \in A(Y)$, it follows from Remark 3 and the continuity of each f^i that there exist m scalars μ_i satisfying:

$$0 \leqq \mu_i \leqq 1, \bar{u}_1 = f^i(\mu_i \hat{x}^i) \text{ for } i = 1, \ldots, m.$$

Defining $\bar{X}$ by $\bar{x}^i = \mu_i x^i$ for $i = 1, \ldots, m$, it follows immediately that $f(\bar{X}) = \bar{u}$, and

$$(3) \quad 0 \leqq \sum_{i=1}^{m} \bar{x}^i \leqq \sum_{i=1}^{m} \hat{x}^i.$$

From (3) and the disposability of Y it then follows that $\bar{X} \in A(Y)$, so that $\bar{u} \in U(E; f)$.

<u>Remark 4</u>. It follows from Lemma 4 and (2) that if R is an m-tuple of preference orderings, each of which is continuous and monotonic, if $f \in F(R)$, and if Y_1 and Y_2 are disposable situations, then:

$$(4) \quad Y_2 >_R Y_1 \text{ iff } U(Y_1; f) \subset U(Y_2; f).$$

In order to prove our next result we shall need the following facts. The first of these is an immediate consequence of our definitions, and the second is an easy consequence of Theorem 2 (which, as mentioned earlier, is proved in Appendix 2).

<u>Remark 5</u>. If $Y \subset E_n^+$ is convex, then A(Y) is convex.

<u>Remark 6</u>. Let R_i be a preference ordering which is continuous, monotonic, weakly convex, and homogeneous. Then there exists a continuous utility function $\bar{f}^i$ representing

R_i and satisfying:

i) $\bar{f}^i$ is positively homogeneous of degree one on E_n^+,

ii) $\bar{f}^i$ is concave on E_n^+.

Lemma 5. Let $E = (R, Y)$ be an economy satisfying:

1) R_i is continuous, monotonic, and weakly convex for $i = 1, \ldots, m$,

2) Y is non-empty, compact, disposable, and convex.

Then if $\bar{f}^i$ is a continuous concave function representing R_i for $i = 1, \ldots, m$, $U(E; \bar{f})$ is non-empty, compact, convex, and disposable.

Proof: Clearly $U(E; \bar{f}) \neq \emptyset$ if $Y \neq \emptyset$, and by Remark 2, $U(E; \bar{f})$ is compact. Similarly the disposability of $U(E; \bar{f})$ is a direct application of Lemma 4.

Recalling that $\bar{f}$ is defined on E_{mn}^+ by:

$$\bar{f}(X) = (\bar{f}^1 (x^1), \bar{f}^2 (x^2), \ldots, \bar{f}^m (x^m)),$$

it follows immediately that $\bar{f}$ is concave on E_{mn}^+. Consequently if u and $\bar{u}$ are contained in $U(E; \bar{f})$ and $\lambda \in [0, 1]$, there exist $X, \bar{X} \in A(Y)$ such that $0 \leqq u \leqq \bar{f}(X)$, $0 \leqq \bar{u} \leqq \bar{f}(\bar{X})$; and we then have:

$$0 \leqq \lambda u + (1-\lambda) \bar{u} \leqq \lambda \bar{f}(X) + (1-\lambda) \bar{f}(\bar{X}) \leqq \bar{f}[\lambda X + (1-\lambda)\bar{X}]$$

[recall that A(Y) is convex]. The disposability of $U(E; \bar{f})$ then implies $\lambda u + (1-\lambda) \bar{u} \in U(E, \bar{f})$. Hence $U(E; \bar{f})$ is convex.[26]

Q.E.D.

It will be observed that, under the conditions of Lemma 5, utility possibility sets have the same formal properties as are usually assumed to hold for production possibility sets. We need only make the verbal substitution of "outputs" for "utilities" and "factors" for "commodities," and "allocations of factors among industries" takes the place of "distributions of commodities among consumers." The possibility of unrestricted transferability of commodities among consumers, which lies at the basis of the Compensation Principle, is the formal counterpart of the assumption that factors are perfectly mobile among industries and indifferent as to occupations.

Suppose we now turn our attention to the Pareto optimal allocations in a given economy, *E*. We first define the following, which can be regarded as a formal characterization of the "contract curve" in the general case; and which will be a principal topic for investigation in the next section. (It should be noted that this definition differs slightly from that introduced in [25]).[27]

Definition 5: Let $E = (R, Y)$ be an economy. We define the set $O(E)$ by:

$$O(E) = \{X \in A(Y) \mid X \text{ is Pareto optimal for } E\}$$

$$= \{X \in A(Y) \mid (\nexists \bar{X} \in A(Y)): \bar{X} \, P \, X\}.$$

Suppose $E = (R, Y)$ is an economy, R_i is continuous ($i = 1, \ldots, m$), and $f \in F(R)$. It is, of course, an immediate consequence of our definitions that an allocation X is in $O(E)$ iff $f(X)$ is an efficient point of $U(E; f)$ (i.e., there exists no $u \in U(E; f)$ such that $u \geq f(X)$). From this we can immediately see that X is Pareto optimal for *E* only if $f(X)$ is a point on the relative boundary of $U(E; f)$ (relative, that is, to E^+_m). On the other hand, under these conditions it is not necessarily true that an allocation $X \in A(Y)$ such that $f(X)$ is on the relative boundary of $U(E;f)$ is Pareto optimal for *E*. To see this, consider the economy $E = (R, Y)$, where $m = n = 2$, Y is of the form $Y = \{\bar{y}\}$ for some $\bar{y} \geqq 0$, and R_1 and R_2 are representable by:

$$f^1(x^1) = x_{11}, \; f^2(x^2) = x_{22}, \text{ respectively.}$$

Then only one point on the relative boundary of $U(E; f)$ corresponds to a Pareto optimal allocation; namely the point $\bar{u} = (\bar{y}_1, \bar{y}_2) = \bar{y}$. However, we can state the following

Theorem 5.[28] Let $E = (R, Y)$ be an economy satisfying:

R_i is strictly monotonic and continuous for $i = 1, \ldots, m$. Then if $f \in F(R)$, we have if $u \in E^+_m$:

$$(\exists X \in O(E)): f(X) = u \text{ iff } u \in B(E; f) \cap \hat{U}(E; f).$$

Proof: Clearly $X \in O(E)$ implies $f(X)$ is on the relative boundary of $\hat{U}(E; f)$, for otherwise there would exist $\bar{u} \in \hat{U}(E; f)$ and $f(\bar{X}) \in U(E; f)$ such that:

$$f(\bar{X}) \geqq \bar{u} > f(X),$$

contradicting the Pareto optimality of X.

In the case where m = 1, it is obvious that if u is in $\hat{U}(E; f) \cap B(E; f)$, then $(\exists X \varepsilon 0(E))$: $f(X) = u$. Consequently, suppose $m \geqq 2$, that $\hat{u} \varepsilon \hat{U}(E; f) \cap B(E; f)$; and, by way of contradiction, that:

(6) $(\exists \bar{u} \varepsilon U(E; f))$: $\bar{u} \geq u$.

Then by definition of $U(E; f)$,

(7) $(\exists \bar{X} \varepsilon A(Y))$: $f(\bar{X}) = \bar{u}$.

We note first that (6) and (7) together imply that $f^{i_o}(\bar{x}^{i_o}) > \hat{u}_{i_o} \geqq 0$ for some $i_o \varepsilon \{1, \ldots, m\}$; which in turn implies, by Remark 3, that:

(8) $(\exists j_o \varepsilon \{1, \ldots, n\})$: $\bar{x}_{i_o j_o} > 0$.

Again using Remark 3, together with the continuity of f^{i_o}, we have:

(9) $(\exists \bar{\mu} \varepsilon]0,1[)$: $f^{i_o}(\bar{\mu}\,\bar{x}^{i_o}) = \frac{1}{2}[f^{i_o}(\bar{x}^{i_o}) + \hat{u}_{i_o}]$.

Define the distribution $\tilde{X}$ by:

$$(10) \quad \tilde{x}^i = \begin{cases} \bar{x}^i + \left(\frac{1-\bar{\mu}}{m-1}\right) \bar{x}^{i_o} & \text{for each } i \varepsilon \{1, \ldots, m\}\backslash\{i_o\}, \\ \bar{\mu}\,\bar{x}^{i_o} & \text{for } i = i_o. \end{cases}$$

Clearly $\sigma(\tilde{X}) \equiv \sum_{i=1}^{m} \tilde{x}^i = \sum_{i=1}^{m} \bar{x}^i \equiv \sigma(\bar{X})$; and, of course, $\tilde{X} \varepsilon E^+_{mn}$. Hence

(11) $\tilde{X} \varepsilon A(Y)$.

Moreover, from (8) and (10) and the fact that $\bar{\mu} \varepsilon]0, 1[$ in (9), we have

$$\tilde{x}^i \geq \bar{x}^i \text{ for each } i \neq i_o,$$

and hence by the strict monotonicity of each R_i,

(12) $f^i(\tilde{x}^i) > f^i(\bar{x}^i) \geqq \hat{u}_i$ for each $i \in \{1, \ldots, m\} \setminus \{i_o\}$.

Since from (9) and (10) we also have

(13) $f^{i_o}(\tilde{x}^{i_o}) = f^{i_o}(\bar{\mu}\,\bar{x}^{i_o}) > \hat{u}_{i_o}$;

it then follows from (12) and (13) that:

(14) $f(\tilde{X}) > \hat{u}$.

However, given the form of $\hat{U}(E;\, f)$, (11) and (14) together contradict the assumption that $\hat{u}$ was on the relative boundary of $\hat{U}(E;\, f)$ (i.e., that $\hat{u} \in B(E;\, f)$). We conclude, therefore, that (6) cannot hold, and hence we have:

(15) $(u \in U(E;\, f)) \colon u \geqq \hat{u} \Rightarrow u = \hat{u}$.

It then follows from the definition of $\hat{U}(E;\, f)$ that

$$(\exists\, \hat{X} \in A(Y)) \colon f(\hat{X}) = \hat{u};$$

and (15) then implies that $\hat{X} \in O(E)$ as well.

5. The Contract Curve and the Evaluation of Real National Income

As we observed in Section 3 (N. B. Theorem 4 and the subsequent discussion), we cannot go very far in comparing situations via the Compensation Principle unless we have more information than just, e.g., that each R_i is individualistic, strictly monotonic, continuous, strictly convex, and homogeneous. It might be, however, that one could obtain the needed information by observation of market behavior. Certainly in the limiting case this might make a more extensive comparison of situations possible, for if we know the exact form of each R_i, we can probably compare many more situations than just those where one situation is a subset of another.

A more reasonable case arises in the evaluation of real national income. Suppose we observe a competitive allocation $\bar{X}$, with price vector $\bar{p} > 0$, and define $\bar{y} = \sigma(\bar{X}) = \sum_{i=1}^{m} \bar{x}^i$. Can we then determine some fairly extensive subset of R_o (where R_o is defined in the paragraph preceding Definition 2 of Section 3), call it R_1, such that if $y \in E_n^+$ and

$\bar{p}\cdot y \leqq \bar{p}\cdot\bar{y}$, then $\{\bar{y}\} >_{R_1} \{y\}$? This is the problem whose investigation we shall now undertake. While our principal results obtained in this connection cannot be said to constitute a very satisfactory answer to the question posed, we feel that they are of some interest; and, perhaps, will set the stage for some further investigations along these lines. Moreover, in the course of developing these results we shall explore some properties of "contract curves" in the general case, for which we have obtained somewhat more conclusive results.

N. B. Recall that in this, as in the preceding section, when we say that R_i is a preference ordering we shall mean that R_i is a complete preordering of E_n^+. We shall also retain the definitions of utility function, $F(R)$, $U(E; f)$, $\hat{U}(E; f)$, and $B(E; f)$ set forth in Definitions 1-4 of the preceding section.

Before beginning our investigation of the "contract curve," $O(E)$, we should note that for many purposes we can conveniently, and without loss of generality, assume that Y is disposable. We state the relevant facts in the following, the proof of which is immediate.

<u>Remark 7</u>. Let $E = (R, Y)$ be an economy satisfying:

R_i is strictly monotonic and continuous for $i = 1, \ldots, m$ and let $f \in F(R)$. Then defining

(1)
$$\hat{Y} = [Y + (-E_n^+)] \cap E_n^+ = \{y \in E_n^+ | (\exists \bar{y} \in Y): y \leqq \bar{y}\},$$
$$\hat{E} = (R, \hat{Y})$$

and taking $\hat{U}(E; f)$ as in Definition 4 of the preceding section, we have:

$$\hat{Y} \text{ is disposable, } U(\hat{E}; f) = \hat{U}(E; f),\ O(E) = O(\hat{E}),$$

and $Y >_R \hat{Y}$.

Suppose $E = (R, Y)$ is an economy satisfying the hypotheses of Remark 7, and in addition:

(2) $(\exists\, y^o \in Y): y^o \geq 0$.

Define the set S^{m-1} [the (m-1)-dimensional unit simplex] by:

$$S^{m-1} = \{a \in E_m^+ \mid \sum_{i=1}^{m} a_i = 1\}.$$

We then define the mapping U(a), U maps S^{m-1} into the power set of $\hat{U}(E;\ f)$ by:

(3) $U(a) = \{u \in \hat{U}(E;\ f) \mid (\exists\lambda \geqq 0):\ u = \lambda a\}.$

(See Figure 3.) Obviously we have:

$(a \in S^{m-1}):\ U(a) \neq \emptyset.$

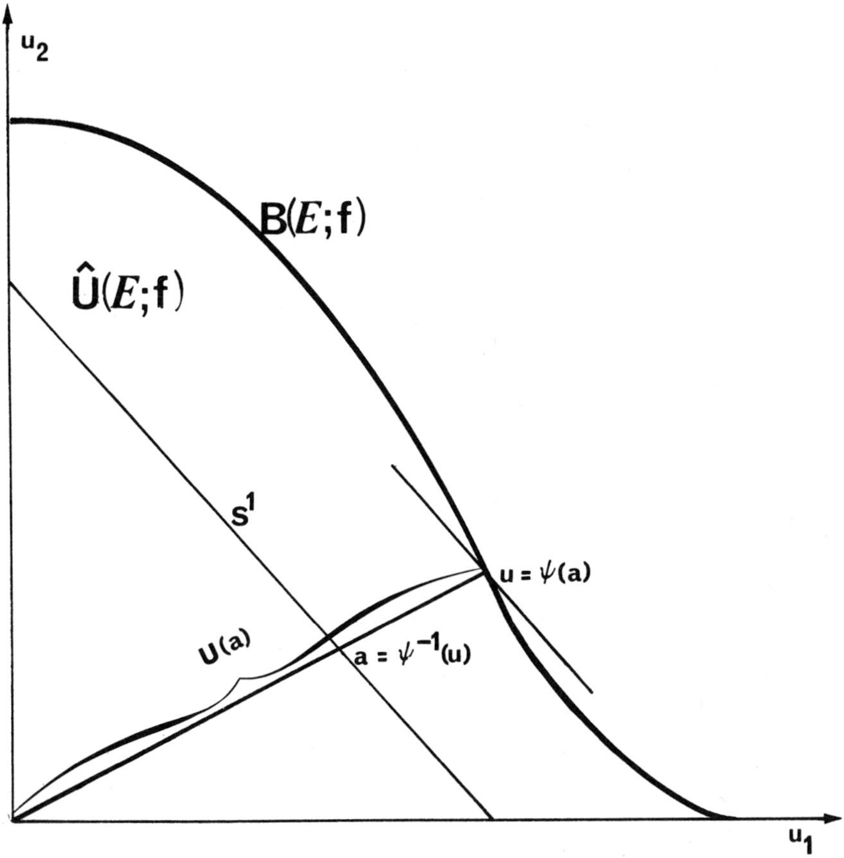

Figure 3

However, we can also show the following.

<u>Lemma 6</u>. Let $E = (R, Y)$ be an economy satisfying:

1) R_i is strictly monotonic and continuous for $i = 1, \ldots, m$;

2) $(\exists\ y^o \in Y):\ y^o \geq 0$;

and let $f \in F(R)$. Then defining $U(a)$ as in (3), above, we have:

$$(a \in S^{m-1})\ (\exists\, u \geq 0):\ u \in U(a).$$

Proof: It is clear that, given hypotheses 1 and 2:

$$(\exists\, \overline{X} \in A(Y)):\ f(\overline{X}) > 0$$

(let, e.g., $\overline{x}^{i} = (1/m)\, y^{o}$ for $i = 1, \ldots, m$). But then it is clear that, given any $a \in S^{m-1}$: $(\exists\, \overline{\lambda} > 0)$: $f(\overline{X}) \geqq \overline{\lambda}\, a$; and then, by definition of $\hat{U}(E;\, f)$, $\overline{\lambda}\, a \in \hat{U}(E;\, f)$. Moreover, $\overline{u} \equiv \overline{\lambda}\, a \in U(a)$, and $\overline{u} \geq 0$.

In order to develop further properties of $U(a)$, we first note the following fact, which will be quite useful in our later development.

Lemma 7. Let $E = (R, Y)$ and f satisfy the assumptions of Lemma 6. Then:

$$(u \in \hat{U}(E;\, f))(\delta > 0)\ (\exists\, \overline{u} \in N(u, \delta) \cap \hat{U}(E;\, f)):\ \overline{u} > 0$$

where $N(u, \delta)$ denotes the open neighborhood of u with radius δ.

Proof: Define $\hat{Y}$ as in Remark 7; that is:

$$\hat{Y} = \{y \in E_n^+ \mid (\exists\, \overline{y} \in Y):\ y \leqq \overline{y}\}.$$

We note that, if $u \in \hat{U}(E;\, f)$, it suffices to prove that, given any $\delta > 0$:

$$(\exists\, \overline{u} \in \hat{U}(E;\, f)):\ \sum_{i=1}^{m} |\overline{u}_i - u_i| < \delta \text{ and } \overline{u} > 0.$$

Since our result is obviously true if $u > 0$, we distinguish two cases.

a) $u = 0$. Recall, as in the proof of Lemma 6, that:

$$(\exists\ \hat{X} \in A(Y)):\ f(\hat{X}) > 0.$$

Defining $\hat{u} = f(\hat{X})$, and $\overline{u}$ by $\overline{u}_i = \text{Min}\, \{\hat{u}_i, (\delta/2m)\}$ for $i = 1, \ldots, m$, we have:

$$\sum_{i=1}^{m} |\overline{u}_i - u_i| = \sum_{i=1}^{m} |\overline{u}_i| \leqq \delta/2 \sum_{i=1}^{m} (1/m) = \delta/2 < \delta.$$

Moreover, $\bar{u} \leqq \hat{u}$, so that by definition of $U(E, f)$, $\bar{u} \in \hat{U}(E; f)$.

b) $u \geq 0$, $u \not> 0$. In this case, let

$$I_1 = \{i \in \{1, \ldots, m\} \mid u_i > 0\},$$

$$I_2 \equiv \{i \in \{1, \ldots, m\} \mid u_i = 0\}.$$

By definition of $\hat{U}(E; f)$, $(\exists X \in A(Y))$: $f(X) \geqq u$, and it is clear that we must have:

(4) $\quad (i \in I_1): f^i(x^i) \geqq u_i > 0, \ (i \in I_2): f^i(x^i) \geqq u_i = 0.$

Using Remark 3 (of the previous section), together with the continuity of each f^i, it is clear that

(5) $\quad (i \in I_1)\ (\exists \mu_i \in]0, 1[): 0 < u_i - f^i(\mu_i x^i) =$

$\quad = \text{Min}\{\delta/2m, u_i/2\}.$

We then define:

(6) $\quad \bar{x}^i = \mu_i x^i, \ \bar{u}_i = f^i(\bar{x}^i)$ for $i \in I_1$.

From (4) and the strict monotonicity of each i, it follows that for $i \in I_1$, $x^i \geq 0$. Hence $\mu_i x^i \geq 0$, and consequently

(7) $\quad (i \in I_1): \bar{u}_i = f^i(\mu_i x^i) > 0.$

Next define

(8) $\quad \hat{x}^i = x^i + (1/m_2) \sum_{k \in I_1} (1-\mu_k)\, x^k$ for each $i \in I_2$

where m_2 is defined as the number of elements in I_2. Since $x^k \geq 0$ for $k \in I_1$, and each $\mu_k < 1$ from (5), it is clear that $\hat{x}^i \geq 0$ for $i \in I_2$. Consequently, using the strict monotonicity of each R_i, Remark 3, and the continuity of each f^i, we see that:

(9) $\quad (i \in I_2)\ (\exists \nu_i \in]0, 1[): 0 < f^i(\nu_i \hat{x}^i) \leqq \delta/2m.$

We now define

(10) $\quad \bar{x}^i = \nu_i \hat{x}^i, \ \bar{u}^i = f^i(\bar{x}^i)$ for $i \in I_2$.

Thus $\overline{X}$ and $\overline{u}$ are defined by (6) and (10), and $\overline{u} = f(\overline{X})$.

From (7) and (9) we have $\overline{u} > 0$, while from (4), (5), (6), (9), and (10) we have

$$\sum_{i=1}^{m} |u_i - \overline{u}_i| = \sum_{i\varepsilon I_1} |u_i - \overline{u}_i| + \sum_{i\varepsilon I_2} \overline{u}_i \leqq \delta/2 < \delta.$$

Finally from (6), (10), and (8):

$$(11)\quad 0 \leqq \sum_{i=1}^{m} \overline{x}^i = \sum_{i\varepsilon I_1} \mu_i x^i + \sum_{i\varepsilon I_2} \nu_i x^i + 1/m_2 \left(\sum_{i\varepsilon I_2} \nu_i \right)$$

$$\left(\sum_{i\varepsilon I_1} (1-\mu_i)\, x^i \right) \leqq \sum_{i\varepsilon I_1} \mu_i x^i + \sum_{i\varepsilon I_2} x^i + \sum_{i\varepsilon I_1} (1-\mu_i) x^i =$$

$$= \sum_{i=1}^{m} x^i .$$

From (11) we see that $\overline{X} \varepsilon A(\hat{Y})$. Hence from Remark 7, we have $\overline{u} \varepsilon \hat{U}(E; f)$.

Q.E.D.

We can now show that U(a) is a <u>continuous</u> point-set mapping; that is, it is both upper semi-continuous (abbreviated u.s.c.) and lower semi-continuous (abbreviated l.s.c.) on S^{m-1} (see Berge [9], pp. 109-110; and Debreu [13], pp. 17-18)[29]. In the sequel, we shall use the generic notation '$\langle a^q \rangle$' to denote an infinite sequence the qth term of which is a^q. If each element of a sequence $\langle a^q \rangle$ is a member of a set X, we shall express this fact by writing '$\langle a^q \rangle \subset X$.'

<u>Lemma 8</u>. Suppose $E = (R, Y)$ and f satisfy the assumptions of Lemma 6 and that, in addition Y is compact. Then the mapping U(a) defined in (3), above, is continuous on S^{m-1}.

<u>Proof</u>:

A) Suppose $\langle a^q \rangle \subset S^{m-1}$, $\overline{a} \varepsilon S^{m-1}$, $\langle u^q \rangle \subset \hat{U}(E; f)$ and $\overline{u} \varepsilon E_m$ are such that:

(12) $a^q \to \overline{a}$, $u^q \varepsilon U(a^q)$ for $q = 1, 2, \ldots,$ and

(13) $u^q \to \overline{u}$.

Since by Remarks 2 and 7, $\hat{U}(E; f)$ is compact, it follows at once from (13) that $\bar{u} \in \hat{U}(E; f)$. We now distinguish two cases.

1) $\bar{u} = 0$. In this case it is obvious that $\bar{u} \in U(\bar{a})$, since:

(14) $(a \in S^{m-1})$: $0 \in U(a)$.

2) $\bar{u} \geq 0$. In this case we may assume, without loss of generality, that:

$$u^q \geq 0 \text{ for } q = 1, 2, \ldots$$

Hence we have from (12) and the definition of U(a):

$$\left(\frac{1}{\sum_{i=1}^{m} u_i^q}\right) u^q = a^q \text{ for } q = 1, 2, \ldots$$

But then, since $(1/\Sigma u_i)\, u$ is a continuous function of u, we have:

$$\bar{a} = \lim_{q\to\infty} a^q = \lim_{q\to\infty} \left[\left(\frac{1}{\sum_{i=1}^{m} u_i^q}\right) u^q\right] = \left(\frac{1}{\sum_{i=1}^{m} \bar{u}_i}\right) \bar{u}$$

Hence $\bar{u} \in U(\bar{a})$, and we conclude that U(a) is u.s.c. on S^{m-1}.

B) Suppose $\bar{a} \in S^{m-1}$, and $W \subset E_m$ is an open set (in E_m) such that:

$$U(\bar{a}) \cap W \neq \emptyset.$$

We distinguish two cases:

1) $0 \in U(\bar{a}) \cap W$. In this case it follows at once from (14) that we may let $V(\bar{a}) = E_m$ to obtain an open set $V(\bar{a})$ such that:

$$(a \in V(\bar{a}) \cap S^{m-1}): U(a) \cap W \neq \emptyset.$$

2) $(u \in U(\bar{a}) \cap W)$: $u \geq 0$. Choose any $\bar{u} \in U(\bar{a}) \cap W$. Then $\bar{u} \geq 0$, and there exists $\delta_o > 0$ such that:

(15) $(u \in E_m^+)$: $\sum_{i=1}^{m} |u_i - \bar{u}_i| < \delta_o \Rightarrow u \in W$.

Note moreover that if we define

(16) $\bar{\lambda} = \sum_{i=1}^{m} \bar{u}_i > 0,$

we can take $0 < \delta_o < 2\,\bar{\lambda}$. Hence, defining the scalar $\tilde{\lambda}$ by:

$$\tilde{\lambda} = 1 - \delta_o/2\,\bar{\lambda} = \frac{2\,\bar{\lambda} - \delta_o}{2\,\bar{\lambda}}$$

we have:

(17) $0 < \tilde{\lambda} < 1.$

Consequently, defining $\tilde{u} = \tilde{\lambda}\,\bar{u}$, we have (see Figure 4)

$\tilde{u} \in E_m^+$ and

$$\sum_{i=1}^{m} |\bar{u}_i - \tilde{u}_i| = \sum_{i=1}^{m} |\bar{u}_i - \tilde{\lambda}\,\bar{u}_i| = (1-\tilde{\lambda}) \sum_{i=1}^{m} \bar{u}_i$$

$$= (\delta_o/2\,\bar{\lambda})\,\bar{\lambda} = \delta_o/2.$$

Hence from (15), we have:

(18) $\tilde{u} \in E_m^+ \cap W.$

Now, define $I_1 = \{i \in \{1, \ldots, m\} |\ \bar{u}_i > 0\}$, and

$$\alpha = \underset{i \in I_1}{\text{Min}}\ \bar{u}_i > 0, \text{ and } r = \alpha\delta_o/4\,\bar{\lambda}.$$

By Lemma 7, we have:

(19) $(\exists \hat{u} \in \hat{U}(E; f)): \sum_{i=1}^{m} |\hat{u}_i - \bar{u}_i| < r \text{ and } \hat{u} > 0.$

Note that (19) implies that:

(20) $\bar{u}_i - r < \hat{u}_i < \bar{u}_i + r$ for $i = 1, \ldots, m$.

On the other hand, if $i \in I_1$, we have:

$$\tilde{u}_i = \tilde{\lambda}\,\bar{u}_i = \bar{u}_i - (\delta_o/2\,\bar{\lambda})\,\bar{u}_i \leqq \bar{u}_i - (\delta_o/2\,\bar{\lambda})\,\alpha$$

(21)

$$= \bar{u}_i - 2\left(\frac{\alpha\delta_o}{4\,\bar{\lambda}}\right) = \bar{u}_i - 2r < \bar{u}_i - r \text{ (for } i \in I_1\text{)}.$$

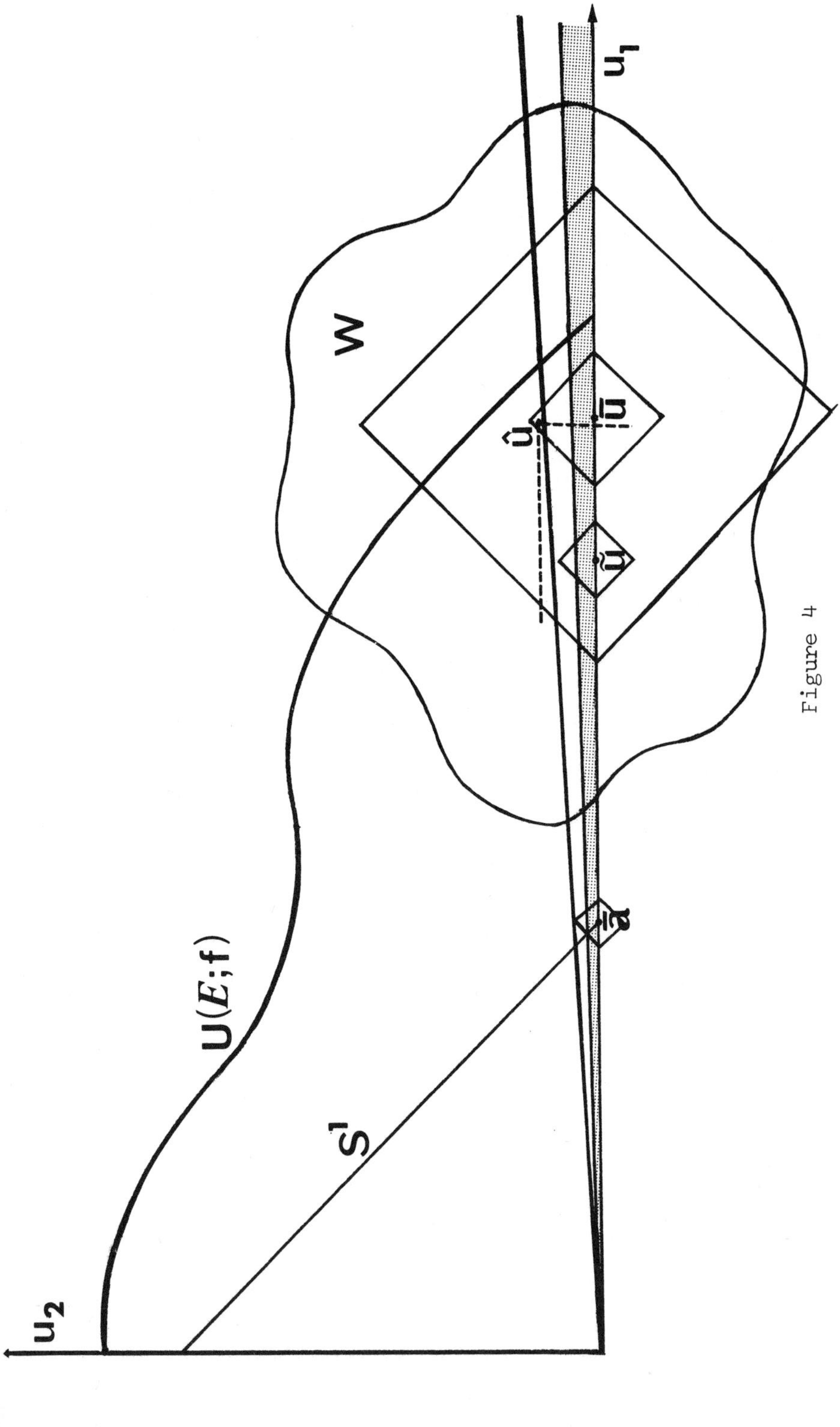

Figure 4

Since $i \notin I_1$ implies $\tilde{u}_i = \tilde{\lambda}\bar{u}_i = 0 < \hat{u}_i$, it then follows from (20) and (21) that (see Figure 4):

(22) $\hat{u} > \tilde{u}$.

Define the function g(u) on E_m^+ by:

$$g(u) = \underset{i}{\text{Max}}\ (u_i / \hat{u}_i).$$

From (22) we have at once that $g(\tilde{u}) < 1$. Hence, since it is clear that g is continuous, and using (15) and the fact that $\sum_{i=1}^{m} |\tilde{u}_i - \bar{u}_i| = \delta_o/2 < \delta_o$, it follows that:

(23) $(\exists\ s > 0)\ (u \in E_m^+)\colon \sum_{i=1}^{m} |u_i - \tilde{u}_i| < s$

$\Rightarrow u \in W$ and $g(u) < 1$.

Now define $V(\bar{a})$ by:

$$V(\bar{a}) = \{a \in S^{m-1} \mid \sum_{i=1}^{m} |a_i - \bar{a}_i| < s/\tilde{\lambda}\ \bar{\lambda}\ ,$$

and for $a \in V(\bar{a})$ let $u(a) = (\tilde{\lambda}\ \bar{\lambda})a$. Then, recalling that $\bar{u} = \bar{\lambda}\bar{a}$, and hence $\tilde{u} = (\tilde{\lambda}\ \bar{\lambda})\bar{a}$, we see that:

$$\sum_{i=1}^{m} |u_i(a) - \tilde{u}_i| = \sum_{i=1}^{m} |(\tilde{\lambda}\ \bar{\lambda})a_i - (\tilde{\lambda}\ \bar{\lambda})\ \bar{a}_i\ |$$

$$= (\tilde{\lambda}\ \bar{\lambda}) \sum_{i=1}^{m} |a_i - \bar{a}_i| < (\tilde{\lambda}\ \bar{\lambda})\ (s/\tilde{\lambda}\ \ \bar{\lambda}) = s.$$

Hence by (23):

(24) $u(a) \in W$, and

(25) $g[u(a)] < 1$.

However, (25) implies $u(a) < \hat{u}$, and since $\hat{u} \in \hat{U}(E; f)$, it follows from the definition of $\hat{U}(E; f)$ that:

(26) $u(a) \in \hat{U}(E; f)$.

Consequently, since each u(a) is a positive scalar multiple of a, we have from (24) and (26) that:

$(a \in V(\bar{a}))\colon U(a) \cap W \neq \emptyset;$

and it follows that U(a) is l.s.c. on S^{m-1}.

Q.E.D.

Proceeding with our investigation of $0(E)$, we now define, for each $a \in S^{m-1}$:

$$(27) \quad \Psi(a) = \operatorname*{Max}_{u \in U(a)} \left(\sum_{i=1}^{m} u_i \right),$$

$$(28) \quad \psi(a) = \Psi(a)\, a, \quad \text{(see Figure 3), and}$$

$$(29) \quad X(a) = f^{-1}[\psi(a)] \cap A(Y) = \{X \in A(Y) \mid f(X) = \psi(a)\}.$$

We then have the following:

<u>Theorem 6.</u> Let $E = (R, Y)$ be an economy satisfying:

1) R_i is strictly monotonic and continuous for $i = 1, \ldots, m$,

2) $(\exists y^o \in Y)\colon y^o \geq 0$,

3) Y is compact.

Then if $f \in F(R)$, and $\hat{U}(E;\, f)$ and $B(E;\, f)$ are defined as in Definition 4 of the previous section we have:

i) $B(E;\, f) = \{u \in U(E;\, f) \mid (\exists X \in 0(E))\colon f(X) = u\}$
$= f[0(E)]$,

ii) $B(E;\, f) = \psi(S^{m-1})$, where ψ is defined in (28) above,

iii) the function Ψ defined in (27) is continuous on S^{m-1},

iv) $\psi(a)$ is continuous on S^{m-1},

v) $B(E;\, f)$ is homeomorphic to S^{m-1},

vi) $0(E) = X(S^{m-1})$, where X(a) is defined in (29),

vii) X(a) is u.s.c. on S^{m-1} and: $(a \in S^{m-1})\colon X(a) \neq \emptyset$,

viii) $0(E)$ is compact.

<u>Proof</u>:

i) This part of our conclusion is an immediate consequence of Theorem 5 since, given that Y is compact, $U(E;\, f)$ and $\hat{U}(E;\, f)$ will be closed sets.

ii) a) If $u \in B(E;\, f)$ then (from hypothesis 2) $u \geq 0$, and it is clear that:

(30) $u = \psi[(\frac{1}{\sum_{i=1}^{m} u_i})\, u]$.

b) If $u = \psi(a)$ for some $a \varepsilon S^{m-1}$, then it is clear that $u \varepsilon B(E; f)$.

iii) The fact that Ψ is continuous on S^{m-1} is an immediate consequence of Berge's "Maximum Theorem" and Lemma 8 (see Berge [9], p. 116).

iv) Since $\psi(a) = \Psi(a)\, a$, this is an immediate consequence of (iii).

v) From (30) above, we see that $\psi^{-1}(u) = (1/ \sum_{i=1}^{m} u_i)u$ for $u \varepsilon B(E; f)$. Consequently, using (ii), we see that ψ is a one-to-one mapping from S^{m-1} onto $B(E; f)$ and that both ψ and ψ^{-1} are continuous. Hence, by definition, $B(E; f)$ and S^{m-1} are homeomorphic.

vi) This follows immediately from (i), (ii), and the definition of $X(a)$.

vii) The fact that $(a \varepsilon S^{m-1})$: $X(a) \neq \emptyset$ follows immediately from (i) and (ii).

Consider now the mapping χ defined on $B(E; f)$ by:

$$\chi(u) = \{X \varepsilon A(Y) \mid f(X) = u\} = f^{-1}(u) \cap A(Y).$$

Suppose $\langle u^q \rangle \subset B(E; f)$, $\bar{u} \varepsilon B(E; f)$, $\langle X^q \rangle \subset A(Y)$, and $\bar{X} \varepsilon E_{mn}$ are such that:

(31) $u^q \to \bar{u}$, $X^q \varepsilon \chi(u^q)$ for $q = 1, 2, \ldots,$ and

(32) $X^q \to \bar{X}$.

We note first that from (32) and Remark 1, we have $\bar{X} \varepsilon A(Y)$. Next, we have from (31):

$$f(X^q) = u^q \text{ for } q = 1, 2, \ldots$$

Consequently, using (31), (32), and the continuity of f, we have:

$$f(\bar{X}) = \lim_{q\to\infty} f(X^q) = \lim_{q\to\infty} u^q = \bar{u}.$$

Therefore, $\bar{X} \varepsilon \chi(\bar{u})$, and we conclude that χ is u.s.c. on

$B(E; f)$. Noting that $X(a) = \chi[\psi(a)]$, our result then follows at once from (iv) and Theorem 1', p. 113, in Berge [9].

viii) This part of our conclusion follows at once from (vi), (vii), and Theorem 3, p. 110, in Berge [9].

Q.E.D.

Notice that, according to (v) of Theorem 6, $B(E, f)$ is a (compact) continuous (m-1)-dimensional surface in E^+_m, a rather surprising result in view of the fact that our hypotheses allow Y to have all sorts of irregularities (as long as it is compact). Our next result shows, in effect, that under the neo-classical assumptions the contract curve in the general case satisfies all the properties usually assumed to hold in the 2 x 2 case.

Theorem 7. Let $E = (R, Y)$ be an economy satisfying all the hypotheses of Theorem 6 and suppose, in addition, that Y is convex. Then we have:

a) if R_i is weakly convex for $i = 1, \ldots, m$, then:

i) $(a \in S^{m-1})$: $X(a)$ is convex,

ii) $O(E)$ is a connected set.[30]

b) if R_i is strictly convex for $i = 1, \ldots, m$,

i) $X(a)$ is a continuous single-valued mapping,

ii) $O(E)$ is homeomorphic to S^{m-1}.

Proof: In the following, let f be an arbitrary member of $F(R)$.

a.i) Suppose $\overline{a} \in S^{m-1}$, that $X, \overline{X} \in X(\overline{a})$, and let $\lambda \in [0, 1]$. Then if $i \in \{1, \ldots, m\}$, we have:

$$f^i(x^i) = f^i(\overline{x}^i) = \Psi(\overline{a})\ \overline{a}_i.$$

Consequently, the weak convexity of each R_i implies:

$$f[\lambda X + (1-\lambda)\ \overline{X}] \geqq \Psi(\overline{a})\ \overline{a} = \psi(\overline{a}).$$

However, it follows from Theorem 6 (vi) that $X, \overline{X} \in O(E)$. Moreover, the convexity of Y implies that $\lambda X + (1-\lambda)\ \overline{X} \in A(Y)$. Consequently we have:

$$f[\lambda X + (1-\lambda)\ \overline{X}] = \psi(\overline{a})$$

and it follows that $\lambda X + (1-\lambda)\ \overline{X} \in X(\overline{a})$.

a.ii) Since S^{m-1} is connected, and for each $a \in S^{m-1}$,

X(a) is convex (and therefore connected) and, finally, X(a) is u.s.c. on S^{m-1}, this becomes an immediate application of Theorem A.2 of Appendix 4.

b.i) Suppose for some $\bar{a} \in S^{m-1}$ there exist distinct points $X, \bar{X} \in X(\bar{a})$. Then from (a.i) we would have:

$$(33) \quad f[1/2\, X + 1/2\, \bar{X}] = \psi(a) = f(X) = f(\bar{X}).$$

However $X \neq \bar{X}$ implies $x^{i_o} \neq \bar{x}^{i_o}$ for some $i_o \in \{1, \ldots, m\}$, and, since $f^{i_o}(x^{i_o}) = f^{i_o}(x^{i_o}) = \Psi(a)\, a_{i_o}$, the strict convexity of R_{i_o} implies:

$$f^{i_o}[1/2\, x^{i_o} + 1/2\, \bar{x}^{i_o}] > f^{i_o}(x^{i_o}),$$

contradicting (33). Hence X(a) is a single-valued mapping, and it then follows at once from (vii) of Theorem 6 that X(a) is continuous on S^{m-1}.

b.ii) We note first that, from Theorem 6 (vi), X(a) maps S^{m-1} onto $0(E)$. Moreover, it is clear that:

$$\alpha(X) \equiv [1/\sum_{i=1}^{m} f^i(x^i)]\, f(X) = X^{-1}(X);$$

and that $\alpha(X)$ is a continuous function on $0(E)$, since f is continuous and

$$(X \in 0(E)): \sum_{i=1}^{m} f^i(x^i) > 0.$$

Hence $0(E)$ is homeomorphic to S^{m-1}.

Q.E.D.

Suppose we now turn our attention to the evaluation of real national income. In this discussion, we shall need to make use of the following definition.

Definition: Let R be an m-tuple of preference orderings. We shall say that a point $(\bar{X}, \bar{p}) \in E_{(m+1)n}$ is a competitive equilibrium for R if:

a) $\bar{X} \in E^+_{mn}$,

b) $(x^i \in E^+_n)$: $\bar{p} \cdot x^i \leqq \bar{p} \cdot \bar{x}^i \Rightarrow \bar{x}^i R_i x^i$ for $i = 1, \ldots, m$.

Our principal result in connection with the evaluation of real national income is the following.

Theorem 8. Suppose R is an m-tuple of preference orderings, and suppose that $(\hat{X}, \hat{p})$ is a competitive equilibrium for R. Define $\hat{y} = \sigma(\hat{X}) = \sum_{i=1}^{m} \hat{x}^i$. Then we have:

i) if each R_i is monotonic, then:

$$(y \in E_n^+): \hat{p} \cdot y \leqq \hat{p} \cdot \hat{y} \Rightarrow XP\hat{X} \text{ for no } X \in A(\{y\}).$$ [31]

ii) if each R_i is strictly convex, then:

$$(y \in E_n^+ \setminus \{\hat{y}\}): \hat{p} \cdot y \leqq \hat{p} \cdot \hat{y} \Rightarrow XR\hat{X}$$

for no $X \in A(\{y\})$ (and hence $y \not>_R \hat{y}$).

iii) if each R_i is monotonic, then

$$(y \in E_n^+): \hat{p} \cdot y < \hat{p} \cdot \hat{y} \Rightarrow XR\hat{X} \text{ for no } X \in A(\{y\})$$

(and hence $y \not>_R \hat{y}$).

iv) if each R_i is strictly monotonic and continuous, if $f \in F(R)$, if $\tilde{y} \in E_n^+$ and if we define $\hat{Y} = \{\hat{y}\}$, $\tilde{Y} = \{\tilde{y}\}$, $\hat{E} = (R, \hat{Y})$, and $\tilde{E} = (R, \tilde{Y})$, we have:

a) $\hat{p} \cdot \tilde{y} \leqq \hat{p} \cdot \hat{y} \Rightarrow (\exists\, \tilde{X} \in O(\tilde{E})): \hat{X}R\tilde{X}$.

b) if $\hat{p} \cdot \tilde{y} < \hat{p} \cdot \hat{y}$, then defining $\hat{u} = f(\hat{X})$, there exist open neighborhoods of $\hat{u}$ and $\hat{X}$, $V(\hat{u})$ and $W(\hat{X})$, respectively, such that:

$$(u \in V(\hat{u}) \cap B(\hat{E}; f))\ (\exists\, \tilde{u} \in B(\tilde{E}; f)): u \geq \tilde{u};$$

$$(X \in W(\hat{X}) \cap O(\hat{E}))\ (\exists\, \tilde{X} \in O(\tilde{E})): f(X) \geq f(\tilde{X}).$$

Proof:

A) Parts (i)-(iii) of our conclusion are really only very thinly disguised versions of the "competitive equilibrium implies Pareto optimality" argument developed in [1], [13], and [23].[32] Accordingly, we shall prove (ii) only, leaving (i) and (iii) to the interested reader.

If each R_i is strictly convex, then, as is well-known,

$$(x^i \in E_n^+ \backslash \{\hat{x}^i\}): \hat{p} \cdot x^i \leqq \hat{p} \cdot \hat{x}^i \Rightarrow \hat{x}^i P_i x^i$$

for i = 1, ..., m. Hence if $\tilde{X} \in E_{mn}^+$ is such that $\sum_{i=1}^{m} \tilde{x}^i \neq \sum_{i=1}^{m} \hat{x}^i$ and $\tilde{X}R\hat{X}$, we must have:

$$\hat{p} \cdot \tilde{x}^i \geqq \hat{p} \cdot \hat{x}^i \text{ for } i = 1, \ldots, m \text{ and}$$

$$(\exists i_o \in \{1, \ldots, m\}): \hat{p} \cdot \tilde{x}^{i_o} > \hat{p} \cdot \hat{x}^{i_o},$$

which implies

$$\hat{p} \cdot \left(\sum_{i=1}^{m} \tilde{x}^i\right) = \sum_{i=1}^{m} \hat{p} \cdot \tilde{x}^i > \sum_{i=1}^{m} \hat{p} \cdot \hat{x}^i = \hat{p} \cdot \hat{y}.$$

We conclude, therefore, that if $y \in E_n^+ \backslash \{\hat{y}\}$ is such that $\hat{p} \cdot y \leqq \hat{p} \cdot \hat{y}$, there exists no $X \in A(\{y\})$ such that $XR\hat{X}$ (and hence $y \not>_R \hat{y}$).

B) Suppose the assumptions of (iv) hold, and define the functions $\hat{\psi}(a)$ and $\tilde{\psi}(a)$ as in (28) above, taking in (3) $E = \hat{E}$ for $\hat{\psi}$ and $E = \tilde{E}$ for $\tilde{\psi}$. Letting

$$\hat{a} = (1/\sum_{i=1}^{m} f^i(\hat{x}^i))\, f(\hat{X}),$$

it is clear that, if $\hat{p} \cdot \tilde{y} \leqq \hat{p} \cdot \hat{y}$, $f(\hat{X}) = \hat{\psi}(\hat{a})$, and, by (i),

$$\tilde{\psi}(\hat{a}) \leqq \hat{\psi}(\hat{a}).$$

Letting $\tilde{X}$ be such that $f(\tilde{X}) = \tilde{\psi}(\hat{a})$, we see from Theorem 6 (i, ii) that we have verified (iv.a).

Suppose now that $\hat{p} \cdot \tilde{y} < \hat{p} \cdot \hat{y}$. Then by (iii) we have at once that:

$$(34) \quad \tilde{\psi}(\hat{a}) \leq \hat{\psi}(\hat{a}) = f(\hat{X}), \text{ and}$$

$$\tilde{\psi}_i(\hat{a}) = \hat{\psi}_i(\hat{a}) \text{ iff } \hat{\psi}_i(\hat{a}) = 0.$$

From (34) we see that, defining $\hat{\Psi}$ and $\tilde{\Psi}$ as in (27) for $\hat{E}$ and $\tilde{E}$, respectively, and

$$\varepsilon_o = \tfrac{1}{2}[\hat{\Psi}(\hat{a}) - \tilde{\Psi}(\hat{a})],$$

we have $\varepsilon_o > 0$. Moreover, it then follows from Theorem 6 that there exists $\delta_o > 0$ such that:

$$(a \in N(\hat{a}, \delta_o) \cap S^{m-1}): \quad |\hat{\Psi}(a) - \hat{\Psi}(\hat{a})| < \varepsilon_o,$$

(35)

$$\text{and } |\hat{\Psi}(a) - \hat{\Psi}(\hat{a})| < \varepsilon_o.$$

Defining $\hat{u} = \hat{\psi}(\hat{a}) = \hat{\Psi}(\hat{a})\hat{a} = f(\hat{X})$, and $V(\hat{u}) = \psi[N(\hat{a}, \delta_o) \cap S^{m-1}]$; it is clear from (35) and Theorem 6 that $V(\hat{a})$ satisfies the first part of (iv.b) of our conclusion (recall that $\hat{\psi}$ is a homeomorphism, so that $\psi[N(\hat{a}, \delta_o) \cap S^{m-1}]$ is open). Moreover, by the continuity of f, there then exists an open neighborhood of $\hat{X}$, $W(\hat{X})$, such that

$$(X \in W(\hat{X}) \cap O(\hat{E})): f(\hat{X}) \in V(\hat{u});$$

and it is clear that $W(\hat{X})$ then satisfies the required properties of the second part of (iv.b).

Q.E.D.

Theorem 8 certainly makes a considerably weaker statement than one would like to make. One would like to be able to infer from the fact that $\hat{p} \cdot y \leqq \hat{p} \cdot \hat{y}$ that $\{\hat{y}\} >_R \{y\}$ under the conditions of Theorem 8. However, in (i) - (iii) we obtain only the statement that $\{y\} \not>_R \{\hat{y}\}$; which, since $>_R$ is not in general a complete preordering of situations, does not imply $\{\hat{y}\} >_R \{y\}$. If all preference orderings are identical and homogeneous the situation is changed, however, as we note in the following.

Theorem 9.[33] Let R be an m-tuple of identical preference orderings, each of which is monotonic, continuous, weakly convex, and homogeneous; and let $(\overline{X}, \overline{p})$ be a competitive equilibrium for R. Then defining $\overline{y} = \delta(\overline{X}) = \sum_{i=1}^{m} \overline{x}^i$, we have:

$$(y \in E_n^+): \overline{p} \cdot y \leqq \overline{p} \cdot \overline{y} \Rightarrow \{\overline{y}\} >_R \{y\}.$$

Proof: We recall first that, from Theorem 2 (see also Remark 6), each R_i can in this case be represented by a function $\overline{g}(x^i)$ (the same function for each i), where $\overline{g}$ is continuous, concave, and positively homogeneous of degree one on E_n^+.

Let $\hat{y} \in E_n^+$ be such that $\bar{p} \cdot \hat{y} \leqq \bar{p} \cdot \bar{y}$, and suppose, by way of contradiction, that:

(36) $\bar{g}(\hat{y}) > \bar{g}(\bar{y})$.

By Lemma 3, there exists $w \in E_m^+$ such that

(37) $\sum_{i=1}^{m} w_i = 1,$

(38) $(w_i\bar{y})\ R_i\ \bar{x}^i$ for $i = 1, \ldots, m$.

Since $(\bar{X}, \bar{p})$ is a competitive equilibrium for R, (38), together with the monotonicity of each R_i, implies:

$$\bar{p} \cdot (w_i\bar{y}) \geqq \bar{p} \cdot \bar{x}^i \text{ for } i = 1, \ldots, m.$$

Hence, since

$$\sum_{i=1}^{m} (w_i\bar{y}) = \bar{y} = \sum_{i=1}^{m} \bar{x}^i,$$

we have:

(39) $w_i(\bar{p} \cdot \bar{y}) = \bar{p} \cdot \bar{x}^i$ for $i = 1, \ldots, m$.

Consider the distribution $\hat{X}$ defined by:

$$\hat{x}^i = w_i\hat{y} \text{ for } i = 1, \ldots, m.$$

Given (36) we have from (38):

(40) $\bar{g}(\hat{x}^i) = w_i\bar{g}(\hat{y}) \geqq w_i\bar{g}(\bar{y}) \geqq \bar{g}(\bar{x}^i)$ for $i = 1, \ldots, m$; and

(41) $(\exists\, i_o \in \{1, \ldots, m\})$: $\bar{g}(\hat{x}^{i_o}) > \bar{g}(\bar{x}^{i_o})$.

However, since $\bar{p} \cdot \hat{y} \leqq \bar{p} \cdot \bar{y}$, we have from (39) and the definition of $\hat{X}$:

(42) $\bar{p} \cdot \hat{x}^{i_o} = w_{i_o}\ \bar{p} \cdot \hat{y} \leqq \bar{p} \cdot \bar{x}^{i_o}$;

and (41) and (42) together contradict the assumption that $(\bar{X}, \bar{p})$ is a competitive equilibrium for R. We conclude, therefore, that:

$$\bar{p} \cdot \hat{y} \leqq \bar{p} \cdot \bar{y} \Rightarrow \bar{g}(\bar{y}) \geqq \bar{g}(\hat{y}),$$

and our conclusion then follows from Theorem 2.

Q.E.D.

In attempting to evaluate the significance of Theorem 8, particularly part iv.b, we are struck by the fact that while this result states that $\hat{y}$ dominates $\tilde{y}$ locally in the KHS sense, the conclusion of part iv.b seems to be more closely related to the following converse of KHS ordering.[34]

Definition 2: Let R be an m-tuple of preference orderings (of E_n^+). We define the BARONE-HICKS-SAMUELSON ORDERING (abbreviated BHS ordering) INDUCED BY R, $>'_R$, on the power set of E_n^+ by:

$$Y_1 >'_R Y_2 \text{ iff } (X \in 0(Y_1))(\exists \overline{X} \in 0(Y_2)):\quad X\ R\ \overline{X}$$

for $Y_1, Y_2 \in E_n^+$ (and where the notation $X \in 0(Y_h)$ is being used as shorthand for "$X \in 0(E_h)$" with $E_h \equiv (R, Y_h)$ for h = 1, 2). (Cf. Barone [7], Hicks [18], Samuelson [32].)

Since the KHS ordering $>_R$ can be given a definition equivalent to that presented in Section 3 by:

(43) $Y_1 >_R Y_2$ iff $(X \in 0(Y_2))(\exists \overline{X} \in 0(Y_1))$: $\overline{X}RX$; it may appear at first glance that the relations $>_R$ and $>'_R$ are equivalent, for a given R. This is not at all the case in general, however, as the following example shows (although it should be noted that $>'_R$ is reflexive and transitive for all $R \in R_o$).

Example: Let m = 2, n = 3, and define R_1 and R_2 by:

$$x^1\ R_1\ \overline{x}^1 \text{ iff } x_{11} + x_{12} \geqq \overline{x}_{11} + \overline{x}_{12},$$

and

$$x^2\ R_2\ \overline{x}^2 \text{ iff } x_{21} + x_{23} \geqq \overline{x}_{21} + \overline{x}_{23},$$

respectively. Consider the singleton situations Y_1, Y_2 and Y_3 defined by:

$$Y_1 = \{(0, 1, 3)\},\ Y_2 = \{(2, 1, 1)\},\ Y_3 = \{(0, 5/2, 5/2)\},$$

respectively. The reader can easily verify that the following statements hold (see Figure 5):

a) $Y_2 >_R Y_1$, but $Y_2 \not>'_R Y_1$,

b) $Y_3 >'_R Y_2$, but $Y_3 \not>_R Y_2$.

Thus we see that $\hat{Y} >'_R Y$ is neither necessary nor sufficient

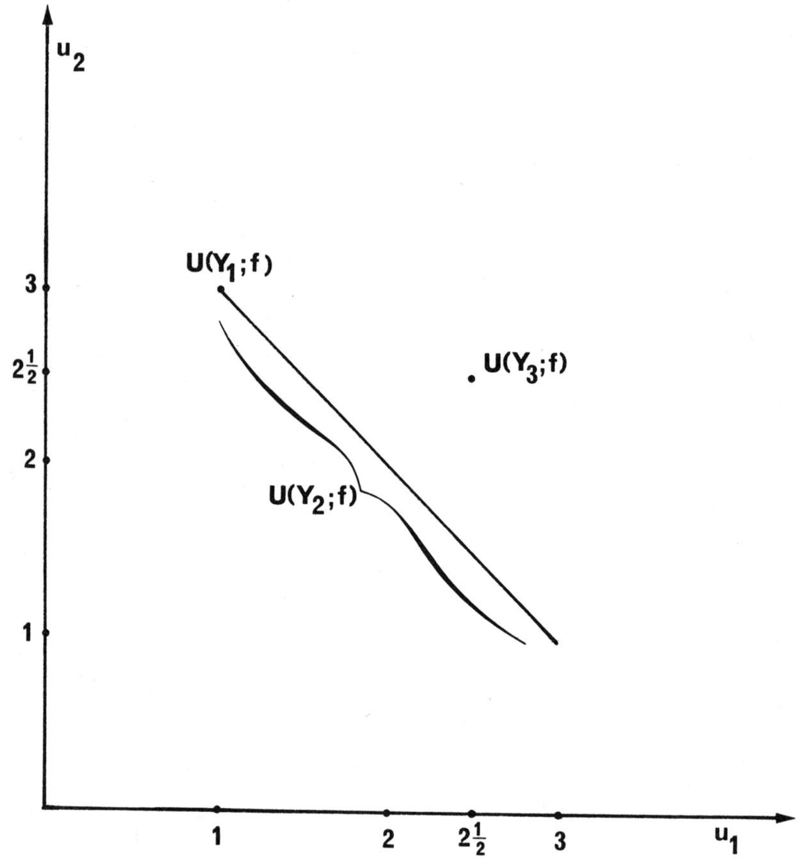

Figure 5

for $\hat{Y} >_R Y$, and conversely. Note, moreover, that the preference orderings used in this example are (individualistic and) monotonic, continuous, convex, and homogeneous.[35]

If the preference orderings are continuous and strictly monotonic the relationship between $>_R$ and $>'_R$ changes drastically, however; a fact which perhaps sheds some light on the significance of Theorem 6.

Theorem 10: Suppose R is an m-tuple of preference orderings, each of which is (individualistic and) continuous and strictly monotonic. Then if $\hat{Y}$ and Y are compact situations, we have

$$\hat{Y} >_R Y \text{ iff } \hat{Y} >'_R Y.$$

Proof:

i) We first note that if either $\hat{Y}$ or Y is the singleton set $\{0\}$, our result is immediate (note that $\hat{Y} = \{0\} \Rightarrow Y = \{0\}$ if either $\hat{Y} >_R Y$ or $\hat{Y} >'_R Y$). Hence we shall suppose throughout the remainder of this proof that both $\hat{Y}$ and Y contain at least one semi-positive vector.

ii) Suppose $\hat{Y} >_R Y$, let $f \in F(R)$ (where F(R) is from Definition 2 of Section 4), and let $\hat{X} \in O(\hat{Y})$. If we define $\hat{a} = \left[\frac{1}{\sum_{i=1}^{m} f^i(\hat{x}^i)}\right] f(\hat{X})$, we have at once from Theorem 6 (i, ii, and v) that there exist $\overline{X} \in O(Y)$, $\overline{\lambda} > 0$ such that:

$$f(\overline{X}) = \overline{\lambda}\hat{a}.$$

However, we must then have $\overline{\lambda} \leqq \sum_{i=1}^{m} f^i(\hat{x}^i)$; for suppose not. If $\overline{\lambda} > \sum_{i=1}^{m} f^i(\hat{x}^i)$, then

$$(44) \quad f(\overline{X}) \geq f(\hat{X}).$$

On the other hand, since $\hat{Y} >_R Y$, we have:

$$(\exists X^* \in A(\hat{Y})): f(X^*) \geqq f(\overline{X});$$

which, together with (44) contradicts the assumption that $\hat{X} \in O(\hat{Y})$. Therefore $\overline{\lambda} \leqq \sum_{i=1}^{m} f^i(\hat{x}^i)$, so that $f(\hat{X}) \geqq f(\overline{X})$, and hence:

$$\overline{X} \in O(Y) \text{ and } \hat{X}R\overline{X}.$$

Therefore, since $\hat{X} \varepsilon O(\hat{Y})$ was arbitrary, we have $\hat{Y} >_R' Y$.

iii) Suppose $\hat{Y} >_R' Y$ and let $\overline{X} \varepsilon O(Y)$. Define

$$\overline{a} = \left[\frac{1}{\sum_{i=1}^{m} f^i(\overline{x}^i)}\right] f(\overline{X}).$$

Again appealing to Theorem 6, we see that there exist $\hat{X} \varepsilon O(\hat{Y})$, $\hat{\lambda} > 0$ such that $f(\hat{X}) = \hat{\lambda}\overline{a}$. Suppose by way of contradiction that $\hat{\lambda} < \sum_{i=1}^{m} f^i(\overline{x}^i)$. Then we would have:

(45) $f(\overline{X}) \geq f(\hat{X})$.

Now, by the fact that $\hat{Y} >_R' Y$,

$(\exists X^* \varepsilon O(Y)): f(\hat{X}) \geqq f(X^*)$;

which together with (45) yields

(46) $f(\overline{X}) \geq f(X^*)$.

However (46) is impossible if $X^* \varepsilon O(Y)$ and $\overline{X} \varepsilon A(Y)$. Hence we conclude that $\hat{\lambda} \geqq \sum_{i=1}^{m} f^i(\overline{x}^i)$, so that $f(\hat{X}) \geqq f(\overline{X})$. Since $\overline{X} \varepsilon O(Y)$ was arbitrary, it follows from (43) that $\hat{Y} >_R Y$.

Q.E.D.

Given an m-tuple of preference orderings R, and a semi-positive vector $y \varepsilon E_n^+$, define

(47) $P(R, y) = \{p \varepsilon S^{n-1} | (\exists X \varepsilon A(\{y\})): (X, p)$ is a competitive equilibrium for R$\}$, (where $S^{n-1} = \{p \varepsilon E_n^+ \mid \sum_{h=1}^{n} p_h = 1\}$).

We then have at once from Theorem 8.iv.a, Theorem 10 and Theorem 9, p. 525, in Arrow [1][36] that if R is an m-tuple of preference orderings, each of which is (individualistic and) strictly monotonic, continuous, and convex; and if:

(48) $(p \varepsilon P(R, \hat{y})): p \cdot \hat{y} \geqq p \cdot \tilde{y}$,

then $\{\hat{y}\} >_R \{\tilde{y}\}$. The informational requirement involved in condition (48) is, of course, quite high; but given only that

$p \cdot \hat{y} \geq p \cdot \tilde{y}$ for a single $p \in P(R, \hat{y})$, we cannot in general conclude that $\{\hat{y}\} >_R \{\tilde{y}\}$ (unless, of course, the corresponding allocation, X, is the only Pareto Optimal allocation of $\hat{y}$[37]). On the other hand, under the more restrictive conditions of Theorem 9, the observation of one price vector $p \in P(R, \hat{y})$ such that $p \cdot \hat{y} \geq p \cdot \tilde{y}$ suffices to conclude $\{\hat{y}\} >_R \{\tilde{y}\}$.[38]

Theorem 9 appears to open up a promising line of investigation. What it states, in effect, is that the observation of a single competitive equilibrium enables one to circumvent the impasse of Theorem 4. Consequently, denoting the set of all m-tuples R satisfying the hypotheses of Theorem 9 by $\mathcal{R}_3$, one is led to speculate that there may exist some subset, $\mathcal{R}_4$, of $\mathcal{R}_o$ such that $\mathcal{R}_3$ is a proper subset of $\mathcal{R}_4$, and such that the following holds.

A) If $R \in \mathcal{R}_4$, if $(\bar{X}, \bar{p})$ and $(\hat{X}, \hat{p})$ are competitive equilibria for R; and if, defining $\bar{y} = \sigma(\bar{X})$ and $\hat{y} = \sigma(\hat{X})$, we have:

(49) $\bar{p} \cdot \hat{y} > \bar{p} \cdot \bar{y}$ and $\hat{p} \cdot \hat{y} > \hat{p} \cdot \bar{y}$,

then $\{\hat{y}\} >_R \{\bar{y}\}$.

There may indeed exist such a subset of $\mathcal{R}_o$ which satisfies (A) for, say, all strictly positive vectors $\bar{y}$ and $\hat{y}$ (satisfying the remaining hypotheses of the conjecture); but the following example, which shows that we cannot simply dispense with the assumption of identical preference orderings in Theorem 9,[39] also demonstrates the fact that the determination of such a subset may be a rather formidable undertaking.

Let $m = n = 2$, $\bar{y} = (9, 4)$, $\hat{y} = (4, 9)$, and R_1 and R_2 be representable by:

$$f^1(x^1) = 3\sqrt{x_{11}} + \sqrt{x_{12}},$$

and

$$f^2(x^2) = \sqrt{x_{21}} + 3\sqrt{x_{22}},$$

respectively. Notice that in this case R_1 and R_2 are (individualistic and) strictly monotonic, continuous, strictly convex, and homogeneous.[40]

Let the price vectors $\bar{p} = \hat{p} = (3, 4)$ be given. We note that at these prices, the consumption paths of the two individuals are given by

$$x_{12} = (\tfrac{1}{16})\, x_{11}, \quad x_{22} = (\tfrac{81}{16})\, x_{21},$$

respectively; which when solved in conjunction with

$$x_{11} + x_{21} = \bar{y}_1 = 9 \qquad x_{11} + x_{21} = \hat{y}_1 = 4$$

$$x_{12} + x_{22} = \bar{y}_2 = 4 \qquad x_{12} + x_{22} = \hat{y}_2 = 9,$$

yield the competitive allocations (see Figure 6):

$$\bar{X} = \begin{bmatrix} \frac{133}{16} & \frac{133}{256} \\ \frac{11}{16} & \frac{891}{256} \end{bmatrix},$$

and

$$\hat{X} = \begin{bmatrix} \frac{9}{4} & \frac{9}{64} \\ \frac{7}{4} & \frac{567}{64} \end{bmatrix}.$$

Clearly $\bar{p} \cdot \hat{y} = \hat{p} \cdot \hat{y} = 48 > \bar{p} \cdot \bar{y} = \hat{p} \cdot \bar{y} = 43$, so that (43) is satisfied in this case; but we see that:

$$f^1(\bar{x}^1) = 3\sqrt{\frac{133}{16}} + \sqrt{\frac{133}{256}} = (\frac{13}{16}) \sqrt{133} \approx 9.37 > f^1(\hat{y}) = 9.$$

Hence, we not only have $\hat{y} \not{P}_R \bar{y}$ in this case, but we also note that it is impossible for the second individual (the gainer in the change from $\bar{X}$ to $\hat{X}$) to compensate the first individual for his loss (in moving from $\bar{X}$ to $\hat{X}$). (Once again we refer the reader to Figure 6).

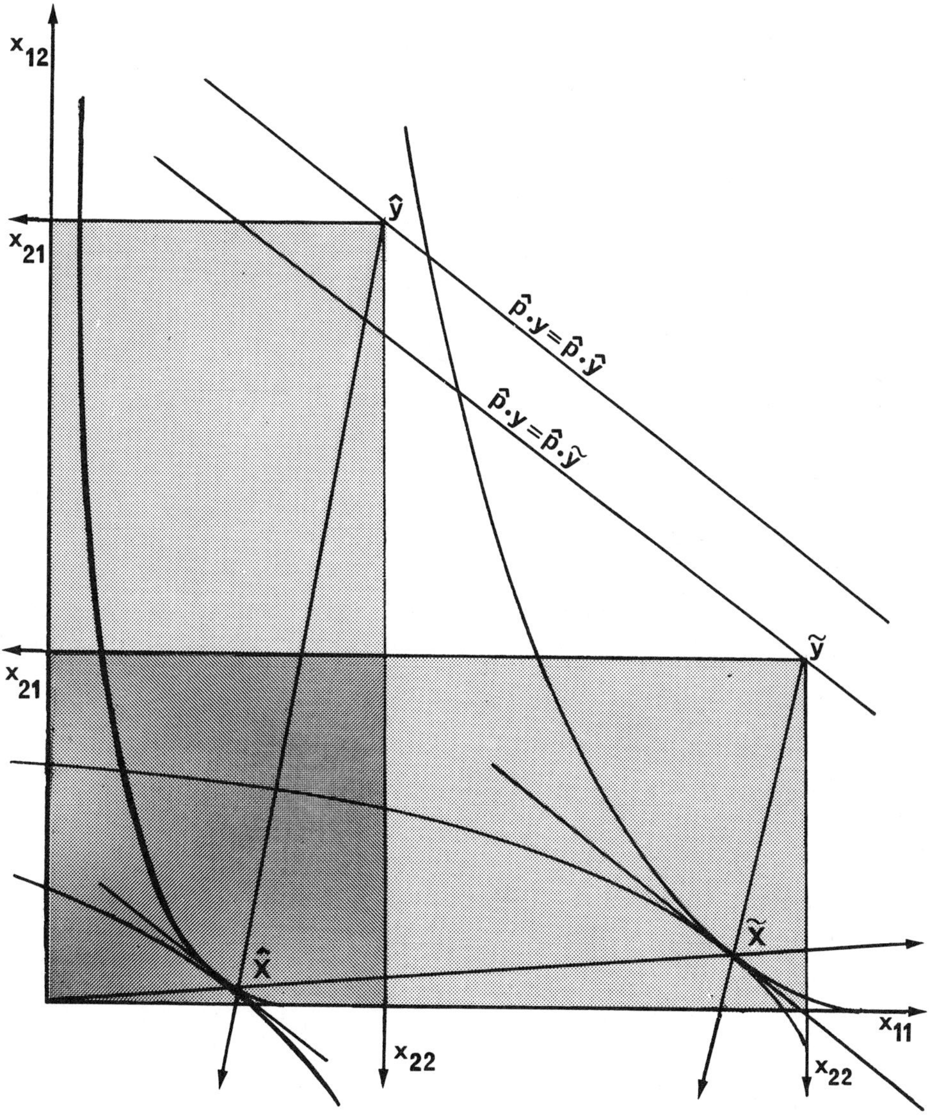
x_{12}
x_{21}
$\hat{y}$
$\hat{p}\cdot y = \hat{p}\cdot\hat{y}$
$\hat{p}\cdot y = \hat{p}\cdot\tilde{y}$
$\tilde{y}$
x_{21}
$\hat{x}$
$\tilde{x}$
x_{11}
x_{22}
x_{22}

Figure 6

APPENDIX 1.

Our concern in this appendix is to show the sense in which the analysis of the text applies to a closed production economy.[41] Consider an economy in which there are m consumers, q commodities, and ℓ producers. Let

> $\mathcal{X}_i \subset E_q$ denote the ith consumer's consumption set for $i = 1, \ldots, m$;
>
> $\mathcal{Y}_h \subset E_q$ denote the hth producer's production set for $h = 1, \ldots, \ell$;

and

> $\omega \in E_q$ represent the economy's aggregate resource endowment.

Defining

$$\mathcal{J} = \prod_{i=1}^{m} \mathcal{X}_i, \quad \mathcal{X} = \sum_{i=1}^{m} \mathcal{X}_i, \mathcal{Y} = \sum_{h=1}^{\ell} \mathcal{Y}_h;$$

we shall suppose that each consumer has a preference ordering, R_i, which is a complete preordering of $\mathcal{J}$. Using the general type of notation followed in the text, we can denote the economy in shorthand notation by:

$$\text{(1)} \qquad \mathcal{E} = ((\mathcal{X}_i, R_i), (\mathcal{Y}_h), \omega);$$

where $(\mathcal{X}_i, R_i)$ denotes the 2m-tuple $(\mathcal{X}_1, R_1; \mathcal{X}_2, R_2; \ldots; \mathcal{X}_m, R_m)$, and $(\mathcal{Y}_h)$ denotes the n-tuple $(\mathcal{Y}_1, \mathcal{Y}_2, \ldots, \mathcal{Y}_n)$ (see Debreu [13], p. 75).

The attainable set for $\mathcal{E}$ is then given by (see Debreu [13], p. 76):

$$\text{(2)} \qquad A(\mathcal{E}) = \{((x^i), (y^h)) \in E_{(m+\ell)q} \mid x^i \in \mathcal{X}_i \text{ for } i = 1, \ldots, m; \; y^h \in \mathcal{Y}_h \text{ for } h = 1, \ldots, q; \; \sum_{i=1}^{m} x^i = \omega + \sum_{h=1}^{q} y^h\}.$$

Suppose there exists an integer n, $1 \leqq n \leqq q$, such that defining $r = q - n$, and denoting the origin in E_r by 0_r, we have:

$$\text{(3)} \qquad (i \in \{1, \ldots, m\})(\exists\, \xi^i \in E_n): \; \mathcal{X}_i = (\xi^i, 0_r) + (E_n^+ \times \{0_r\})$$

This assumption undoubtedly deserves a few words of explanation.

If we write (3) in the form $\mathcal{X}_i = \xi^i + E^+_q$, the assumption would probably be clear enough. In this alternative form, the assumption indicates that each consumer has some minimal quantities of some commodities which he must consume in order to survive, and maximal quantities of other commodities which he can supply; and, moreover, that he can supply the maximal quantities (e.g., of labor) while simultaneously consuming the minimal amounts of the commodities necessary for his survival. Clearly this assumption does not make too much sense unless each consumer supplies only one type of labor, but perhaps the state employment offices would tell us that this isn't too unreasonable an assumption, at least for the short run.

The situation when r is positive (≥ 1) is essentially similar, except here we are allowing for r "intermediate goods" which consumers do not consume. One could argue that this sort of thing is really a property of the preference orderings. However, the existence of an integer n such that $1 \leq n < q$ and (supposing preferences to be individualistic for the moment):

$$(x^i_{(1)}, x^i_{(2)}) \; R_j (\bar{x}^i_{(1)}, \bar{x}^i_{(2)})$$

(where we write $x^i = (x^i_{(1)} \; x^i_{(2)})$ with $x^i_{(1)} \varepsilon \, E^+_n$ and $x^i_{(2)} \varepsilon \, E^+_{q-n}$ for each $x^i \varepsilon \, E^+_q$) implies

$$((\hat{x}^i_{(2)}, \tilde{x}^i_{(2)}) \varepsilon \, E_{q-n}): \; (x^i_{(1)}, \hat{x}^i_{(2)}) \; R_i (\bar{x}^i_{(1)}, \tilde{x}^i_{(2)}),$$

implicitly assumes a kind of free disposability if (2) is used as our definition of the attainable set for $\mathcal{E}$. More importantly:

1.) using the convention that, if n = q, we take (3) to mean:

$$(\exists \; \xi^i \varepsilon \, E_q): \; \mathcal{X}_i = \xi^i + E^+_q,$$

the situation in which there are no such intermediate goods becomes a special case of (3).

2.) assumptions such as monotonicity make more sense and are easier to formulate and deal with, given assumption (3).

Given (3) we shall denote points in $\mathcal{Z}$ by

$$Z = [X, 0],$$

where 0 denotes the m x r null matrix.

Define

$\xi = [\xi_{ij}]$ (where we write $\xi^i = (\xi_{i1}, \ldots, \xi_{in})$ for $i = 1, \ldots, m$);

$\overline{R}_i$ on E^+_{mn} by $X\overline{R}_i \overline{X}$ iff $[X + \xi, 0]R_i[\overline{X} + \xi, 0]$ for $X, \overline{X} \in E^+_{mn}$, $i = 1, \ldots, m$;

$$\hat{Y} = \{y \in E_q \mid (\exists((x^i), (y^h)) \in A(\mathcal{E})): \sum_{h=1}^{\ell} y^h = y\}.$$

We note first that if $y \in \hat{Y}$,

$$(\exists[X, 0] \in Z): \quad (\sum_{i=1}^{m} x^i, 0_r) = \omega + y.$$

Hence it is clear that $\omega + \hat{Y}$ is of the form

$$\omega + \hat{Y} = Y' \times \{0_r\} \text{ for some } Y' \subset E_n;$$

and moreover, defining

$$Y = Y' - \sum_{i=1}^{m} \xi^i,$$

we have $Y \subset E^+_n$. Consequently the economy

$$E(\mathcal{E}) = (\overline{R}, Y)$$

is of the form analyzed in the text. Moreover, given that the Compensation Principle depends only on consumer's preferences (and not, e.g., on the distribution of production), any conclusions to be made with the use of the Compensation Principle regarding an economy $\mathcal{E}$ of the form (1) and satisfying (3) will depend only on $E(\mathcal{E})$, as defined above. Hence the analysis of the text can be taken to apply to economies of the form (1) as long as condition (3) is satisfied.

APPENDIX 2.

The purpose of this appendix is to prove Theorem 3, stated in Section III of the text.

We first state the following result, which is due to Yokoyama (see [38], pp. 40-42).[42] In our remaining discussion we shall dispense with superscripts and subscripts, and write simply R, f, etc., in place of R_i, f^i, respectively.

THEOREM (YOKOYAMA): Given that a preference ordering R is monotonic, it is continuous if and only if it satisfies:

(1) Given that $X, \overline{X}, \hat{X} \in E^+_{mn}$ are such that $XR\overline{X}$ and $\overline{X}R\hat{X}$, $(\exists\ \overline{\lambda} \in [0, 1])$: $[\lambda X + (1 - \lambda)\hat{X}]I\overline{X}$.

We now state and prove a result due to Wold (see Wold [37], pp. 223-26).[43]

THEOREM (WOLD): If R is a preference ordering which is monotonic and continuous, there exists a real-valued function $\overline{f}$ defined on E^+_{mn} and satisfying:

i.) $\overline{f}$ represents R on E^+_{mn}, that is:

$(X, \overline{X} \in E^+_{mn})$: $\overline{f}(X) \geqq \overline{f}(\overline{X})$ iff $XR\overline{X}$,

ii.) $\overline{f}$ is continuous on E^+_{mn}.

PROOF: For purposes of this and the following proof, define $q = mn$, and denote points in E_q by $x = (x_h)(h = 1, \ldots, q)$. Define the vector $e \in E_q$ by:

$$e = ((1/q)^{\frac{1}{2}}, (1/q)^{\frac{1}{2}}, \ldots, (1/q)^{\frac{1}{2}}),$$

and the set $L \subset E^+_q$ by:

$$L = \{x \in E_q \mid (\exists \lambda \geqq 0): x = \lambda e\}.$$

Denoting the norm of x by $||x||$ for $x \in E_q$, i.e.,

$$||x|| = (\sum_{h=1}^{q} (x_h)^2)^{\frac{1}{2}};$$

we note that:

(2) $$||e|| = 1$$

and if $x = \lambda e \in L$, we have:

(3) $$||x|| = ||\lambda e|| = \lambda||e|| = \lambda.$$

We now define the function π, where π: $E^+_q \rightarrow L$, as follows. Let $x \in E^+_q$. Then there exists $\overline{x} \in L$ such that $\overline{x} > x$, and hence by monotonicity $\bar{x}Px$. Moreover, since $x \geqq 0$, we have $x R 0$. Hence by (1):

(4) $(\exists \hat{x} \in L)$: $\hat{x}Ix$,

and it follows immediately from the definition of L and the transitivity and monotonicity of R that $\hat{x}$ is unique. We define

$$\hat{x} = \pi(x),$$

where $\hat{x}$ is from (4).

We now define the function $\bar{f}$ on E_q^+ by:

(5) $\bar{f}(x) = ||\pi(x)||$.

We note that, since $\pi(x)$ is of the form $\pi(x) = \bar{\lambda}e$, with $\bar{\lambda} \geqq 0$,

(6) $\bar{f}(x) = ||\pi(x)|| = ||\bar{\lambda}e|| = \bar{\lambda}$;

and therefore:

(7) $\pi(x) = \bar{f}(x)e$.

We wish now to show that $\bar{f}$ represents the preference ordering R. Suppose first that $xR\bar{x}$. Then since $\pi(x)Ix$ and $\pi(\bar{x})I\bar{x}$ we have by the transitivity and weak monotonicity of R and (7):

$$\bar{f}(x) \geqq \bar{f}(\bar{x})$$

(note that otherwise $\pi(\bar{x}) > \pi(x)$, by (7)). On the other hand, if $\bar{f}(x) \geqq \bar{f}(\bar{x})$, then by (7):

$$\pi(x) \geqq \pi(\bar{x})$$

and therefore $\pi(x)R\pi(\bar{x})$; which by transitivity implies $xR\bar{x}$.

To show that $\bar{f}$ is continuous on E_q^+, let α be a real number, and consider the sets:

(8) $\bar{f}^{-1}(]-\infty, \alpha])$, $\bar{f}^{-1}([\alpha, +\infty[)$.

If $\alpha < 0$, the set on the left in (8) is empty, while the set on the right is E_q^+; both of which are closed sets. If $\alpha \geqq 0$, define $x = \alpha e$. Then by (6), $\bar{f}(x) = \alpha$, and therefore

$$\bar{f}^{-1}(]-\infty, \alpha]) = xR, \ \bar{f}^{-1}([\alpha, +\infty[) = Rx;$$

which by the continuity of R are both closed sets. Hence $\overline{f}$ is continuous on E_q^+.

Q.E.D.

We shall refer to the utility function constructed in the previous proof as the "Wold function." For convenience we now provide a re-statement, as well as a proof, of Theorem 2.

THEOREM 2: Let R be a preference ordering of E_q^+ which is monotonic, continuous, weakly convex, and homogeneous. Then there exists a continuous real valued utility function $\overline{f}$ representing R on E_q^+, and satisfying:

i.) $\overline{f}$: $E_q^+ \rightarrow E_1^+$, $\overline{f}(0) = 0$,

ii.) $\overline{f}$ is positively homogeneous of degree one on E_q^+,

iii.) $\overline{f}$ is concave on E_q^+.

PROOF: Taking $\overline{f}$ to be the Wold function, we have by Wold's theorem that $\overline{f}$ is continuous and represents R on E_q^+. Moreover, (i) follows immediately from (6) and (7).

ii.) Let $x \in E_q^+$ and $\lambda \in E_1^+$. Then since $xI\pi(x)$, we have by homogeneity:

$$[\lambda x]I[\lambda\ \pi\ (x)];$$

and hence

$$\pi(\lambda x) = \lambda\pi(x).$$

However, by (7), $\pi(x) = \overline{f}(x)e$, and therefore

$$\lambda\pi(x) = \lambda\overline{f}(x)e.$$

Consequently

$$\overline{f}(\lambda x) = ||\pi(\lambda x)|| = ||\lambda\pi(x)|| = ||\lambda\overline{f}(x)e|| = \lambda\overline{f}(x);$$

and we see that $\overline{f}$ is positively homogeneous of degree one on E_q^+.

iii.) Define

$$\overset{o}{E}{}_q^+ = \{x \in E_q^+ |\ x > 0\}.$$

Then by the monotonicity of R, we have $(x \in \overset{o}{E}{}_q^+)$: $x\ P\ 0$;

and therefore by (i):

(9) $(x \in \overset{o}{E}{}^{+}_{q})$: $\bar{f}(x) > 0$

Noting that the weak convexity of R implies that $\bar{f}$ is quasi-concave, we see that from (9) and Theorem 3, p. 208, of Berge [9] it follows that $\bar{f}$ is concave on E^{+}_{q}.

Q.E.D.

APPENDIX 3.

In this appendix we shall prove the assertions made regarding the function g(y) in the proof of Theorem 4 (Section III). We shall need to begin with some preliminary considerations.

DEFINITIONS: Let $f:D \to E_1$, where $D \subset E_n$. Then we shall say that:

1.) f if NON-DECREASING on D if whenever x, y ε D and $x \geqq y$, we have $f(x) \geqq f(y)$.

2.) f is INCREASING on D if f is non-decreasing on D and whenever x, y ε D and $x > y$, we have $f(x) > f(y)$.

3.) f is STRICTLY INCREASING on D if whenever x, y ε D and $x \geq y$, we have $f(x) > f(y)$.

DEFINITIONS: Let $f:D \to E_n$, where $D \subset E_m$ is convex. Then we shall say that:

4.) g is SEMI-STRICTLY CONCAVE on D if whenever x, y ε D and $x \neq y$, we have:

$$(\lambda \in]0, 1[): g[\lambda x + (1-\lambda)y] \geq \lambda g(x) + (1-\lambda)g(y).$$

5.) g is STRICTLY CONCAVE on D if whenever x, y ε D and $x \neq y$, we have:

$$(\lambda \in]0, 1[): g[\lambda x + (1-\lambda)y] > \lambda g(x) + (1-\lambda)g(y).$$ [44]

The following result is a rather trivial extension of a theorem in Berge [9].[45]

LEMMA A.1. Suppose:

1.) $f:C \to E_1$, where $C \subset E_m$ is convex,

2.) f is non-decreasing and quasi-concave on C,

3.) $g:D \to E_m$, where $D \subset E_n$ is convex,

4.) g is concave on D,

5.) $g(D) \subset C$.

Then the function ϕ defined on D by

$$\phi(x) = f[g(x)]$$

is quasi-concave on D. Moreover, if we have either:

i.) f is increasing on C and g is strictly concave on D, or

ii.) f is strictly increasing on C and g is semi-strictly concave on D;

then ϕ is strictly quasi-concave on D.

PROOF: We shall prove the special result (i) only, since the other proofs are similar and quite easy.

Suppose $\phi(x) \geqq \phi(y)$, $x \neq y$, and that $\lambda \in]0, 1[$. Then we have

$$g[\lambda x + (1-\lambda)y] > \lambda g(x) + (1-\lambda)g(y),$$

since g is strictly concave. Therefore, since f is increasing and quasi-concave on C, we have respectively:

$$\phi[\lambda x + (1-\lambda)y] = f(g[\lambda x + (1-\lambda)y]) > f[\lambda g(x) + (1-\lambda)g(y)]$$

$$\geqq \text{Min}\{f[g(x)], g[g(y)]\} = \text{Min}\{\phi(x), \phi(y)\} = \phi(y).$$

Q.E.D.

LEMMA A.2: Suppose:

1.) $f:D \to E_1$, $g:D \to E_1$, where $D \subset E_n$ is convex;

2.) f is concave and strictly quasi-concave on D,

3.) g is concave on D,

4.) f and g satisfy the following condition:

$\bar{x}, \bar{y} \in D$, $\bar{x} \neq \bar{y}$ and

$$(\lambda \in]0, 1[): \quad f[\lambda\bar{x} + (1-\lambda)\bar{y}] = \lambda f(x) + (1-\lambda)f(\bar{y})$$

$$\text{and} \quad g[\lambda\bar{x} + (1-\lambda)\bar{y}] = \lambda g(\bar{x}) + (1-\lambda)g(\bar{y})$$

together imply:

$$\text{either } g(\bar{x}) = g(\bar{y}) \text{ or } f(\bar{x}) - f(\bar{y}) \neq g(\bar{y}) - g(\bar{x}).$$

Then the function h defined on D by

$$h(x) = f(x) + g(x)$$

is concave and strictly quasi-concave on D.

PROOF: It is well known that h is concave on D. Hence it suffices to prove that if $x, y \in D, x \neq y$, and $h(x) \geqq h(y)$, then:

$$(\lambda \in]0, 1[): h[\lambda x + (1-\lambda)y] > h(y).$$

We distinguish three cases:

i.) $h(x) > h(y)$. Then by the concavity of h, if $\lambda \in]0, 1[$, we have:

$$h[\lambda x + (1-\lambda)y] \geqq \lambda h(x) + (1-\lambda)h(y) > \lambda h(y) + (1-\lambda)h(y) = h(y)$$

ii.) $h(x) = h(y)$ and $f(x) = f(y)$. Then by the strict quasi-concavity of f and the concavity of g, if $\lambda \in]0, 1[$, we have:

$$h[\lambda x + (1-\lambda)y] = f[\lambda x + (1-\lambda)y] + g[\lambda x + (1-\lambda)y]$$
$$> f(y) + \lambda g(x) + (1-\lambda)g(y) = f(y) + g(y) = h(y).$$

iii.) $h(x) = h(y)$ and $f(x) \neq f(y)$. Here we have

$$f(x) - f(y) = g(y) - g(x) \neq 0.$$

Hence by hypothesis 4, either:

(1) $$(\exists \bar{\lambda} \in]0, 1[): f[\bar{\lambda}x + (1-\bar{\lambda})y] > \bar{\lambda} f(x) + (1-\bar{\lambda}) f(y),$$

or

(2) $$(\exists \hat{\lambda} \in]0, 1[): g[\hat{\lambda}x + (1-\hat{\lambda})y] > \hat{\lambda} g(x) + (1-\hat{\lambda}) g(y).$$

We then see that if either (1) or (2) holds, we can use the concavity of f and g to assert:

(3) $$\begin{aligned}(\exists \tilde{\lambda} \in]0, 1[): & h[\tilde{\lambda}x + (1-\tilde{\lambda})y] \\ & > \tilde{\lambda} f(x) + (1-\tilde{\lambda}) f(y) + \tilde{\lambda} g(x) + (1-\tilde{\lambda}) g(y) \\ & = \tilde{\lambda} [f(x) + g(x)] + (1-\tilde{\lambda}) [f(y) + g(y)] \\ & = \tilde{\lambda} h(x) + (1-\tilde{\lambda}) h(y) = h(x) = h(y).\end{aligned}$$

Define

$$z = \tilde{\lambda}x + (1-\tilde{\lambda})y.$$

Then from (3) we have:

$$h(z) > h(x) \text{ and } h(z) > h(y).$$

Hence from case (i), we have:

(4) $(\lambda \, \varepsilon \,]\,0, 1\,[): \; h[\lambda x + (1-\lambda)z] > h(x) = h(y),$

(5) $(\lambda \, \varepsilon \,]\,0, 1\,[): \; h[\lambda y + (1-\lambda)z] > h(y).$

However, (3), (4), (5), and our definition of z together imply:

$$(\lambda \, \varepsilon \,]\,0, 1\,[): \; h[\lambda x + (1-\lambda)y] > h(y).$$

Q.E.D.

THEOREM A.1: Suppose:

1.) $f^i: D \to E_1$ for $i = 1, \ldots, m$; where $D \subset E_n^+$ is convex;

2.) f^i is concave on D for $i = 1, \ldots, m$,

3.) $(\exists \, i_o \, \varepsilon \{1, \ldots, m\})$: f^{i_o} satisfies the following condition:

if x, y ε D and

$$(\lambda \, \varepsilon \, [0, 1]): \; f^{i_o}[\lambda x + (1-\lambda)y] = \lambda f(x) + (1-\lambda)y,$$

then

$$(\exists \, \mu \geqq 0): \; y = \mu x \text{ or } x = \mu y.$$

4.) $(\exists \, i_1 \, \varepsilon \{1, \ldots, m\})$: f^{i_1} is strictly quasi-concave on D,

5.) for each i $(i = 1, \ldots, m)$, either:

a.) f^i is nonnegative and homogeneous of degree $r_i \geqq 0$ on D, or

b.) f^i is non-decreasing on D.

The $f(x) \equiv \sum_{i=1}^{m} f^i(x)$ is concave and strictly quasi-concave on D.

PROOF: Define $M = \{1, \ldots, m\}$, and

$$I = \{i \, \varepsilon \, M | \; f^i \text{ is non-decreasing on } D\}, \; J = M \backslash I.$$

i.) We first note that if x, y ε D are such that $x \neq y$ and:

(6) $(\lambda \, \varepsilon \, [0, 1]): \; f^{i_o}[\lambda x + (1-\lambda)y] =$
$\lambda f^{i_o}(x) + (1-\lambda) f^{i_o}(y),$

then by hypothesis 3, we may assume, without loss of generality:

(7) $(\exists \, \mu \geqq 0): \; y = \mu x.$

We distinguish two cases.

a.) $0 \leqq \mu \leqq 1$. Then by (7) we have $x \geqq y$. Hence

(8) $$(i \in I): \; f^i(x) \geqq f^i(y),$$

while:

(9) $$(j \in J): \; f^j(x) - f^j(y) = (1 - \mu^{r_j})f^j(x) \geqq 0.$$

b.) $\mu > 1$. In this case we have by (7), $y \geqq x$, and hence:

(10) $$(i \in I): \; f^i(x) \leqq f^i(y),$$

and

(11) $$(j \in J): \; f^j(x) - f^j(y) = (1 - \mu^{r_j})f^j(x) \leqq 0.$$

Comparing (8) and (9) and (10) and (11), we see that if (6) holds, then:

(12) $$[f^i(x) - f^i(y)][f^j(x) - f^j(y)] \geqq 0 \text{ for } i, j = 1, \ldots, m.$$

ii.) Define $K = M \setminus \{i_1\}$, and $f^K(x) = \sum_{I \in K} f^i(x)$. Clearly $f^K(x)$ is concave on D, $f^{i_1}(x)$ is concave and strictly quasi-concave on D and $f(x) = f^K(x) + f^{i_1}(x)$.

Suppose now that $x, y \in D$ are such that $x \neq y$ and:

$$(\lambda \in [0, 1]): \; f^K[\lambda x + (1-\lambda)y] = \lambda f^K(x) + (1-\lambda)f^K(y),$$

$$\text{and } f^{i_1}[\lambda x + (1-\lambda)y] = \lambda f^{i_1}(x) + (1-\lambda)f^{i_1}(y).$$

Then since each f^i is concave, it follows that:

$$(\lambda \in [0, 1]): \; f^{i_o}[\lambda x + (1-\lambda)y] = \lambda f^{i_o}(x) + (1-\lambda) f^{i_o}(y),$$

i.e., that (6) holds. But then by (12):

$$[f^K(x) - f^K(y)][f^{i_1}(x) - f^{i_1}(y)] \geqq 0.$$

We conclude, therefore, that f^{i_1} and f^K satisfy the hypotheses of Lemma 2; and hence by Lemma 2, f(x) is concave and strictly quasi-concave on D.

Q.E.D.

Define the function Ψ on E_n^+ as in the proof of Theorem 4 of the text; that is:

(13) $$\Psi(x) = [\sum_{j=1}^{n} (x_j)^{\frac{1}{2}}]^2 .$$

We then have the following.

LEMMA A.3: The function $\Psi(x)$ defined in (13) is:

i.) continuous,
ii.) positively homogeneous of degree one,
iii.) strictly increasing,
iv.) strictly quasi-concave, and
v.) concave

on E_n^+. Moreover,

vi.) $x, \bar{x} \in E_n^+$ are such that

$$(\lambda \in [0, 1]): \Psi[\lambda x + (1-\lambda)\bar{x}] = \lambda\Psi(x) + (1-\lambda)\Psi(\bar{x}),$$

if and only if

$$(\exists\mu \geqq 0): \text{ either } x = \mu\bar{x} \text{ or } \bar{x} = \mu x.$$

PROOF: Properties (i) - (iii) are obvious.

iv.) This property is probably "well-known", since Ψ is a special case of a C.E.S. production function. We can, however, provide a direct proof, as follows.

The functions $g^j(x_j) = (x_j)^{\frac{1}{2}}$ are strictly concave for $j = 1, \ldots, n$. Hence the function $g(x) \equiv \sum_{j=1}^{n} g^j(x_j)$ is strictly concave on E_n^+. Moreover, the function $f(y)$ defined on E_1^+ by $f(y) = y^2$ is strictly increasing and, because of this, is strictly quasi-concave on E_1^+. Hence it follows from Lemma 1 that $\Psi(x) = f[g(x)]$ is strictly quasi-concave on E_n^+.

v.) Since Ψ is strictly increasing on E_n^+, we have:

$$(x \in E_n^+ \setminus \{0\}): \quad \Psi(x) > \Psi(0) = 0.$$

From properties (ii) and (iv), we then have by Theorem 3, p. 208, and the Remark on p. 213 of Berge [9], Ψ is concave on E_n^+.[46]

vi.a.) Suppose $x, \bar{x} \in E_n^+$ are such that $\bar{x} = \mu x$ for some $\mu \geqq 0$. Then we have: $(\lambda \in [0, 1])$: $\Psi[\lambda x + (1-\lambda)\bar{x}] =$

$$\left(\sum_{j=1}^{n} [\lambda x_j + (1-\lambda)\bar{x}_j]^{\frac{1}{2}}\right)^2 = \left(\sum_{j=1}^{n} [\lambda x_j + (1-\lambda)\mu x_j]^{\frac{1}{2}}\right)^2 =$$

$$\{[\lambda + (1-\lambda)\mu]^{\frac{1}{2}} \times [\sum_{j=1}^{n} (x_j)^{\frac{1}{2}}]\}^2 = \lambda[\sum_{j=1}^{n} (x_j)^{\frac{1}{2}}]^2$$

$$+ (1-\lambda)[\sum_{j=1}^{n} (\mu x_j)^{\frac{1}{2}}]^2 = \lambda\Psi(x) + (1-\lambda)\Psi(\bar{x}).$$

b.) Suppose $x, \bar{x} \in D$ are such that:

$(\lambda \in [0, 1])$: $\Psi[\lambda x + (1-\lambda)\bar{x}] = \lambda\Psi(x) + (1-\lambda)\Psi(\bar{x})$.

Then, in particular, we must have:

$$\tfrac{1}{2}\Psi(x + \bar{x}) = \Psi[\tfrac{1}{2}(x + \bar{x})]$$
$$= \Psi[\tfrac{1}{2}x + \tfrac{1}{2}\bar{x}] = \tfrac{1}{2}\Psi(x) + \tfrac{1}{2}\Psi(\bar{x})$$

where the second equality is by (ii); which implies:

$$\left(\sum_{j=1}^{n} (x_j + \bar{x}_j)^{\frac{1}{2}}\right]^2 = \left[\sum_{j=1}^{n} (x_j)^{\frac{1}{2}}\right]^2 + \left[\sum_{j=1}^{n} (\bar{x}_j)^{\frac{1}{2}}\right]^2.$$

It then follows from Theorem 24, p. 30, of [16], that

$$(\mu \geqq 0): \quad x = \mu\bar{x} \text{ or } \bar{x} = \mu x.$$

Q.E.D.

Let $y \in E_n^+ \setminus \{0\}$, and define the set $J(y)$ and the function $\mu_y(x)$ by:

(14) $$J(y) = \{j \in \{1, \ldots, n\} \mid y_j > 0\},$$

and

(15) $$\mu_y(x) = \underset{j \in J(y)}{\text{Min}} \left\{\frac{x_j}{y_j}\right\} \quad \text{for } x \in E_n^+.$$

Then we have the following.

<u>LEMMA A.4</u>: For each $y \in E_n^+ \setminus \{0\}$, the function $\mu_y(x)$ defined in (15) above, is:

i.) nonnegative,
ii.) increasing,
iii.) positively homogeneous of degree one,
iv.) continuous, and
v.) concave

on E_n^+.

PROOF: Properties (i) - (iii) are obvious.

iv.) Let $\bar{x} \varepsilon E_n^+$, and define:

$U_j(\bar{x}) = \{x \varepsilon E_n^+ | x_j \geqq \mu_y(\bar{x}) \cdot y_j\}$, and

$L_j(\bar{x}) = \{x \varepsilon E_n^+ | x_j \leqq \mu_y(\bar{x}) \cdot y_j\}$, for each $j \varepsilon J(y)$.

Then we note that each $L_j(\bar{x})$ and $U_j(\bar{x})$(being in each case a lower half-space) is closed. Therefore:

$$\mu_y^{-1} ([\mu_y(x), +\infty [) = \{x \varepsilon E_n^+ | \mu_y(x) \geqq \mu_y(\bar{x})\}$$

$$= \bigcap_{j \varepsilon J(y)} U_j(\bar{x}),$$

and

$$\mu_y^{-1} (] -\infty, \mu_y(\bar{x})] = \bigcup_{j \varepsilon J(y)} L_j(\bar{x}),$$

are both closed sets. Hence $\mu_y(x)$ is continuous on E_n^+.

v.) Suppose $x, \bar{x} \varepsilon E_n^+$ and $\lambda \varepsilon [0, 1]$. Then we have:

$$\frac{\lambda x_j + (1-\lambda)\bar{x}_j}{y_j} = \lambda(\frac{x_j}{y_j}) + (1-\lambda)(\frac{\bar{x}_j}{y_j})$$

$$\geqq \underset{j \varepsilon J(y)}{\text{Min}} (\frac{x_j}{y_j}) + (1-\lambda) \underset{j \varepsilon J(y)}{\text{Min}} (\frac{\bar{x}_j}{y_j}) \text{ for each } j \varepsilon J(y).$$

Hence

$$\mu_y[\lambda x + (1-\lambda)\bar{x}] = \underset{j \varepsilon J(y)}{\text{Min}} \left(\frac{[\lambda x_j + (1-\lambda)\bar{x}_j]}{y_j}\right)$$

$$\geqq \lambda \mu_y(x) + (1-\lambda)\mu_y(\bar{x});$$

and we see that $\mu_y(x)$ is concave on E_n^+.

Q.E.D.

Suppose now that $y \in E_n^+ \setminus \{0\}$ and $\alpha \in E_1^+ \setminus \{0\}$. We then define the function $g(x)$ on E_n^+ by

(16) $$g(x) = \Psi(x) + \alpha\, \mu_y(x),$$

where Ψ is defined in (13) and $\mu_y(x)$ is defined in (15), above. We then have the following.

LEMMA A.5: If $y \in E_n^+ \setminus \{0\}$ and $\alpha \in E_1^+ \setminus \{0\}$, the function $g(x)$ in (16), above, is:

i.) nonnegative,
ii.) continuous,
iii.) positively homogeneous of degree one,
iv.) strictly increasing,
v.) concave, and
vi.) strictly quasi-concave

on E_n^+.

PROOF: This result is an immediate application of Lemmas A.3 and A.4 and Theorem A.1.

Q.E.D.

APPENDIX 4.

Insofar as we know, the following theorem is new: albeit not very startling. It appears, however, that it could occasionally be useful in dealing with problems in economic theory.

THEOREM A.2: If X and Y are topological spaces, and

1.) $\Gamma: X \to 2^Y$,
2.) X is connected,
3.) Γ is u.s.c. on X and satisfies:
$(x \in X)$: Γx is connected (and non-empty), then

$$\Gamma(X) \equiv \bigcup_{x \in X} \Gamma x \quad \text{is a connected subset of } Y.$$

PROOF: Suppose $Z \equiv \Gamma(X)$ is separated (i.e., not connected). Then there exist open (in the relative topology for Z) sets U and V such that:

$$U, V \neq \emptyset;\; U \cap V = \emptyset,\; U \cup V = Z.$$

But we then note that for every $x \in X$ we must have either:

$$\Gamma x \subset U \text{ or } \Gamma x \subset V;$$

since otherwise $U \cap \Gamma x$ and $V \cap \Gamma x$ give a separation of Γx, contradicting the assumption that each such set is connected. It then follows that the sets:

$$\Gamma^{+}U \equiv \{x \varepsilon X \mid \Gamma x \subset U\},$$

and

$$\Gamma^{+}V \equiv \{x \varepsilon X \mid \Gamma x \subset V\}$$

are such that:

$$\Gamma^{+}U,\ \Gamma^{+}V \neq \emptyset \text{ (since } U,\ V \neq \emptyset),$$

(1) $$(\Gamma^{+}U) \cup (\Gamma^{+}V) = X,$$

$$(\Gamma^{+}U) \cap (\Gamma^{+}V) = \emptyset \text{ (since } U \cap V = \emptyset).$$

However, by Theorem 2, p. 110, of Berge [9], $\Gamma^{+}U$ and $\Gamma^{+}V$ are both open sets; given that Γ is u.s.c. on X. Hence (1) contradicts the connectedness of X, and we conclude that $Z \equiv \Gamma X$ is connected.

Q.E.D.

FOOTNOTES

*The research upon which this paper is based was supported in part by National Science Foundation grant NSF-GS-544, and in part by the School of Business and Public Administration of the University of Missouri, Columbia. The authors are grateful to Professors Claude Colantoni, Stanley R. Johnson, and Charles Plott for helpful comments and suggestions.

[1]The set-theoretic notation used in this paper is quite standard, with the possible exception that we denote the set-theoretic difference of, say A and B, by $A\setminus B$; that is:

$$A\setminus B = \{a \in A \mid a \notin B\}.$$

[2]We follow Debreu [13] in using the Bourbaki term "preordering," rather than the term "quasiordering," which is probably more commonly used in mathematical publications in the U.S. In order to avoid such awkward circumlocutions as "preference preorderings" and "Pareto preordering," however, we shall follow the convention adopted in Chipman [10] of using "ordering" as a generic term applying to any transitive binary relation (cf. [10], p. 197).

[3]Completeness, as defined here, implies reflexivity; so that condition (b) is actually superfluous. However, we shall want to deal with preorderings which are not necessarily complete (i.e., with binary relationships satisfying (b) and (c), but not necessarily (a)), making a statement of reflexivity desirable. Again we have bowed to Debreu's usage [13] in using the term "completeness" instead of, e.g., the probably less confusing term "connexity."

[4]We use the following logical quantifier notation. If X is a set, the expression:

$(x \in X)$: x satisfies ...,

is read: "for every x in X it is true that x satisfies ...;" while the expression

$(\exists x \in X)$: x satisfies ...

is read: "there exists an x in X such that x satisfies ..."

[5]On this see, for instance, Baldwin [4,5] and Samuelson [33]. See also Nikaido [26, 27] (N.B. [26], Sec. 5).

[6]This assumption was introduced by Arrow in [1], and was there described as "selfish" behavior. In his book [2] this term was replaced by the less ethically loaded word "individualistic."

[7]We follow Debreu [13] in denoting the open interval from a to b by "]a,b[", rather than the more usual "(a,b)."

[8]Cf. Pareto [28]. In the first part of this article (pp. 48-57) Pareto employed the criterion of adding together different people's utilities. However, in the second part he introduced (p. 60) what is now called the "Pareto principle;" although only (by his own admission, p. 58) at the insistence of his friends Pantaleoni and Barone.

The term "Pareto principle" was introduced by K.J. Arrow in the (second edition of) [2], p. 96. The term "Pareto optimum" is evidently due to I.M.D. Little [24], p. 101. (See also Arrow [3].) The term "Pareto optimal" was erroneously attributed to Frisch in Chipman [11] p. 736. We are indebted to K.J. Arrow, who questioned this attribution in private correspondence.

[9]See Theorem 1 of the text.

[10]The acceptance of this ordering as a criterion for social choice among situations was called the "Kaldor Principle" by Arrow [2], p. 39). The ordering used here is, however, broader than the usual interpretation, and corresponds to the Compensation Principle as formulated by Samuelson. Cf. Kaldor [21], Hicks [17], and Samuelson [32].

[11]There appear to be some important applications where this is true, however; and in fact, it appears that most if not all applications of the Compensation Principle that have been considered so far in the literature of welfare economics have been precisely of this class. Thus, Baldwin [4] considers a country's consumption possibility sets Y_1, Y_2, Y_3 corresponding to autarky, unrestricted free trade, and discriminatory trade, respectively, and shows that $Y_1 \subset Y_2 \subset Y_3$. See also Baldwin [5,6] and Samuelson [32, 33]. (These authors have also stressed the limited scope of such comparisons in specific practical applications, incidentally.)

[12]Where, as is usual, we say that g represents $\dot{R}_i$ on E_n^+ if g satisfies:

$$g(x^i) \geqq g(\bar{x}^i) \text{ iff } x^i \; \dot{R}_i \; \bar{x}^i.$$

[13]We say that g is positively homogenous of degree one on E_n^+ if:

$$(x \in E_n^+)(\lambda \geqq 0): \quad g(\lambda x) = \lambda g(x).$$

[14]This result could probably be credited to Gorman [15]. See also Eisenberg [14].

[15]Lemma 2, incidentally, is presumably "well-known;" and is stated and proved here only for the sake of completeness.

[16]We should also note that from Theorem 1 we have at once:

$(R_1 \subset R_0)$: $R_1 \neq \emptyset$ implies $>_{R_1}$ is a preordering of situations.

[17]Where for $Y \subset E_n$, we let $\overline{Y}$ denote the closure of Y.

[18]An exception to this statement which is of some interest is presented in Theorem 9 of Section 5, however.

[19]Or at least unless we are willing to make considerably more stringent assumptions about the properties of each R_i than economists have generally been willing to make. However, see Theorem 9 of Section 5.

[20]First introduced in [31], but not fully developed until his fundamental paper [32].

[21]More exactly, the individualism assumption is nearly always (the only exception being Remark 2 of the text) either needed for our method of proof, or such that it cannot simply be dispensed with if the result is to remain correct, or both.

[22]See Debreu [13], Theorem (1), p. 56. Note that in the construction of Debreu's proof, f^1 can be taken to map into an arbitrary (non-degenerate) closed finite interval.

[23]Actually, a functional analyst would say they are the same thing in any case.

[24]Clearly this result does not require that the R_i's be individualistic.

[25]If $A \subset E_n^+$, we shall say that $x \in E_m^+$ is a <u>relative boundary point of A</u> iff given any open set V such that $x \in V$, we have:

$$V \cap A \neq \emptyset \text{ and } V \cap [E_m^+ \setminus A] \neq \emptyset.$$

[26]If is actually well known that, under these circumstances, the set

$$A = \{u \in E_m \mid (\exists X \in A(Y)): \quad u \leqq \overline{f}(X)\}$$

is convex (cf. Hurwicz [20], Theorem V. 3.1, p. 91; and Uzawa [35], Theorem 2). Hence

$$U(E; \overline{f}) = A \cap E_m^+$$

being the intersection of two convex sets, is itself convex.

[27]It should also be noted that the contract curve is usually (and was by Edgeworth) defined so as to include only those Pareto optimal allocations which are Pareto superior to a given distribution of initial endowments. This definition is not applicable here, however, since we are not taking a distribution of initial endowments as given.

[28]It may be that this result is already apparent to anyone who has read, and understands, Gorman [15] thoroughly.

[29]It should be noted that, under the conditions here (that is where the range space of the mapping is compact), the definitions used by these two authors are equivalent.

[30]That is there do not exist open sets V_1 and V_2 such that:

$$[V_1 \cap 0(E)] \cap [V_2 \cap 0(E)] = \emptyset, \; V_1 \cap 0(E) \neq \emptyset,$$

$$V_2 \cap 0(E) \neq \emptyset \text{ and } [V_1 \cap 0(E)] \cup [V_2 \cap 0(E)] = 0(E).$$

[31]Professor Koopmans' "locally non-saturating" assumption could, of course, be used here in place of monotonicity. See Koopmans [23], p. 47.

[32]Parts (i)-(iii) are certainly not new results in any case. In fact (i)-(iii) were stated by Hicks in more or

less this form [18], and the proof we give was sketched by Kennedy [22]. See also Samuelson [30, 32].

[33]This theorem can be credited to Gorman. See [15], p. 73, and also Eisenberg [14].

[34]Essentially this same ambiguity, which amounts to a reversal of the quantifiers in the definition of the KHS ordering, persists throughout the literature on the evaluation of real national income. We expand and clarify this point in [12].

[35]Moreover, the first commodity is "always desired" by the two consumers. If we drop this property of the preference orderings, and consider non-singleton situations, we can simplify our example in the following way. Letting $m = n = 2$, take $f^1(x^1) = x_{11}$ and $f^2(x^2) = x_{22}$. Letting $Y_1 = \{(1, 3)\}$, $Y_2 = \{y \in E_2^+ | 1 \leqq y_1 \leqq 3 \text{ and } y_2 = 4 - y_1\}$, $Y_3 = \{(5/2, 5/2)\}$, respectively, we obtain exactly the same relationships as in the original example; and, in fact, the same diagram as in Figure 5.

[36]See also [25], pp. 41-44.

[37]Or unless $P(R, \hat{y})$ is a singleton. See n. 38, below.

[38]Of course if the utility function common to the m consumers can be taken to be continuously differentiable, then $P(R, \hat{y})$ will be a singleton; so this then would become a special case of (48) of the text.

[39]Although Professor Eisenberg's Theorem 2 ([14], p. 341) may seem to suggest this.

[40]Note that the functions f^1 and f^2 used here are strictly monotonic transformations of functions of the C.E.S. class (having σ, the elasticity of substitution, equal to 2).

[41]On this same general point, see Nikaido [26, 27]. N.B. [26], Section 5, pp. 141-144.

[42]It should be noted that Professor Yokoyama uses the assumption of strict monotonicity, rather than the weaker monotonicity assumption used here. Moreover, his "Wold axiom of continuity" is slightly different from our condition (1). However, a careful reading of his proof will reveal that his result holds under the assumptions used here.

[43]The proof presented here is only very slightly different from Professor Wold's, although his assumptions are somewhat different from ours. We present a proof primarily because we shall need to use the Wold construction of the function $\overline{f}$ very explicitly in the sequel.

[44]As usual we shall say that $g(x) = (g_1(x), \ldots, g_n(x))$ is concave iff each g_i if concave. This is, of course, equivalent to the statement that g is concave iff whenever $x, y \in D$, $\lambda \in [0, 1]$, we have

$$g[\lambda x + (1-\lambda)y] \geqq \lambda g(x) + (1-\lambda)g(y).$$

Note that a sufficient condition for g to be semi-strictly concave is for each g_i to be concave, while at least one g_i is strictly concave.

[45]Theorem 1, p. 207.

[46]Notice that by this same reasoning, it follows that each member of the class of C.E.S. production functions is concave on E_n^+.

REFERENCES

[1] Arrow, Kenneth J.: "An Extension of the Basic Theorems of Classical Welfare Economics," in Proceedings of the Second Berkeley Symposium on Mathematical Statistics and Probability (edited by Jerzy Neyman). Berkeley and Los Angeles: University of California Press, 1950, 507-532. Reprinted in Readings in Mathematical Economics (edited by Peter Newman), Vol. 1 Baltimore: The Johns Hopkins Press, 1968, 365-390.

[2] ______: Social Choice and Individual Values. New York: John Wiley & Sons, Inc., 1951. 2nd edition, 1963.

[3] ______: "Little's Critique of Welfare Economics," American Economic Review, 41 (December 1951), 923-934.

[4] Baldwin, Robert E.: "Equilibrium in International Trade: A Diagrammatic Analysis," Quarterly Journal of Economics, 62 (November 1948), 748-762.

[5] ______: "The New Welfare Economics and Gains in International Trade," Quarterly Journal of Economics, 66 (February 1952), 91-101. Reprinted in Readings in International Economics (edited by Richard E. Caves and Harry G. Johnson). Homewood, Ill.: Richard D. Irwin, Inc., 1968, 204-212.

[6] ______: "A Comparison of Welfare Criteria," Review of Economic Studies 21 (1953-54), 154-161.

[7] Barone, Enrico: "Il ministerio della produzione nello stato colletivista," Giornale degli Economisti [2], 37 (August, October 1908), 267-293, 391-414. English translation: "The Ministry of Production in the Collectivist State," in Collectivist Economic Planning (edited by F. A. Hayek). London: Routledge & Kegan Paul Ltd., 1935, 245-290. Reprinted in Readings in Mathematical Economics (edited by Peter Newman), Vol. I. Baltimore: The Johns Hopkins Press, 1968, 319-364.

[8] Baumol, William J.: "Community Indifference," Review of Economic Studies, 14 (1946-47), 44-48.

[9] Berge, Claude: Topological Spaces. New York: The Macmillan Co., 1963. (English translation of Espaces topologiques, fonctions multivoques. Paris: Dunod, 1959.)

[10] Chipman, John S.: "The Foundations of Utility," Econometrica, 28 (April 1960), 193-224.

[11] ______: "A Survey of the Theory of International Trade: Part 2, The Neo-Classical Theory," Econometrica, 33 (October 1965), 685-760.

[12] Chipman, John S., and James C. Moore: "The End of the 'New Welfare Economics'," University of Minnesota, Center for Economic Research, Report Series, No. 5.

[13] Debreu, Gerard: Theory of Value. New York: John Wiley & Sons, Inc., 1959.

[14] Eisenberg, E.: "Aggregation of Utility Functions," Management Science, 7 (July 1961), 337-350.

[15] Gorman, W. M.: "Community Preference Fields," Econometrica, 21 (January 1953), 63-80.

[16] Hardy, G. H., J. E. Littlewood, and G. Polya: Inequalities, 2nd edition. Cambridge: Cambridge University Press, 1952.

[17] Hicks, J. R.: "The Foundations of Welfare Economics," Economic Journal, 49 (December 1939), 696-712.

[18] ______: "The Valuation of the Social Income," Economica, N.S., 7 (May 1940), 105-124.

[19] Hotelling, Harold: "The General Welfare in Relation to Problems of Taxation and of Railway and Utility Rates," Econometrica, 6 (July 1938), 242-269. Reprinted in Readings in Welfare Economics (edited by Kenneth J. Arrow and Tibor Scitovsky), Homewood, Ill.: Richard D. Irwin, Inc., 1969, 284-308.

[20] Hurwicz, Leonid: "Programming in Linear Spaces," Chapter 4 in Studies in Linear and Non-Linear Programming (edited by K. J. Arrow, L. Hurwicz, and H. Uzawa), Stanford: Stanford University Press, 1958, 38-102.

[21] Kaldor, Nicholas: "Welfare Propositions in Economics and Inter-Personal Comparisons of Utility," Economic Journal, 49 (September 1939), 549-552. Reprinted in Readings in Welfare Economics (edited by Kenneth J. Arrow and Tibor Scitovsky), Homewood, Ill.: Richard D. Irwin, Inc., 1969, 387-389.

[22] Kennedy, Charles: "An Alternative Proof of a Theorem in Welfare Economics," Oxford Economic Papers, N.S., 6 (February 1954), 98-99.

[23] Koopmans, Tjalling C.: Three Essays on the State of Economic Science (I. "Allocation of Resources and the Price System"). New York: McGraw-Hill Book Company, Inc., 1957.

[24] Little, I.M.D.: A Critique of Welfare Economics. Oxford: Clarendon Press, 1950. 2nd edition, 1957.

[25] Moore, James C.: "On Pareto Optima and Competitive Equilibria, Part 1: Relationships Among Equilibria and Optima," Krannert School of Industrial Administration, Institute Paper No. 268, Purdue University, Lafayette, Indiana, March 1970.

[26] Nikaido, Hukukane: "On the Classical Multilateral Exchange Problem," Metroeconomica, 8 (August 1956), 135-145. Reprinted in Readings in Mathematical Economics (edited by Peter Newman), Vol. I, Baltimore: The Johns Hopkins Press, 1968, 116-126.

[27] ______: "A Supplementary Note to 'On the Classical Multilateral Exchange Problem,'" Metroeconomica, 9 (December 1957), 209-210. Reprinted in Readings in Mathematical Economics (edited by Peter Newman), Vol. I., Baltimore: The Johns Hopkins Press, 1968, 127-128.

[28] Pareto, Vilfredo: "Il massimo di utilità dato dalla libera concorrenza," Giornale degli Economisti [2], 9 (July 1894), 48-66.

[29] ______: "Teoria matematica del commercio internazionale," Giornale degli Economisti [2], 10 (April 1895), 476-498.

[30] Samuelson, Paul A.: "The Gains from International Trade," Canadian Journal of Economics and Political Science, 5 (May 1939), 195-205. Reprinted in Readings in the Theory of International Trade (edited by Howard S. Ellis and Lloyd A. Metzler), Homewood, Ill.: Richard D. Irwin, Inc., 1950, 239-252.

[31] ______: Foundations of Economic Analysis. Cambridge, Mass.: Harvard University Press, 1947.

[32] ______: "Evaluation of Real National Income," Oxford Economic Papers, N.S., 2 (January 1950), 1-29. Reprinted

in Readings in Welfare Economics (edited by Kenneth J. Arrow and Tibor Scitovsky), Homewood, Ill.: Richard D. Irwin, Inc., 1969, 402-433.

[33] ______: "The Gains from International Trade Once Again," Economic Journal, 72 (December 1962), 820-829.

[34] Scitovsky, Tibor de: "A Note on Welfare Propositions in Economics," Review of Economic Studies, 9 (1941-42), 77-88. Reprinted in Readings in Welfare Economics (edited by Kenneth J. Arrow and Tibor Scitovsky), Homewood, Ill.: Richard D. Irwin, Inc., 1969, 390-401.

[35] Uzawa, Hirofumi: "The Kuhn-Tucker Theorem in Concave Programming," Chapter 3 in Studies in Linear and Non-Linear Programming (edited by K. J. Arrow, L. Hurwicz, and H. Uzawa). Stanford: Stanford University Press, 1958, 32-37.

[36] Viner, Jacob: Studies in the Theory of International Trade. New York: Harper & Brothers, 1937.

[37] Wold, Herman O. A.: "A Synthesis of Pure Demand Analysis," Part II, Skandinavisk Aktuarietidskrift, 26 (1943), 220-263.

[38] Yokoyama, Tamotsu: "Continuity Conditions of Preference Ordering," Osaka Economic Papers, 4 (February 1956), 39-45.

INTERRELATED CONSUMER PREFERENCE AND VOLUNTARY EXCHANGE

by

Theodore C. Bergstrom*
Washington University

It is traditional in the theory of economic choice to assume that an individual economic agent chooses his economic activities in such a way to maximize a preference ordering which depends only on his own consumption. This assumption, while an immensely useful simplification, does cause some embarrassment when economists desire to explain such phenomena as gifts and inheritances, compulsory schooling, forced savings plans such as Social Security, and even the often discussed notion of a "household".

The first section of this paper suggests some weaker assumptions on the nature of individualism which preserve much of the individualistic flavor of Western economics, yet allow one to consider some of the effects of interrelated consumer preferences. These assumptions provide a useful taxonomy for the analysis of consumer interrelationships.

In the second section we define an exchange equilibrium which allows mutually voluntary bilateral gifts between interrelated pairs of consumers. It is demonstrated that if all interrelatedness is between "monogamous" pairs of consumers who are "benevolent" but somewhat "selfish", then equilibrium exists and is Pareto optimal. These results may provide a useful starting point for a theory of the "household".

Section I. Interrelated Consumer Preferences

There are assumed to be m commodities and n consumers. Let N be the set of all consumers. Define the consumption set, X_i, of Consumer i so that X_i is that subset of Euclidean m space which consists of all commodity bundles which could be consumed by i. Define the allocation set, X, so that $X \equiv \prod_{i \in N} X_i$. An allocation is a point $u \in X$ where $u = (u_1, \ldots, u_n)$ and u_i is the commodity bundle allocated to Consumer i.

Each consumer, $i \in N$, is assumed to have a complete preordering, R_i, defined on X. This is called the preference ordering of i.[1] The relations, P_i and I_i, are defined in the usual way.

Two consumers are said to be interrelated if at least

one of them expresses strict preference between some pair of allocations which differ only in what the other receives.

Definition 1. Consumer i is related to Consumer j if there exists a pair of allocations u and v in X such that $u_k = v_k$ for all $k \neq j$ and uP_iv. Consumers i and j are interrelated if either i is related to j, or j is related to i.

Definition 2. Preferences of Consumer i are separable with respect to Consumer j if for all allocations, u and v, such that $u_k = v_k$ for every $k \neq j$ and all allocations u' and v' such that $u'_k = v'_k$ for every $k \neq j$ and such that $u'_j = u_j$ and $v'_j = v_j$, it is implied that uR_iv if and only if $u'R_iv'$. Preferences of i are separable between individuals if preferences of i are separable with respect to every consumer.

This is the notion of separability familiar in consumer theory. It can be shown that if preferences of i are separable between individuals and representable by a continuous utility function, $F_i(x)$, then $F_i(x)$ can be written as $F_i(g_{i1}(x_1),\ldots,g_{in}(x_n))$. Separability between individuals rules out such Veblenesque effects as the desire to imitate the consumption of others or desire for a commodity solely because of its scarcity.

When preferences are separable between individuals, one can define a private preference ordering, $\gtrsim_i$, on the consumption set, X_i, of each individual. In particular if uR_iv for some pair of allocations, u and v, which differ only in the consumption bundles allocated to i, it will be said that $u_i \gtrsim_i v_i$. It is easily verified that if preferences are separable between individuals, then the relation, $\gtrsim_i$, is a complete quasi-ordering on X_i.

Definition 3. The private preference ordering, $\gtrsim_i$, is defined as follows. If u and v are allocations such that $u_j = v_j$ for all $j \neq i$, then $u_i \gtrsim_i v_i$ if and only if uR_iv. The relations of strict private preference, $>_i$, and private indifference, $\sim_i$, are defined in the natural way.

Definition 4. Consumer i is nonmalevolently related to j if preferences of i and j are separable between individuals and if for every pair of allocations u and v in X such that $u_j \gtrsim_j v_j$ and such that $u_k = v_k$ for all $k \neq j$, it is implied that uR_iv.

If Consumer i is nonmalevolently related to j then for any two allocations, u and v, which contain the same bundles for everyone except j, if j privately prefers his bundle in u to his bundle in v then i will consider u at least as good as v. Nonmalevolence rules out the possibility that i disagrees with j about what kinds of goods j should consume.

Definition 5. Consumer i is benevolently related to j if preferences of consumers i and j are separable between individuals and if for all allocations, u and v, such that $u_k = v_k$ for $k \neq j$; $u_j >_j v_j$ if and only if uP_iv.

It can be shown that if preferences of i are separable between individuals and representable by a continuous utility function and if consumer i is nonmalevolently (benevolently) related to consumer j, then the utility function of i can be represented by a function $F_i(g_1(x_1),\ldots,g_n(x_n))$, where $g_j(.)$ represents the private preferences, $\gtrsim_j$, of j and F_i is a nondecreasing (increasing) function of $g_j(.)$.

Definition 6. Consumer i is locally nonsatiated on X_j if for all $u \varepsilon X$, in every open neighborhood of u_j in X_j there is an $x_j \ \varepsilon \ X_j$ such that vP_iu where v is an allocation such that $v_k = u_k$ for $k \neq j$ and $v_j = x_j$.

Remark. If i has transitive and continuous preferences and is locally nonsatiated on X_j, then i is benevolently related to j if and only if i is nonmalevolently related to j.

Proof: The only way in which a nonmalevolently related i could not be benevolently related to j would be if for some $u \varepsilon X$ and some $v_j \ \varepsilon \ X_j$, it is true that $u_j >_j v_j$ and $(u_1 \ldots u_j \ldots u_n) I_i \ (u_1 \ldots v_j \ldots u_n)$. Continuity of R_j in the product topology implies continuity of $\gtrsim_j$. Hence if the $u_j >_j v_j$, there is some open neighborhood, $N(v_j)$, of v_j in X_j such that $x_j \ \varepsilon \ N(v_j)$ implies that $u_j >_j x_j$. By local nonsatiation of i on X_j, there is some $\bar{x}_j \ \varepsilon \ N(v_j)$ such that $(u_1 \ldots \bar{x}_j \ldots u_n)$ $P_i(u_1 \ldots u_j \ldots u_n)$. But $u_j >_j \bar{x}_j \ \varepsilon \ N(v_j)$. This contradicts nonmalevolence. Therefore nonmalevolence implies benevolence. That benevolence implies nonmalevolence follows trivially from the definitions. The remark is now proved.

Definition 7. Consumer i is egocentric with respect to consumer j if preferences of i are separable between individuals and if for any pair of allocations, u and v, such that $u_k = v_k$ where $k \neq i$ and $k \neq j$; if uR_jv and $u_i \gtrsim_i v_i$ then uR_iv.

Remark. If consumer i is egocentric with respect to consumer j, he is nonmalevolent with respect to j.

Proof: Simply apply the definition of egocentricity where $u_i = v_i$.

Theorem 1.

(a) Consumer i is egocentric with respect to consumer j if and only if for all allocations, u and v, such that $u_k = v_k$ where $k \neq i$ and $k \neq j$; if vP_iu and uR_jv then $v_i >_i u_i$.

(b) If consumer i is egocentric with respect to j and j is nonmalevolent with respect to i, and if u and v are allocations such that vP_iu and uR_jv, then $u_j \gtrsim_j v_j$ and $v_i >_i u_i$.

Proof:

To prove Part (a), simply observe that since the relation, R_i, is complete, the statement, "If uR_jv and $u_i \gtrsim_i v_i$ then uR_iv" is logically equivalent to the statement "If uR_jv and vP_iu then $v_i >_i u_i$." Therefore the statement in Theorem 1(a) is equivalent to the definition of egocentricity.

Consider two allocations u and v such that $u_k = v_k$ where $k \neq i$ and $k \neq j$ and such that vP_iu and uR_jv. Part (a) of Theorem 1 implies that $v_i >_i u_i$. If consumer j is nonmalevolent, it is easily shown that if $v_j >_j u_j$ then vP_ju. But by assumption, uR_jv. Therefore $u_j \gtrsim_j v_j$. This proves Part (b). QED

One's intuition about the nature of egocentricity is aided by Theorem 1. If two persons are egocentric with respect to each other, then whenever they disagree about the relative merits of two allocations, the disagreement is such that each person prefers the allocation in which his own bundle ranks higher in his private preference, $\gtrsim_i$. If two persons disagree because each wants the other to have the better part, then they violate the assumptions of egocentricity. (A delightful fictional account of a pair of non-egocentric individuals is found in O. Henry's short story, The Gift of the Magi.)

To consider an example, suppose there were only one commodity and two persons, an egocentric rich man and an egocentric poor man. If each prefers to have more of the commodity rather than less, given the consumption of the other, then the rich man might give to the poor man, but one would never find that the rich man wants to change places with the poor man while the poor man is unwilling to do so.

This can be illustrated by the figure below. There is just one good to be allocated between two consumers. Each consumer privately prefers more of the good. Both are benevolent. Possible allocations are represented by points on the line 0 - 1. The distance to the left of any point measures the amount consumed by A. The distance to the right

Figure 1: Egocentric preference

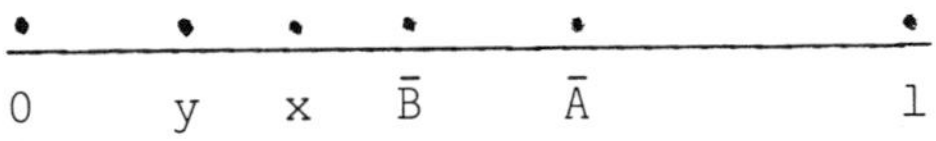

Figure 2: Non-egocentric preference

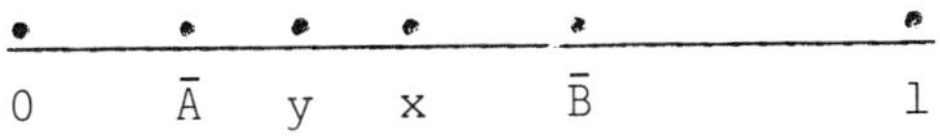

of the point measures the amount consumed by B. Consumer A prefers the point $\bar{A}$ to all other allocations on the line. Consumer B prefers $\bar{B}$ to all other allocations on the line. Each ranks other allocations inversely with their distance from his favorite point. We show that when $\bar{A}$ and $\bar{B}$ are located as in Figure 1, preferences are egocentric. Suppose xR_By and $x_A >_A y_A$. Then x must be to the right of y. The only way this can happen when xR_By is if both points are to the left of $\bar{B}$. But if this is the case, both points are also to the left of $\bar{A}$ and therefore, xR_Ay. Consumer A must be egocentric with respect to B. Likewise one can show that B is egocentric with respect to A. To see that preferences are not egocentric if $\bar{A}$ and $\bar{B}$ are located as in Figure 2, consider points x and y between $\bar{A}$ and $\bar{B}$ such that x is to the right of y. Then xR_By and $x_A >_A y_A$ but yP_Ax, which could not happen if A were egocentric with respect to B.

It is sometimes useful to have a slightly stronger version of egocentricity.

Definition 8. Consumer i is strongly egocentric with respect to j if i is egocentric with respect to j and if in addition, for any allocations, u and v, such that $u_k = v_k$ where $k \neq i$ and $k \neq j$; uR_jv and $u_i >_i v_i$ imply that uP_iv.

It is not in general true that egocentricity, even with continuity of preferences, implies strong egocentricity. If, for example, two consumers are in complete agreement about the relative merits of every pair of allocations, then they are egocentric with respect to each other but neither need be strongly egocentric with respect to the other.

It turns out that if preferences are egocentric and continuous and if for any allocation, u, there is some allocation, w, close to u (in a sense defined below) such that Consumers i and j disagree about whether u is better than w, then preferences are strongly egocentric. These notions are made precise below.

Definition 9. There is local conflict of interest between Consumers i and j, if in every open neighborhood of every allocation, u, there is an allocation, w, such that $w_k = u_k$ where $k \neq i$ and $k \neq j$, and such that $wP_j u$ and $uP_i w$.

Theorem 2.

If preferences of Consumer i are continuous and egocentric with respect to Consumer j, and if there is local conflict of interest between i and j, then preferences of i are strongly egocentric with respect to j.

Proof:

Suppose that u and v are allocations such that $u_k = v_k$ where $k \neq i$ and $k \neq j$ and suppose that $uR_j v$ and $u_i >_i v_i$. Since preferences of i are continuous, there is an open neighborhood, N(u), of u, such that if $w \epsilon N(u)$ then $w_i >_i v_i$. Since there is local conflict of interest, there is some $w \epsilon N(u)$ such that $wP_j u$ and $uP_i w$. Since $w \epsilon N(u)$, $w_i >_i v_i$. Since $wP_j u$ and $uR_j v$, $wR_j v$. Egocentricity therefore implies that $wR_i v$. But $uP_i w$. Therefore $uP_i v$. QED

The following theorem states some properties of strongly egocentric preferences.

Theorem 3.

If preferences of Consumer j are nonmalevolent with respect to Consumer i then the following statements are logically equivalent.

(a) Consumer i is strongly egocentric with respect to Consumer j.

(b) For any allocations, u and v, such that $u_k = v_k$ where $k \neq i$ and $k \neq j$; if $vR_i u$ and $uR_j v$, then $v_i \gtrsim_i u_i$ and $u_j \gtrsim_j v_j$.

(c) Consumer j is strongly egocentric with respect to Consumer i.

Proof:

Completeness of R_i implies that the statement, "If $uR_j v$ and $u_i >_i v_i$ then $uP_i v$", is logically equivalent to the statement, "If $vR_i u$ and $uR_j v$ then $v_i \gtrsim_i u_i$." Nonmalevolence of j toward i implies that if $vR_i u$, $uR_j v$, and $v_i \gtrsim_i u_i$ then $u_j \gtrsim_j v_j$. The equivalence of Statements (a) and (b) follows immediately.

Since Statement (b) is symmetric with respect to i and j, it is immediate that Statement (c) is also equivalent to Statements (a) and (b).

QED

Section II. Households and Competitive Gift Equilibrium

It is well known that a competitive equilibrium as ordinarily defined will not in general be Pareto optimal if there is consumer interrelatedness. Where all consumer interrelatedness is nonmalevolent, it is of interest to consider an exchange equilibrium in which bilateral gifts are allowed. Such an equilibrium will be defined below.

Definition 10. A household is a set of interrelated consumers such that each member of the set is interrelated with some other member and no member of the set is interrelated with any consumer not in the set. (The definition of interrelatedness is such that an individual is interrelated with himself. Therefore the set containing a completely "selfish" individual is a single member household.)

Definition 11. If each member, i, of a household, H, commands an initial vector, w_i, of commodity holdings, then the allocation, x, is a household equilibrium for H at the prices, p, if $p \sum_{i\varepsilon H} x_i \leqq p \sum_{i\varepsilon H} w_i$ and if for every $i\varepsilon H$ and for every allocation, x', such that $p \sum_{i\varepsilon H} x'_i \leqq p \sum_{i\varepsilon H} w_i$; if $x'P_i x$ then $px'_i > pw_i$.

If an allocation is a household equilibrium at the prices, p, then it must be that the total value of goods consumed by members of the household does not exceed the total value of the initial holdings of household members. If some member of the household prefers another allocation to a household equilibrium, it must be either that the total cost of goods consumed by members of the household exceeds total household wealth or that the bundle preferred by that member costs more than the value of his personal initial holdings. It is possible that in equilibrium, some members of the household consume bundles of higher value than their holdings. If this is to happen, other members of the household must voluntarily consume bundles of lower value than their initial holdings.

Definition 12. A competitive gift equilibrium (c.g.e.) for an exchange economy is an allocation $\bar{x}$ and a set of prices, $\bar{p}$, such that:

(a) The allocation $\bar{x}$ is a household equilibrium at prices, $\bar{p}$, for every household.

(b) $\sum_{i \varepsilon N} \bar{x}_i = \sum_{i \varepsilon N} w_i$, where N is the set of all consumers.[2]

Even if all consumer interrelatedness is nonmalevolent, a competitive gift equilibrium does not necessarily exist. In fact there may be households for which there is no household equilibrium at any price vector. Furthermore, a c.g.e. need not be Pareto optimal. (See Bergstrom [2]) A special case of interrelated preferences for which a c.g.e. exists and is Pareto optimal will be presented below.

Theorem 4.

Let the allocation, x, be a household equilibrium for household, H, at prices, p. Suppose that for all $i \varepsilon H$, preferences of i are locally nonsatiated on X_i. Then if $x'R_i x$ for all $i \varepsilon H$, it must be that $p \sum_{i \varepsilon H} x'_i \geq \sum_{i \varepsilon H} w_i$.

Proof:

Suppose that $x'R_i x$ for all $i \varepsilon H$ and that $p \sum_{i \varepsilon H} x'_i <$ $p \sum_{i \varepsilon H} w_i$. Then for some $j \varepsilon H$, $px'_j < pw_j$. Since j is locally nonsatiated on X_j there is an $\overset{o}{x}_j$ near x'_j such that $p\overset{o}{x}_j < pw_j$, $p\overset{o}{x}_j + \sum_{\substack{i \varepsilon H \\ i \neq j}} x'_j < p \sum_{i \varepsilon H} w_i$, and such that $\hat{x}P_j x'$ where $\hat{x}$ is an allocation such that $\hat{x}_j = \overset{o}{x}_j$ and $\hat{x}_k = x'_k$ for all consumers, $k \neq j$. Since $s'R_j x$, it follows that $\hat{x}P_j x$. But this contradicts the assertion that x is a c.g.e. Therefore if $x'R_i x$ for all $i \varepsilon H$ then $p \sum_{i \varepsilon H} x'_i \geq p \sum_{i \varepsilon H} w_i$. QED

An easy consequence of Theorem 4 is that if x is a household equilibrium for household, H, at prices, p, then $p \sum_{i \varepsilon H} x_i =$ $p \sum_{i \varepsilon H} w_i$.

In the remainder of this section, attention will be confined to the case where no consumer is interrelated with more than one other consumer. In this case, no household consists of more than two consumers. Theorem 5 states a property of equilibrium for a household which contains two benevolent and egocentric members.

Theorem 5.

Let H be a household with exactly two members, A and B. Assume that consumers A and B are benevolent and egocentric with respect to each other, that preferences of A are locally nonsatiated on X_A and that preferences of B are locally nonsatiated on X_B. Let x be a household equilibrium for H at prices, p. If $x'P_Ax$ and $x'R_Bx$, or if $x'R_Ax$ and $x'P_Bx$, then $p(x'_A + x'_B) > p(w_A + w_B)$.

Proof:

Suppose that $x'P_Ax$, $x'R_Bx$, and that $p(x'_A + x'_B) \leqq p(w_A + w_B)$. Since x is a household equilibrium, it must be that $px'_A > pw_A$. Therefore $px'_B < pw_B$. But, since x is a household equilibrium, this implies that xR_Bx'. Since consumers A and B are egocentric with respect to each other, it follows from Theorem 1b that $x'_A >_A x_A$ and that $x_B \gtrsim_B x'_B$.

If $px'_B < px_B$ then, since B is locally nonsatiated on X_B, there is an $\overset{\circ}{x}_B$ near x'_B such that $p\overset{\circ}{x}_B < px_B$, $p(x_A + \overset{\circ}{x}_B) < p(w_A + w_B)$, and such that $\hat{x}P_Bx$ where $\hat{x}$ is an allocation in which $\hat{x}_B = \overset{\circ}{x}_B$, and $\hat{x}_i = x_i$ for all consumers, i, other than B. But this cannot be if x is a c.g.e. Therefore $px'_B \geqq pw_B$. Suppose that $px'_A \leqq px_A$. Let $\hat{x}$ be an allocation such that $\hat{x}_A = x'_A$ and such that $\hat{x}_i = x_i$ for all consumers, i, other than A. Then $p(\hat{x}_A + \hat{x}_B) \leqq p(w_A + w_B)$ and $p\hat{x}_B \leqq pw_B$. But since Consumer B is benevolent toward A, and since $\hat{x}_A = x'_A >_A x_A$ and $\hat{x}_B = x_B$, it must be that $\hat{x}P_Bx$. This cannot be, since x is a c.g.e. Therefore $px'_A > px_A$. It follows that $p(x'_A + x'_B) > p(x_A + x_B)$. Since x is a household equilibrium, $p(x_A + x_B) = p(w_A + w_B)$. Therefore $p(x'_A + x'_B) > p(w_A + w_B)$.

If $x'R_Ax$ and $x'P_Bx$, an analogous proof shows that $p(x'_A + x'_B) > p(w_A + w_B)$.

QED

Observe that in Theorem 5 it is assumed that both consumers are benevolent. It might seem plausible that continuity, interrelatedness, and egocentricity (which implies nonmalevolence) would be sufficient for the conclusion of Theorem 5. This turns out not to be the case unless it is also assumed that there is some point in the consumption set of each consumer which is cheaper at the equilibrium prices than his equilibrium consumption.

Theorem 5 may be helpful for interpreting the meaning of a household equilibrium for two-member households. If x is a household equilibrium at prices, p, then Theorem 5 implies that for any allocation, x', such that $p(x'_A + x'_B) \leqq p(w_A + w_B)$; if $x'P_A x$ then $px'_A > 0$ and $xP_B x'$. Thus, if the total cost to the household of allocation x' does not exceed the total wealth of the household and if Consumer A prefers x' to x then it must be that the allocation x' is achieved only if Consumer B makes a gift of value, px'_A, to Consumer A. But B prefers not to make such a gift.

Theorem 6.

If no household contains more than two consumers, if members of each household are egocentric and benevolent with respect to each other, and if preferences of each consumer, i, are locally nonsatiated on X_i, then a competitive gift equilibrium is Pareto optimal.

Proof:

Suppose that $\bar{x}$ is a c.g.e. and suppose that x is Pareto superior to $\bar{x}$. Then $\bar{x}$ is a household equilibrium for every household at prices, $\bar{p}$. If a consumer belongs to a single member household, this means that at $\bar{x}$ he is maximizing his preferences subject to an ordinary private competitive budget constraint. Just as in the traditional proof of the optimality of competitive equilibrium, it must be that when i is the only member of a household, if $xR_i\bar{x}$ then $\bar{p}x_i \geqq \bar{p}w_i$ and if $xP_i\bar{x}$ then $\bar{p}x_i > \bar{p}w_i$.

Since $xR_i\bar{x}$ for all $i \varepsilon N$ and since $xP_j\bar{x}$ for some $j \varepsilon N$, it follows from Theorem 4 that $\bar{p} \sum_{i \varepsilon H} x_i \geqq \bar{p} \sum_{i \varepsilon H} w_i$ for every household, H. From Theorem 5, it follows that for some household, H, $\bar{p} \sum_{i \varepsilon H} x_i > \bar{p} \sum_{i \varepsilon H} w_i$. Therefore $\bar{p} \sum_{i \varepsilon N} x_i > \bar{p} \sum_{i \varepsilon N} w_i$. This cannot be if x is a feasible allocation. Therefore $\bar{x}$ is Pareto optimal.

QED

It is, of course, not very useful to know that a completitive gift equilibrium if Pareto optimal unless we also know that such an equilibrium exists. In the usual proofs of the existence of competitive equilibrium, the crucial step is to show that there is a nonempty, upper-semi-continuous aggregate demand correspondence. Theorem 8 states conditions under which there if such a correspondence when there if pairwise consumer interrelatedness. With the use of Theorem 8, it is a quite mechanical exercise to adapt any of the familiar proofs of Arrow and Debreu [1], Debreu [3], McKenzie [4] or Rader [5], to prove the existence of a competitive gift equilibrium.

Definition 13. The joint household demand correspondence, f_H, of household, H, is a correspondence $f_H : E^m \to \sum_{i \varepsilon H} X_i$ such that for $p \varepsilon E^m$, $f_H(p) = \{ \sum_{i \varepsilon H} x_i | x$ is a household equilibrium for H at prices, p$\}$. Let H be the set of all households. Then the <u>aggregate demand correspondence, f</u>, is a correspondence such that for $p \varepsilon E^m$, $f(p) = \sum_{H \varepsilon H} f_H(p)$.

The set, $f_H(p)$, will be nonempty if at prices, p, there is a household equilibrium for H. If consumers are not egocentric, $f_H(p)$ may be empty at some prices. In the example illustrated in Figure 2 of Section I, if the initial allocation of wealth is represented by a point between $\bar{A}$ and $\bar{B}$, then there is no household equilibrium when the price of the good is positive. The only point which A likes at least as well as every x such that $px_A \leqq pw_A$ and $p(x_A + x_B) \leqq p(w_A + w_B)$ is $\bar{A}$. The only point which B likes at least as well as every x such that $px_B \leqq pw_B$ and $p(x_A + x_B) \leqq p(w_A + w_B)$ is $\bar{B}$.

<u>Theorem 7.</u>

If household, H, has exactly two members, A and B, with compact, convex consumption sets X_A and X_B respectively, if preferences of A and B are weakly convex, continuous and egocentric and if preferences of A and B are locally nonsatiated on X_A and X_B respectively, then for any price vector, p, such that $px_A \leqq pw_A$ for some $x_A \varepsilon X_A$ and such that $px_B \leqq pw_B$ for some $x_B \varepsilon X_B$, the set $f_H(p)$ is nonempty.

Proof:

The set $f_H(p)$ will be nonempty if there exists a household equilibrium for H at prices, p. Since Consumers A and B are interrelated with no consumers outside the household, the level of preference of A and B depends only on what is consumed by A and B. One can therefore treat preferences of A and B as if they were defined only on (X_A, X_B). Let $x^A(p) \equiv (x_A^A(p), x_B^A(p))$ be an allocation such that $x^A(p)$ maximizes R_A on the set $\{(x_A, x_B) | p(x_A + x_B) \leqq p(w_A + w_B)\}$. Let $x^B(p) \equiv (x_A^B(p), x_B^B(p))$ be an allocation such that $x^B(p)$ maximizes R_B on $\{(x_A, x_B) | p(x_A + x_B) \leqq p(w_A + w_B)\}$.

Suppose that $px_A^A(p) < pw_A$. It will be shown that in this case $x^A(p)$ is a household equilibrium at prices, p. Consider (x_A', x_B') such that $p(x_A' + x_B') \leqq p(w_A + w_B)$ and $(x_A', x_B') P_B (x_B^A(p), x_B^A(p))$. The definition of $x^A(p)$ implies that $x^A(p) R_A (x_A', x_B')$. Since preferences are egocentric, it must be that $x_B' >_B x_B^A(p)$. If $px_B' < px_B^A(p)$, then continuity of preferences together with Assumption 5, ensure that for some $\mathring{x}_B$ near x_B', $\mathring{x}_B >_B x_B^A(p)$ and $p\mathring{x}_B < px_B^A(p)$. But since A is nonmalevolent, $(x_A^A(p), \mathring{x}_B)R_A(x_A^A(p), x_B^A(p))$. Since A is locally nonsatiated on X_A, there is an $\mathring{x}_A$ near $x_A^A(p)$ such that $(\mathring{x}_A, \mathring{x}_B)P_A(x_A^A(p), x_B^A(p))$ and such that $p(\mathring{x}_A + \mathring{x}_B) < p(w_A + w_B)$. This contradicts the definition of $x^A(p)$. Therefore if $(x_A', x_B')\ P_B x^A(p)$ and if $p(x_A' + x_B') \leqq p(w_A + w_B)$ then $px_B' \geqq px_B^A(p)$. But since $px_A^A(p) < pw_A$, $px_B^A(p) > pw_B$. Therefore $px_B' > pw_B$. It follows that when $px_A^A(p) < pw_A$, $x^A(p)$ is a household equilibrium at prices, p. An analogous proof shows that if $px_B^B(p) < pw_B$, then $x^B(p)$ is a household equilibrium at prices, p.

The remaining case is where $px_A^A(p) \geqq pw_A$ and $px_B^B(p) \geqq pw_B$. Consider an allocation, $(\bar{x}_A, \bar{x}_B)$, such that $\bar{x}_A$ maximizes $\gtrsim_A$ on $\{x_A | px_A \leqq pw_A\}$ and $\bar{x}_B$ maximizes $\gtrsim_B$ on $\{x_B | px_B \leqq pw_B\}$. Suppose that $(x_A, x_B)\ P_A(\bar{x}_A, \bar{x}_B)$, $p(x_A + x_B) \leqq p(w_A + w_B)$ and $px_A \leqq pw_A$. Then $x^A(p)\ R_A(x_A, x_B)$. Since preferences are weakly convex, if $(x_A(\lambda), x_B(\lambda)) = \lambda(x_A^A(p), x_B^A(p)) + (1-\lambda)(x_A, x_B)$ for λ such that $0 \leqq \lambda \leqq 1$, then $(x_A(\lambda), x_B(\lambda))R_A(x_A, x_B)\ P_A(\bar{x}_A, \bar{x}_B)$. But $px_A^A(p) \geqq pw_A$ and $px_A \leqq pw_a$. Therefore for some $\hat{\lambda}$ such that $0 \leqq \hat{\lambda} \leqq 1$, $px_A(\hat{\lambda}) = pw_A$ and $px_B(\hat{\lambda}) \leqq pw_B$. But this implies that $\bar{x}_A \gtrsim_A x_A(\hat{\lambda})$ and $\bar{x}_B \gtrsim_B x_B(\hat{\lambda})$. Nonmalevolence implies that $(\bar{x}_A, \bar{x}_B)\ R_A(x_A(\hat{\lambda}), x_B(\hat{\lambda}))$. But this is a contradiction. It follows that if $p(x_A + x_B) \leqq p(w_A + w_B)$ and if $px_B \leqq pw_A$, then $(\bar{x}_A, \bar{x}_B)\ R_A(x_A, x_B)$. An analogous proof shows that if $p(x_A + x_B) \leqq p(w_A + w_B)$ and if $px_B \leqq pw_B$, then $(\bar{x}_A, \bar{x}_B)\ R_B(x_A, x_B)$. Therefore $(\bar{x}_A, \bar{x}_B)$ is a household equilibrium at prices, p. QED

<u>Theorem 8.</u>

If the following assumptions hold:

(1) For all $i \varepsilon N$, X_i is a convex, compact subset of Euclidean m space.

(2) For all $i \varepsilon N$, R_i is a weakly convex, continuous quasi-ordering on $X = \prod_{i \varepsilon N} X_i$.

(3) For all $i \varepsilon N$, Consumer i is locally nonsatiated on X_i and preferences of Consumer i are egocentric with respect to every other consumer.
(4) No household contains more than two consumers.
(5) The set of prices, P, is a closed convex set not containing zero, such that for all $i \varepsilon N$, and for all $p \varepsilon P$, there exists an $x_i \varepsilon X_i$ such that $px_i < pw_i$.

then the aggregate demand correspondence $f : P \rightarrow \sum_{i \varepsilon N} X_i$ is upper semi-continuous and for every $p \varepsilon P$, f(p) is a nonempty convex set.

Proof:

Since X_i is compact and R_i is continuous for all $i \varepsilon N$, it must be that if H has only one member then $f_H(p)$ is nonempty for all $p \varepsilon P$. According to Theorem 7, if H has two members, $f_H(p)$ is nonempty for all $p \varepsilon P$.

If a household has only one member, one can immediately apply the method used by Debreu [3, p. 63] to show that f_H is upper semi-continuous. Suppose that a household has two members, A and B.

Let $g_A(p) = \{x | p(x_A + x_B) \leqq p(w_A + w_B)$ and xR_Ax' if $p(x_A' + x_B') \leqq p(w_A + w_B)$ and $px_A' \leqq pw_A\}$. Let $g_B(p) = \{x | p(x_A + x_B) \leqq p(w_A + w_B)$ and xR_Bx' if $p(x_A' + x_B') \leqq p(w_A + w_B)$ and $px_B' \leqq pw_B\}$. Assumption 5 and the continuity of R_A and R_B ensure that $g_A(p)$ and $g_B(p)$ are upper semi-continuous correspondences. Since $f_H(p) = g_A(p) \cap g_B(p)$, f_H is also u.s.c.

Weak convexity of preferences guarantees that $f_H(p)$ is a convex set for every $p \varepsilon P$. Since $f(p) = \sum_{H \varepsilon \mathcal{H}} f_H(p)$, f is u.s.c. and has nonempty convex image sets for every $p \varepsilon P$. QED

The final theorem and its corollary are counterparts to the "Second Optimality Theorem of Welfare Economics". It is shown that when consumer interrelatedness is restricted to monogamous pairs and is egocentric that a large class of Pareto optima can be sustained as competitive gift equilibria.

Theorem 9.

If $\bar{x}$ is a Pareto optimal allocation for an exchange economy with an aggregate vector of commodity holdings, w, and if

(1) For all $i \varepsilon N$, R_i is a convex quasi-ordering on X_i and Consumer i is locally nonsatiated on X_i.

(2) No household contains more than two consumers.

(3) All consumer interrelatedness is egocentric.

then there exists a price vector $\bar{p}$ and budgets, $(b_1,\ldots,b_n)$, such that: if i belongs to a single member household and if $xP_i\bar{x}_i$ then $px_i \geqq b_i$; if A and B belong to a two member household then for x such that $p(x_A + x_B) < b_A + b_B$, if $xP_A\bar{x}$ then $px_A \geqq b_A$, and if $xP_B\bar{x}$ then $px_B \geqq b_B$.

Corollary.[3]

If the assumptions of Theorem 9 are true, if preferences are continuous, and if for every $i\varepsilon N$, there exists an $\overset{o}{x}_i \;\varepsilon\; X_i$ such that $\bar{p}\overset{o}{x}_i < \bar{p}\bar{x}_i$ where $\bar{p}$ is a price vector satisfying Theorem 8, then $\bar{x}$ is a competitive gift equilibrium at prices $\bar{p}$ where for all $i\varepsilon N$, consumer i is given a budget, $b_i = \bar{p}\bar{x}_i$.

Proof of Theorem 9:

Since preferences are convex, the set, $V \equiv \{ \sum_{i\varepsilon N} x_i \mid \mathbf{x}$ is Pareto superior to $\bar{x}\}$ is convex. Since $\bar{x}$ is Pareto optimal, $w \notin V$. Minkowski's separation theorem implies that there exists a (non-zero) $\bar{p}$ such that if $\sum_{i\varepsilon N} x_i \;\varepsilon\; V$ then $\bar{p} \sum_{i\varepsilon N} x_i \geqq \bar{p}w = \bar{p} \sum_{i\varepsilon N} \bar{x}_i$. It is easily shown, since preferences are non-malevolent, that for all $i\varepsilon N$, if $x_i >_i \bar{x}_i$ then $\bar{p}x_i \geqq \bar{p}\bar{x}_i$. If consumer i belongs to a single member household it is immediate that if $xP_i\bar{x}$, then $\bar{p}x_i \geqq \bar{p}\bar{x}_i$.

Suppose that A and B belong to the same two member household. Since A and B are interrelated with no consumers outside the household, it follows that if $\bar{p}(x_A + x_B) < \bar{p}(\bar{x}_A + \bar{x}_B)$ then $\bar{x}P_A x$ or $\bar{x}P_B x$. Suppose $p(x_A + x_B) < \bar{p}(\bar{x}_A + \bar{x}_B)$ and $xP_A\bar{x}$. Then $\bar{x}P_B x$. Since preferences are egocentric $x_A > \bar{x}_A$. But it was shown above that this implies that $\bar{p}x_A \geqq \bar{p}\bar{x}_A$. Likewise if $p(x_A + x_B) < \bar{p}(\bar{x}_A + \bar{x}_B)$ and $xP_B\bar{x}$, it must be that $\bar{p}x_B \geqq \bar{p}\bar{x}_B$. Therefore if each consumer $i\varepsilon N$, is given a budget $b_i = \bar{p}\bar{x}_i$, the conclusion of the theorem holds.

QED

Proof of Corollary:

If consumer i belongs to a single member household, the proof that $\bar{x}$ is a household equilibrium at $\bar{p}$ for his household is the same as that offered in Debreu [3, p. 96].

Suppose that A and B are members of a two person household and that $\bar{p}$ is a price vector satisfying Theorem 9. Suppose that $\bar{p}(x_A + x_B) \leqq \bar{p}(\bar{x}_A + \bar{x}_B)$, $\bar{p}x_A \leqq \bar{p}\bar{x}_A$ and $xP_A\bar{x}$.

By assumption there is an $\overset{\circ}{x}_A \in X_A$ such that $\bar{p}\overset{\circ}{x}_A < \bar{p}\bar{x}_A$. Consider the allocation, $x(\lambda)$ where $x_B(\lambda) = x_B$ and $x_A(\lambda) = \lambda x_A + (1-\lambda)\overset{\circ}{x}_A$. Continuity implies that for λ close to one, $x(\lambda)P_A\bar{x}$. But $\bar{p}x_A(\lambda) < \bar{p}\bar{x}_A$ and $\bar{p}(x_A(\lambda) + x_B(\lambda)) < \bar{p}(\bar{x}_A + \bar{x}_B)$. This contradicts Theorem 8. Therefore if $\bar{p}(x_A + x_B) \leqq \bar{p}(\bar{x}_A + \bar{x}_B)$ and $\bar{p}x_A \leqq \bar{p}\bar{x}_A$ then $\bar{x}R_Ax$. An analogous statement can be made for B. The corollary follows immediately.

QED

<u>Conclusion</u>:

The purposes of this paper have been twofold. Restrictions on the nature of consumer interrelatedness such as separability between individuals, nonmalevolence, and egocentricity (in decreasing order of generality) are suggested. The relations between these assumptions are explored, as are some of their implications for individual behavior. Perhaps the most interesting and least intuitively understandable of these assumptions is that of egocentricity which limits the degree of generosity of our consumers. Theorems 1, 2, and 3 help to clarify the meaning of this assumption.

It is established that a competitive gift equilibrium can be shown to exist when the only consumer interrelatedness is between pairs of egocentric consumers. In this case there is also a two way correspondence between the set of competitive gift equilibria and the set of Pareto optima.

Things become more difficult (and perhaps more interesting) when preferences are less monogamous. An allocation mechanism which is Pareto efficient when there are large networks of interrelated consumers is discussed in Bergstrom [2].

FOOTNOTES

[1] Implicit in the interpretation of R_i as the preference relation of consumer i is that his ranking of situations depends only on the quantities of commodities consumed by each consumer. If there is more than one way in which the same commodity bundle can be used by a given consumer, the traditional theory is salvaged by arguing that the R_i's are derived from the solutions of the underlying problem of how best to use each commodity bundle. This underlying problem is solved unambiguously by each consumer and the resultant activities are compared. If there is consumer interrelatedness, and if two consumers disagree about how one of them should consume a particular bundle, more care is required in the interpretation of R_i.

[2] Here and in the sequel we deal only with an exchange economy. This theorem and subsequent theorems can be extended to a production economy of the sort described by Debreu [3]. Attention is restricted here to an exchange economy solely as a matter of notational convenience.

[3] An alternative and perhaps more satisfactory theorem on the correspondence between Pareto optima and competitive equilibrium is proved by Rader [4]. Rader's assumptions and method of proof can be readily adapted to this problem.

REFERENCES

* I owe a debt of thanks to Professor Trout Rader of Washington University for many helpful comments and suggestions.

[1] Arrow, K.J., and G. Debreu, "Existence of an Equilibrium for a Competitive Economy", Econometrica XXII, (July, 1954), 265-90.

[2] Bergstrom, T., "A 'Scandinavian Consensus Solution' for Efficient Income Distribution among Benevolent Consumers", (mimeographed).

[3] Debreu, G., Theory of Value (New York, John Wiley & Sons, 1959).

[4] McKenzie, L.W., "On the Existence of General Equilibrium: for a Competitive Market", Econometrica XXVII, (January, 1959) 54-57.

[5] Rader, J.T., "Pairwise Optimality and Non-Competitive Behavior," in Papers in Quantitative Economics, edited by J. P. Quirk and A. M. Zarley (Lawrence, Kansas, University of Kansas Press, 1968) 101-128.

PARETO OPTIMALITY AND COMPETITIVE EQUILIBRIUM

IN A GENERAL EQUILIBRIUM MODEL OF ECONOMIC GROWTH

by

Mohamed Ali El-Hodiri*
University of Kansas

1. Introduction

In this paper we show that a growth program is "Pareto Optimal" if and only if it could be characterized by a "competitive equilibrium." The assumptions under which this is achieved are, essentially, non-increasing returns to scale concavity, of utility functions and independence on the consumption and production sides. We assume also that all decisions are taken at the beginning of the planning period, and that utility functionals are represented by integrals of instantanious utility functions. Thus we restrict our attention to a very special class of economies, and so we shall not pretend that our result is usable in the planning of economic development. Our result, however, is a step forward from static welfare economics, see e.g. Karlin [3], as time enters the analysis in some sense. Our view of the next step, is where utility functionals don't assume a special form and where an adaptive set up is the frame work for decision making.

This paper is an extension of my paper with Professor Takayama [1], where we did not allow for capital accumulation. The price we pay for the presence of capital accumulation is in terms of concavity assumptions.

2. Formulation of the Problem

Consider an economy with n goods, m production processes, ℓ investment processes and B consumers. Let $g_{ij}(t, u_j)$ denote the outcome, in terms of good i of operating process j at level u_j at time t. We follow the convention that $g_{ij} \leq 0$ if good i is a net input to process j and $g_{ij} > 0$ if good i is a net output of process j. The presence of t as an argument of g_{ij} indicates the possibility of technological change and the fact that g_{ij} depends only on u_j assumes the absence of externalities. Investment processes represent some grouping of investment projects (an alternative name would be: project types). They are described by way of requirement functions and addition-to-capacity functions.

Let $s_{ik}(t, v_k)$ be the requirement in terms of good i, when process k is operated at level v_k at time t, and let $S_{kj}(t, v_k)$ be the gross addition to the capacity of production process j when investment process k is operated at level v_k at time t. The capacity of a production process, $z_j(t)$, is defined to be the maximum level at which the process could be operated. Denote consumer β's consumption of good i at time t by c_i^{β}, and let $c_i = (c_i^1, \ldots, c_i^B)$. Assume all decision makers' planning period to be [0,T]. The rate of change in the capacity of production process j is given by:

(1) $\dot{z}_j = \sum_k S_{kj}(t, v_k) - \alpha_j z_j$

where α_j is the constant rate of depreciation in the capacity of process j.

Definition 1. A program is: vector functions: $u(t) = (u_1(r), \ldots, u_m(r))$, $v(t) = (v_1(r), \ldots, v_\ell(t))$, $c(t) = (c_1(t), \ldots, c_n(t))$; an initial capacity $z(0) = (z_1(r_o), \ldots, z_m(t_o)) = z_o$ and a terminal capacity $z(T) = z_T$. Let a program be denoted by $\Pi = (u, v, c, z, z_T)$.

Definition 2. A program is said to be feasible if:

(i) Equation (1) is satisfied subject to $z^o \varepsilon Z^o$ and $z^1 \varepsilon Z^1$, where Z^o and Z^1 are initial and terminal sets of capacities, with Z^1 representing the "goals" of the plan.

(ii) No more of any good is used than what is available.

(2) $\sum_j g_{ij}(t,u_j) - \sum_k s_{ik}(t,v_k) - \sum_\beta c_i \geq 0$

(iii) No process is operated beyond its capacity.

(3) $u_j \leq z_j$

(iv) Consumption and levels of processes are never negative.

(4) $c_i \geq 0$, $v_j \geq 0$, $u_j \geq 0$.

Now let $\phi^{\beta}(t,c^{\beta})$ be the instantaneous utility function of consumer β, where $c^{\beta} = (c_1^{\beta}, \ldots, c_n^{\beta})$. We assume that the consumers' ordering of consumption paths is represented by the functional

$$I^{\beta}[C^{\beta}] = \int_o^T \phi^{\beta}(t, c^{\beta})dt.$$

Definition 3. A feasible program $\hat{\Pi}$ is said to be Pareto optimal if there does not exist a feasible program Π' such that $I^{\beta}[C'^{\beta}] \geq I^{\beta}[\hat{C}^{\beta}]$, $\beta = 1, \ldots, B$; with strict inequality for at least one β.

Before we introduce the definition of a competitive equilibrium path we first define the "cumulative return on a unit of capacity." Suppose capacity of type j depreciates at the rate α_j, then a unit of capacity added at time t becomes $e^{\alpha_j(t-\tau)}$ at time τ. If the rental per unit of capacity j at time τ is $r_j(\tau)$, then the return accumulated from time τ to time T is $\int_t^T e^{\alpha_j(t-\tau)} r_j(\tau)d\tau$.

Definition 4. A program $\overset{o}{\Pi}$ is said to be a competitive equilibrium program if there exist prices of goods $P \varepsilon E_n^+$, rentals of capacity $R \varepsilon E_m^+$, where P(t) and r(t) are piecewise continuous on [O, T], such that:

(i) Consumers maximize their instantaneous utility among bundles that cost no more, i.e. $u^{\beta}(c^{\beta},t)$ is maximized at $\overset{o}{c}{}^{\beta}$ subject to $P.\overset{o}{C}{}^{\beta} \geq P.C^{\beta}$, at each point of time.

(ii) Producers of current goods maximize their profits, i.e. $\sum_i P_i g_{ij}(u_j,t) - r_j u_j$ is maximized at each point of time.

(iii) Producers of investment goods maximize their profits which is defined as the difference between comulative returns on capacity added by investment minus the costs of production, i.e.,

$$\sum_j \left(\int_t^T e^{\alpha_j(t-\tau)} r_j(\tau)d\tau \right) S_{kj}(V_k,t) - \sum_i P_i S_{ij}(V_k,t) \text{ is}$$

maximized at each point of time.

(iv) Supply of current output is no less than demand; in case of excess supply of any good its price is zero, i.e.,

$$E_i = \sum_j y_{ij}(u_j,t) - \sum_\beta c_i^\beta - \sum_k S_{ik}(t,v_k) \geq 0 \text{ and } P_iE_i = 0.$$

(v) Utilized capacity is no more than available capacity; in case of excess capacity the rental is zero, i.e.,

$$z_j(t) - u_j(t) \geq 0 \text{ and } r_j(z(t) - u_j(t)) = 0.$$

Before we state our proposition, we list the assumptions under which it holds.

A.1. The functions g_{ij}, S_{kj}, s_{ik}, ϕ^β have continuous first order partial derivatives in all their arguments.

A.2. The functions g_{ij}, S_{kj}, $-s_{ik}$, ϕ^β are concave for any given t, positive g_{ij}. When $g_{ij} < 0$ g_{ij} is convex.

A.3. An increase in the level of an investment process never decreases the capacity of any production process. For each process j there exists an investment process k such that increasing the level of k adds to the capacity of j, i.e., S_{kj} is monotone nondecreasing, for each j there exists a k such that S_{kj} is strictly monotone increasing.

A.4. There exists a good that is a necessity in the sense that each consumer consumes a positive amount of that good; furthermore the "marginal utility" of that good is never zero, i.e., there exists a good i_o that

(i) $c_{io}^\beta(t) > 0$ $\qquad t \in [0,T]$

(ii) $\phi_{io}^\beta = \partial \dfrac{\phi^\beta}{\partial c_{io}^\beta} \neq 0$ $\qquad t \in [0,T],\ c_{io}^\beta > 0.$

A.5. For each point in time, for any good i there exists a consumer that acquires a positive amount of that good, i.e., given $\bar{t} \in [0,T]$, and $\underline{i} \in \{1, 2, \ldots, n\}$; $\bar{\beta} \in \{1, \ldots, B\}$. $c_{\underline{i}}^\beta(\bar{t}) > 0$.

A.6. The set Z_o is a single point, and the set Z_1 is an open set.

3. Characterization of the Solution.

Proposition: Assuming A.1-A.6, a program $\hat{\Pi}$ is Pareto optimal if and only if it is a competitive equilibrium.

Proof:

(1) A program is $\hat{\Pi}$ Pareto optimal if it is a solution to all of the following maximization problems $M(\beta^*)$, $\beta^* = 1, 2, \ldots, B$, where $M(\beta^*)$ is:

$$\max I^{\overset{*}{\beta}}[c^{\overset{*}{\beta}}] \text{ subject to}$$

$$I^{\beta}[c^{\beta}] \geq I^{\beta}[\hat{c}^{\beta}], \; \beta \neq \overset{*}{\beta}$$

and to conditions (1) through (5).

To establish (1), we first suppose $\hat{\Pi}$ is not a solution to the individual maximization problems $M(\overset{*}{\beta})$. Then, for at least one $\overset{*}{\beta}$, there exists a feasible program $\hat{\Pi}$ such that:

$$I^{\overset{*}{\beta}}[\bar{c}^{\overset{*}{\beta}}] > I^{\overset{*}{\beta}}[\hat{c}^{\overset{*}{\beta}}]$$

$$I^{\beta}[\bar{c}^{\beta}] \geq I^{\beta}[\hat{c}^{\beta}], \; \beta \neq \overset{*}{\beta}.$$

But this contradicts the Pareto optimality of $\hat{\Pi}$.

On the other hand, suppose $\acute{\Pi}$ is a solution to the problems $M(\beta^*)$ which is not a Pareto optimum. Then there exists a feasible program $\bar{\Pi}$ such that

$$I^{\beta}[\bar{c}^{\beta}] \geq I^{\beta}[c'^{\beta}],$$

with strict inequality for at least one β. Thus $\acute{\Pi}$ does not solve at least one of the problems $M(\beta^*)$, which is a contradiction. This completes the proof of (1).

(2) A program $\hat{\Pi}$ is a solution to a problem $M(\beta^*)$ if: there exist positive constants $y_{\beta}^{\beta^*}$ and non-negative functions $\mu_i^{\beta^*}(t)$, $\nu^{\beta^*}(t)$ such that: for all $t \in [0,T]$,

2.1. $\mu_i^{\beta^*} \hat{g}'_{ij} - \nu_j^{\beta^*} \leq 0$, where $\hat{g}'_{ij} = \dfrac{\partial g_{ij}}{\partial u_j} \Big| \hat{\Pi}$, with equality if $\hat{u}_j > 0$.

2.2. $\sum_j (\int_t^T e^{\alpha_j(t-\tau)} \nu_j^{\overset{*}{\beta}}(\tau)\, d\tau)\, \hat{S}'_{kj} - \sum_i \mu_i^{\overset{*}{\beta}} \hat{s}'_{ik} \leq 0$, where

$\hat{S}'_{kj} = \frac{\partial S_{kj}}{\partial v_k} |\hat{\Pi}$, $\hat{s}'_{ik} = \frac{\partial s_{ik}}{\partial v_k} |\hat{\Pi}$, with equality when $\hat{v}_k > 0$.

2.3. $y_\beta^{\beta*} \hat{\phi}_i^\beta - \mu_i^{\beta*} \leq 0$, where $\hat{\phi}_i^\beta = \frac{\partial S_{ik}}{\partial c_i^\beta} |$, with equality when $\hat{c}_i^\beta > 0$.

2.4. $\mu_i^{\beta*}(\Sigma_i g_{ij}(t, \hat{u}_j) - \Sigma_k s_{ik}(t, \hat{v}_k) - \Sigma_\beta \hat{c}_i^\beta) = 0$,

$\nu_j^{\beta*} (\hat{z}_j - \hat{u}_j) = 0$.

To prove (2) we utilize the fact that each problem $M(\beta*)$ is an optimal control problem. A necessary[1] (see Hestenes [2]) condition for $\hat{\Pi}$ to be a solution to the problem $M(\beta*)$ is: there exist non-negative constants $y_\beta^{\beta*}$, functions $q_j^{\beta*}(t)$ and non-negative functions $\mu_k^{\beta*}(t)$, $\nu_j^{\beta*}(t)$, which are never all zeros, where $\mu_i^{\beta*}(t)$, $\nu_j^{\beta*}(t)$ are piecewise continuous and $q_j^\beta(t)$ are piecewise continuously differentiable; such that if we define:

$$H = y_\beta^{\beta*} \phi^{\beta*}(c^{\beta*}) + \sum_{\beta \neq \beta} y_\beta^{\beta*}(\phi^\beta(c^\beta) - \phi^\beta(\hat{c}^\beta)) +$$

$$\Sigma_j q_j^{\beta*}(t) (\Sigma_k S_{kj}(t, v_k) - \alpha_j z_j) + \sum_i \mu^{\beta*}(\Sigma_j g_{ij}(t, u_j) -$$

$$\sum_\beta c_i^\beta) + \sum_j \nu_j^{\beta*}(z_j - u_j),$$

(i) $\dot{q}_j^{\beta*} = -\hat{H}_{z_j} = \frac{\partial H}{\partial z_j}\Big|_{\Pi=\hat{\Pi}} = \alpha_j q_j^{\beta*} - \nu_j^{\beta*}$, $q(T) = 0$,

$(t \in [0,T]$, all $j)$

[1]The regularity conditions for the Hestenes theorem are satisfied (due to A.1.), in particular the Jacobian of constraints 2-4 has full rank (it contains submatrix of order n + m whose determinant is 1).

$$\text{(ii)}\ \hat{H}_{c_i^\beta} = \left.\frac{\partial H}{\partial c_i^\beta}\right|_{\Pi = \hat{\Pi}} = y_\beta^{\beta*}\hat{\phi}_i - \mu_i^{\beta*} \leq 0 \ (t \,\varepsilon\, [0, T],$$

all i and all β)

$$\text{(iii)}\ \hat{H}_{v_k} = \left.\frac{\partial H}{\partial v_k}\right|_{\Pi = \hat{\Pi}} = \sum_j q_u^{\beta*}\hat{S}'_{kj} - \sum_i \mu_i^{\beta*} s'_{ik} \leq 0$$

(t ε [0, T], all k)

$$\text{(iv)}\ \hat{H}_{u_j} = \left.\frac{\partial H}{\partial u_j}\right|_{\Pi = \hat{\Pi}} = \sum_i \mu_i^{\beta*}\hat{g}_{ij} - \nu_j^{*} \leq 0 \ (t \,\varepsilon\, [0,T], \text{ all } j)$$

with equality holding if c_i, v_k, u_j are positive, respectively.

$$\text{(v)}\ \mu_i^{\beta*}\left(\sum_j g_{ij}(t, \hat{u}_j) - \sum_k s_{ik}(t, \hat{v}_k) - \sum_\beta \hat{c}_i^\beta\right) = 0,$$

$$\nu_j^{\beta*}(\hat{z}_j - \hat{u}_j) = 0.$$

Solving (i) we find that $q_j^{\beta*}(t) = \int_t^T e^{\alpha_j(t-\tau)} \nu^{\beta*}(\tau)d\tau$ (utilizing $q_j^{\beta*}(T) = 0$ and the fact that (i) is a linear differential equation). Substituting in (iii)

$$\text{(iii)}'\ \sum_j\left(\int_t^T e^{\alpha_j(t-\tau)} \nu_j^{\beta*}(\tau)d\tau\right)\hat{S}'_{kj} - \sum_i \mu_i^{\beta*}\hat{s}'_{ik} \leq 0,$$

(t ε [0, T], all k).

Our necessary conditions are equivalent to (ii), (iii), (iv) and (v). Note that $\int_t^T e^{\alpha_j(t-\tau)} \nu^\beta \geq 0$.

We now show that $y_\beta^{\beta*}$ are positive for all β. For suppose one of them, say $y_{\overline{\beta}}^{\beta*}$, is zero. Then by assumption A.4 (i) and by (ii) above, we have

$$0 = y^{\beta}_{\bar{\beta}} \hat{\phi}^{\beta}_{i_o} - \mu^{\beta*}_{i_o} = -\mu^{\beta*}_{i_o}, \text{ i.e. } \mu^{\beta*}_{i_o} = 0, \text{ while}$$

$$0 = y^{\beta*}_{\beta} \hat{\phi}_{i_o} - \mu^{\beta*}_{i_j} = y^{\beta*}_{\beta} \hat{\phi}_{i_o} \; (\beta \neq \bar{\beta}).$$

By assumption A.4. (ii), this implies $y^{\beta*}_{\beta} = 0$ $(\beta \neq \bar{\beta})$ and thus $y^{\beta*}_{\bar{\beta}}$ = 0 (all β). By A.5. (i) for each commodity i, there exists a consumer β such that $y^{\beta*}_{\beta} \hat{\phi}^{\beta}_{i} - \mu_i = 0$. Thus all the μ_i's are zeros. Substituting in (iii) we have $\sum_j q_j(t)\hat{S}'_{kj} \leq 0$. By A.3., $\hat{S}'_{kj} \geq 0$, we noted above that $q_j(t) \geq 0$. Thus $\sum_j q_j(t)\hat{S}'_{kj} = 0$, which (since $q_j S'_{kj} \geq 0$) implies $q_j(t)\hat{S}'_{kj} = 0$ for all k and j. By assumption A.3., for each j there exists a k such that $S'_{kj} > 0$. Thus $q_j(t) = 0$ for all j. This means $\int_t^T e^{\alpha_j(t-\tau)} \nu_j(\tau)\, d\tau \overset{t}{\equiv} 0$. But, since the integrand is non-negative, this implies $e^{\alpha_j(t-\tau)} \nu^{\beta*}_j(\tau) = 0$ a.e. for $\tau \in [t, T]$. But $e^{\alpha_j(t-\tau)} > 0$. Thus $\nu^{\beta*}_j(\tau) = 0$ a.e. for $\tau \in [t, T]$ for $\tau \in [0, T]$. Thus $\nu^{\beta*}_j(t) = 0$ on a subset on [0, T] of positive linear measure, say τ, for all j. Thus there exists a $t \in T$ for which $y^{\beta*}_{\beta}$, $u^{\beta*}_i$, $\nu^{\beta*}_j$ and $q^{\beta*}_j$ are simultaneously zeros. This contradiction proves the assertion that $y^{\beta*}_{\beta} > 0$. Conditions 2.1., 2.2., 2.3. and 2.4. are implied by as (ii), (iii), (iv) and (v) respectively.

Turning now to sufficiency, suppose conditions 2.1. - 2.4. hold. Then conditions (i) to (iv) are satisfied. By assumptions A.1. and A.2., the sufficiency theorem of Mangasarian [4] applies. Thus 2.1. - 2.3. are sufficient for $\hat{\Pi}$ to be a solution to problem M(β*).

(3) If $\hat{\Pi}$ is a Pareto optimum then $\hat{\Pi}$ is a competitive equilibrium. Since $\hat{\Pi}$ is a Pareto optimum, we have, by (1) and (2): conditions 2.1. - 2.3. hold for $\beta* = 1, 2, \ldots, B$. Summing those sets of relations over β*, we get:

3.1. $\left(\sum_{\beta*=1}^{B} \mu^{\beta*}_i\right) \hat{g}_{ij} - \left(\sum_{\beta*} \nu^{\beta*}_j\right) \leq 0$, with equality if $\hat{u}_j > 0$.

3.2. $\sum_j \int_t^T e^{-\alpha_j(t-\tau)} \sum_{\beta^*} \nu_j^{\beta^*}(\tau)d\tau)\ \hat{S}'_{kj} - \sum_i (\sum_{\beta^*} \mu_i^{\beta^*})\ \hat{s}'_{ij} \leq 0,$

with equality if $\hat{v}_k > 0$.

3.3. $(\sum_{\beta^*} y_\beta^{\beta^*})\ \hat{\phi}_i^\beta - \sum_{\beta^*} \mu_i^{\beta^*} \leq 0$, with equality if $\hat{c}_i^\beta > 0$.

3.4. $(\sum_{\beta^*} \mu_i^{\beta^*})\ (\sum_j g_{ij}(t, \hat{u}_j) - \sum_k s_{ik}(t, \hat{v}_k) - \sum_\beta \hat{c}_i^\beta) = 0,$

$(\sum_{\beta^*} \nu_j^{\beta^*})\ (\hat{z}_j - \hat{u}_j) = 0.$

Now define $p_i = \sum_{\beta^*} \mu_i^{\beta^*}$, $r_j = \sum_{\beta^*} \nu_j^{\beta^*}$, and $y^\beta = \sum_{\beta^*} y_\beta^{\beta^*}$.

Substituting in 3.1. - 3.4., we get:

3.1.' $\sum_i p_i \hat{g}'_{ij} - r_j \leq 0.$

3.2.' $\sum_j (\int_t^T e^{\alpha_j(t-\tau)} r_j(\tau)d\tau)\hat{S}'_{kj} - \sum_i p_i \hat{s}_{ij} \leq 0.$

3.3.' $y^\beta \hat{\phi}_i^\beta - p_i \leq 0.$

3.4.' $p_i(\sum_j g_{kj}(t, \hat{u}_j) - \sum_k s_{ik}(t, \hat{v}_k) - \sum_\beta c_i^\beta) = 0,$

$r_j(\hat{z}_j - \hat{u}_j) = 0.$

Condition (i) in the definition of competitive equilibrium is satisfied by 3.3.' and the concavity ϕ^β. For when we have, for $c_i^\beta \geq 0$, $y^\beta\phi^\beta(t, \hat{c}^\beta) - \sum_i p_i\hat{c}_i^\beta \geq y^\beta\phi^\beta(t, c^\beta) - \sum p_i c_i^\beta$, where $y^\beta > 0$. This, in turn, implies:

$$\phi^\beta(t, \hat{c}^\beta) \geq \phi^\beta(t, c^\beta), \text{ for } c_i^\beta \geq 0 \text{ with } \sum_i p_i c_i^\beta \leq \sum p_i \hat{c}_i^\beta.$$

Conditions (ii) and (iii) follow similarly from (3.1)' and (3.2)' respectively. The first parts of conditions (iv) and (v) follow from the feasibility of $\hat{\Pi}$. The second parts of conditions (iv) and (v) follow from (3.4)'.

(4) If $\hat{\Pi}$ is a competitive equilibrium then $\hat{\Pi}$ solves all maximization problems $M(\beta^*)$. Since $\hat{\Pi}$ is a competitive equilibrium, there exist functions, $p_i(t) \geq 0$, $r_j(t) \geq 0$, that are piecewise continuous such that:

4.1. $\hat{\phi}_i^\beta - p_i \leq 0$, with equality when $\hat{c}_i^\beta > 0$, (since $\phi^{\beta}(c^{\beta}) - \Sigma p_i c_i^{\beta}$ is maximized by (i), and such that (3.1)', (3.2)' and (3.4)' are satisfied (this follows from (ii), (iii), (iv) and (v) in the definition of competitive equilibrium). Now take $y_{\beta}^{\beta*} = 1$ for all β and $\beta*$, $\mu_i^{\beta*} = p_i$ for all $\beta*$ and i, $\nu_i^{\beta*} = r_j$ for all j and $\beta*$ and $q_j^{\beta} = \int_t^T e^{\alpha_j(t-\tau)} r_j(\tau)d\tau$ for all j and $\beta*$. Consider a problem $M(\bar{\beta}*)$. With our choice of multipliers we have the conditions of (2) above. Thus by A.2., (2) applies. Since $\bar{\beta}*$ is arbitrary this establishes (4).

(5) If $\hat{\Pi}$ is a competitive equilibrium then it is a Pareto optimum. This follows from (4) and (1). By (3) and (5) our proposition is proved.

REFERENCES

*A single consumer version of this paper was presented at the Joint Seminar in Theoretical and Applied Economics, Colorado, February 1969. I am grateful to Professor L. S. Fan for useful comments on the present draft.

[1] El-Hodiri, Mohamed and Akira Takayama, Price Implications of Pareto Optimality in a Dynamic General Equilibrium Model of Economic Growth, Research Paper No. 26, Research Papers in Theoretical and Applied Economics, Dept. of Economics, University of Kansas.

[2] Hestenes, Magnus, On Variational Theory and Optimal Control Theory, SIAM Journal on Control, vol. 3 (1965), 23-48.

[3] Karlin, S., Mathematical Methods and Theory in Games, Programming and Economics, vol. 1, Addison Wesley, Reading, Mass., 1959.

[4] Mangasarian, O. L., Sufficient Conditions for Optimal Control of Nonlinear Systems, SIAM Journal on Control, vol. 4, 1966, 139-152.

SPATIAL PRICE EQUILIBRIUM, LOCATION ARBITRAGE AND LINEAR PROGRAMMING

by

S. R. Johnson*
University of Missouri

I. Preliminary Comments

In this paper a method for studying competitive price equilibrium between markets separated by transportation costs is introduced. The method has applicability to both spatial and intertemporal allocation problems in which the separation of markets can be entirely characterized in terms of one-way transportation costs.[1] For purposes of exposition, however, the problem is discussed here only in its spatial context.[2] In the problem to be studied we are given at each of two or more localities linear domestic demand and supply functions for a particular product. These domestic supply and demand functions depend only on the local price. Constant per unit transportation costs for carrying the product between localities are specified. This information together with an assumed equilibrating process is used in determining the final competitive equilibrium of prices in all the markets, quantities of the product supplied and demanded at each price, and exports and imports.

Methods currently available for solving the spatial price equilibrium problem depend on the maximization of net social pay-off [7] and the minimization of economic rent [8].[3] Both methods involve areas between or under domestic demand and supply functions. As a result the solutions are only indirectly related to behavioral assumptions about firms and/or individuals engaged in the transfer of the product between markets. An alternative approach to the spatial price equilibrium problem based directly on the activity of location arbitrage is explored in this paper. It results in a linear programming algorithm which is computationally simple and yields transportation cost efficient solutions which under certain conditions are competitive price equilibria.

In the discussion to follow, the problem is first examined for the two locality case. Restricting the problem to two localities is useful both for formalizing the ideas related to the equilibrating process and for relating the location arbitrage approach to the earlier works of Samuelson and Smith. Following discussion of the two locality case the linear programming algorithm based on location arbitrage is formulated for an arbitrary number of localities and investigated for its effectiveness in identifying competitive price equilibria. Lastly, some cursory results which follow from other assumed structures for the arbitrage industry and other specifications of transport costs and supply and demand functions are examined.

II. Spatial Price Equilibrium for Two Localities

To begin, it is assumed that there exist firms and/or individuals which engage in intermarket product arbitrage.[4] Price equilibrium between product markets is brought about by profit maximizing actions of these firms which engage in the transfer of the product from markets with lower domestic prices to markets with higher domestic prices. Costs to the arbitraging firms are those incurred in transporting the product between localities. Based on this intermarket price equilibrating process, demand and supply functions for locality arbitrage can be deduced from domestic demand and supply functions and transportation costs. Given these demand and supply functions for moving the product between localities, and the condition that product arbitraging firms are competitive, the existence of a spatial price equilibrium is easily demonstrated.

Linear supply and demand functions for the two localities are given in Equation 2.1.

$$(2.1) \quad Q_i^d = a_i - b_i P_i \text{ and } Q_j^s = c_j + d_j P_j$$

Q_j^s and $Q_i^d \geqq 0$ are quantities of the product supplied and demanded in the jth and i^{th} localities $(i,j = 1,2)$; a, b, c, and d are non-negative constants; and $P \geqq 0$ is the product price. Let F_{ij} $(= -F_{ji})$ equal the quantity of the product transferred from locality i to locality j. Then the domestic price equilibrium identities for the markets are:

$$(2.2) \quad Q_i^d = Q_i^s + \sum_{j=1}^{2} F_{ji}.$$

Substitution of locality demand and supply from equations, 2.1, into the equilibrium identities, 2.2, yields expressions for domestic equilibrium prices in terms of constants in the domestic supply and demand equations and intermarket product flows.[5] Differences between expressions for equilibrium prices in the localities are interpreted as the industry demands for location arbitrage. For two localities the demands for location arbitrage are:[6]

(2.3) $P_i - P_j = A_i - A_j - B_i \sum_{j=1}^{2} F_{ji} + B_j \sum_{i=1}^{2} F_{ij}.$

Since $P_i - P_j = -[P_j - P_i]$ just one of the two possible arbitrage demand functions contains all of the information for relating domestic equilibrium price differentials to product flows. Hence, by using $F_{ij} = -F_{ji}$, the demand for location arbitrage can always be taken as a decreasing function of the appropriate product flow.

The supply for location arbitrage is based upon the constant transport costs T_{ij} and T_{ji}. If these constant costs contain a normal rate of return then the industry supply for location arbitrage is perfectly price elastic. Letting $T_{ij} = T_{ji}$ be the supply price for location arbitrage and assuming the industry is competitive, the intermarket equilibrium condition is:

(2.4) $T_{ij} \geqq P_i - P_j.$

The inequality is included to account for the situation in which the intercept of the supply function exceeds that of the arbitrage demand function. The greater than inequality is associated with the subtraction of domestic equilibrium prices which yields an arbitrage demand function with a positive intercept.[7] If the relationship between initial domestic equilibrium prices and transportation costs is such that the inequality holds, then profit maximizing firms would not engage in arbitrage. In the more interesting case, with the difference between initial domestic equilibrium prices in excess of transport costs, firms engage in product arbitrage--collecting rents--until the domestic price differential is just equal to the transport cost.

The implied actions of the arbitrage firms suggest a solution algorithm which is quite simple for two localities. Assume the isolated equilibrium price in locality 1 is greater than the isolated equilibrium price in locality 2; i.e., $P_1^* > P_2^*$. The appropriate intermarket equilibrium condition is $T_{21} \geqq P_1 - P_2$. Consider the linear programming problem 2.5.

(2.5) Minimize $F_{21}T_{21}$

Subject to $T_{21} \geqq P_1 - P_2 = A_1 - A_2 - (B_1 + B_2)F_{21}$

$F_{21} \geqq 0.$

If the difference in the initial domestic equilibrium prices is less than the cost of transporting the product between markets, then the optimum is $F_{21} = 0$. Alternatively, if the initial domestic equilibrium price is greater than the transportation cost then the criterion is minimized at the value of F_{21} for which the demand and supply constraint holds as an equality. In each case, the solution of the programming model is identical to the industry equilibrium under the assumptions governing the behavior of the arbitraging firms and the form of competition in the arbitrage industry.[8]

III. Geometry of the Two Locality Case

The equilibrating process can be illustrated geometrically for the two locality case. In addition to developing an intuitive basis for the subsequent generalization of the arbitrage model to multiple localities, the illustration provides a convenient vehicle for integrating the related works of Samuelson and Smith. The illustration employs excess demand and supply functions for the two localities.[9] Equation 3.1 defines the locality excess demand and supply functions in terms of the notation used in the arbitrage model.

$$(3.1) \qquad ES_i = -ED_i = Q_i^s + \sum_{j=1}^{2} F_{ji} - Q_i^d$$

In Figure 1, the excess supply and demand functions for the two localities along with average transport cost functions are plotted in a back-to-back diagram similar to the one used by Samuelson in illustrating the same problem [7, p. 288]. Initial domestic equilibrium prices in the two markets are, again, P_1^* and P_2^*. The difference between domestic equilibrium prices as related to intermarket flows is given by $ES_1 - ES_2$ or alternatively, AC. AC is the function defined as the demand for location arbitrage in Equation 2.3. The average cost of transport or, incorporating our earlier assumptions regarding costs, the supply price of location arbitrage is OD. Intermarket equilibrium prices are P_1 and P_2.

Solutions obtained from arbitrage model and Samuelson's social pay-off criterion are identical in the two locality case. Net social pay-off (NSP) is defined by Samuelson [7] as the area of ABD. That is,

$$(3.2) \qquad NSP = \int_0^{F_{21}} ES_1 dt - \int_0^{F_{21}} ES_2 dt - T_{21}F_{21}.$$

FIGURE 1. PRICE EQUILIBRIUM BETWEEN TWO LOCALITIES

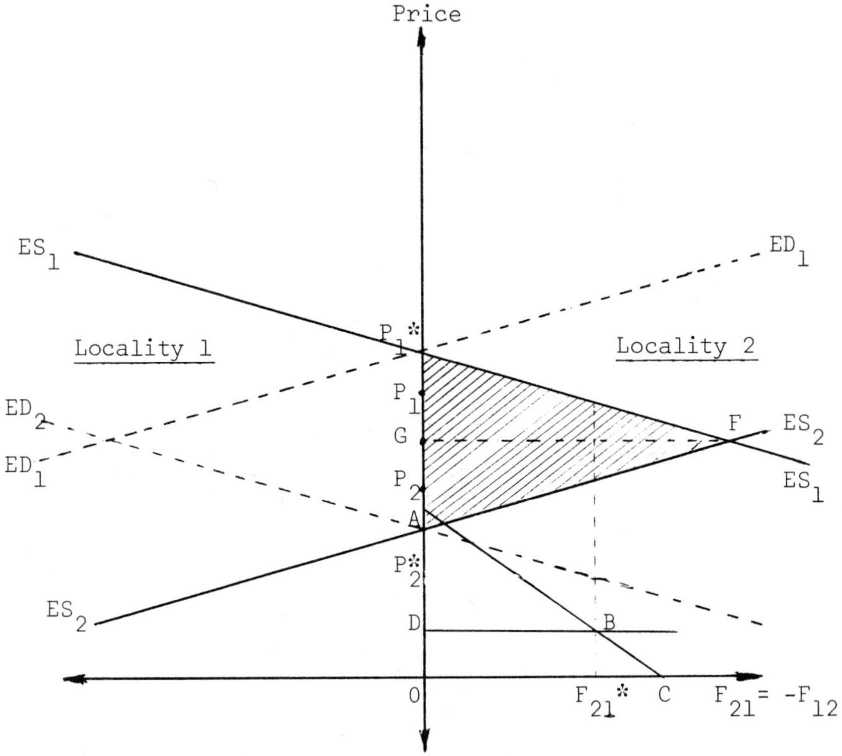

Maximizing this expression subject to the condition that $F_{21} \geqq 0$ gives first order conditions which imply a solution identical to that suggestion by the arbitrage approach.[10] It is particularly clear that the solutions are identical when we recognize that the value of the integral (3.2) at F^*_{21} is the area ADB in Figure 1.

Economic rent in the two markets is the criterion used by Smith. In the notation of Equations 2.1, the function minimized is:

$$(3.3)\quad R = \int_{P_1}^{\infty} Q_1^d dp_1 + \int_0^{P_1} Q_1^s\, dp_1 + \int_{P_2}^{\infty} Q_2^d dp_2 + \int_0^{P_2} Q_2^s dp_2.$$

The function is minimized subject to conditions $P_1, P_2 \geqq 0$ and $P_1 - P_2 + T_{12} \geqq 0$, $P_2 - P_1 + T_{21} \geqq 0$ [8, p. 27-27]. The criterion function can be rewritten taking advantage of the initial equilibrium prices P_1^* and P_2^* as:

$$(3.4) \quad R = R_1^* + R_2^* + \int_{P_1^*}^{P_1} [Q_1^s - Q_1^d]\, dp_1 + \int_{P_2}^{P_2^*} [Q_2^d - Q_2^s]\, dp_2.$$

The bracketed terms are differences between domestic supply and demand functions expressed in terms of price.[11] Geometrically, the quantity to be minimized is the area between the excess supply and demand functions for the two markets. That is, on making the appropriate conversion to the diagram in Figure 1, FP_1^*G and FP_2^*G or alternatively the area ACO. Setting intermarket transfers so as to minimize this area subject to the conditions relating prices and the non-negativity restrictions on P_1 and P_2, gives either solution at B ($F_{21} = F_{21}^*$) or at $F_{21} = 0$. Hence, it follows that each approach to the intermarket equilibrating processes leads to the same solution in the two locality case. The similarity of the three approaches for the two locality case is somewhat misleading. As we shall show in Section V, additional conditions are required to show the solutions are the same for arbitrary numbers of localities.

IV. Generalization of the Linear Programming Algorithm

Suppose that instead of two, there are $i,j = 1,2 \ldots,n$ localities. Domestic supply and demand functions are given by 2.1, where i and j take on the appropriate values. Market equilibrium conditions, 2.2, are altered to provide for the possible flows by increasing the index of summation on i and j from 2 to n. Expressions for intermarket price differentials are then obtained by the same procedure as in the two locality case. For n locations, these subtractions give n(n-1) price differentials. Since $F_{ij} = -F_{ji}$, one-half of the equations contain all of the information relating price differentials to product flows. That is, in the pair wise comparison of domestic equilibrium prices $P_i - P_j = [P_j - P_i]$. Let the redundant equations be those in which higher isolated equilibrium prices are subtracted from lower ones. The inequality signs then hold as in Equation 2.4. That is, for each price differential we can write that the supply price of location arbitrage is greater than or equal to the demand. If we assume the localities are ordered according to their initial equilibrium prices (the high subscript corresponding to the high price and so forth), then the n(n-1)/2 equilibrium conditions for the arbitrage markets can be written:

$$(4.1) \qquad T_{ji} \geqq P_i - P_j \text{ for } i > j.$$

Transport cost incurred in satisfying the equilibrium conditions is:

$$(4.2) \qquad \sum_{i=1}^{n} \sum_{j>i} F_{ij} T_{ij}.$$

If we assume the set of equations 4.1 has the appropriate rank the only difficulty in casting 4.1 and 4.2 in the form, a linear programming problem is the non-negativity condition which would be required of the F_{ij}'s. This condition is easily met if an additional assumption regarding the transportation costs is made. This assumption relates to the cost of transporting the product through a locality k in route from i to j.[12]

$$(4.3) \qquad T_{ij} \leqq T_{ik} + T_{kj}$$

Direct shipment between localities has the lowest unit cost. From 4.3 and 4.1, it follows that the minimum of the total transport cost required to satisfy the system 4.1 occurs at non-negative values for all F_{ji}. To show this, we observe that for each of the equations in 4.1, one of the F_{ji} can be restricted to be non-negative in sign. To be specific, from Equation 2.3, it follows that each equation, $T_{j'i'} \geqq P_{i'} - P_{j'}$, in the set 4.1 includes one $F_{i'j'}$ and $F_{j'i'}$ which are of opposite signs -- $F_{j'i'}$ has a positive sign and $F_{i'j'}$ has the negative sign. Since $P_{i'} \geqq P_{j'}$, it follows that an increase in the positive value of $F_{i'j'}$ [F_{ij} $(= -F_{ji}) = 0$ for $i \neq i'$ and $j \neq j'$] would increase the discrepancy between P_i and P_j. This increase in $P_{i'} - P_{j'}$ can only be adjusted by letting some of the other $F_{ij} \neq 0$. But this is equivalent to a transshipment which is ruled out as an optimizing activity by condition 4.3. Hence, we can set $F_{ij} = -F_{ji}$ and restrict F_{ji} to be non-negative. From 4.3, it follows that there are no advantages in combining additional sets of equations for conditions on the F_{ji}.[13] Thus, the transportation cost minimizing programming problem which produces the competitive price equilibrium can be written:

$$\text{(4.4)} \quad \text{Minimize} \sum_{i=1}^{n} \sum_{j>i} F_{ji} T_{ij}$$

$$\text{Subject to} \quad T_{ji} \geqq P_i - P_j, \quad i > j$$

$$F_{ji} \geqq 0, \quad i > j.$$

The programming problem 4.4 has a solution with at most $n(n-1)/2$ of the $F_{ji} > 0$ on the condition that the constraint set formed by the arbitrage equilibrium conditions has a rank equal to the number of equations. Reductions in the rank of the constraint set are both necessary and sufficient conditions for reductions in the possible number of $F_{ji} > 0$. More precise statements as to the number of non-zero flows depend upon the particular problem or more information of the form included in Equation 4.3. Identification of numbers of non-zero product flows becomes a more specialized problem as the number of localities increases beyond three.

V. Transportation Cost Efficiency and Price Equilibrium

In the two locality case it was shown that both the Samuelson net social payoff criterion and the transportation cost minimizing algorithm lead to the competitive price equilibrium. In this section conditions are examined under which the two models lead to a competitive price equilibrium for arbitrary numbers of localities. To begin, it is known that the social payoff criterion leads to a competitive price equilibrium for arbitrary numbers of localities [5, 9]. First order necessary conditions for the maximization of net social payoff are $[P_i - P_j = T_{ij}]\, F^*_{ij} = 0$. At the optimum for the transportation cost minimizing problem $P_i - P_j = T_{ij}$ for $F_{ij} \geqq 0$ and for $P_i - P_j < T_{ij}$, $F_{ij} = 0$. That is, the transportation cost minimizing algorithm selects one of the set of F_{ij} for which the first order conditions from the Samuelson model are met. Hence, if the transportation cost minimizing problem has an optimum then there exists at least one set of F_{ij} for which $[P_i - P_j = T_{ij}]\ F^*_{ij} = 0$.[14]

Optimal flows implied by the two problems are not, in general, identical. The solution to the transportation cost problem does, however, locate a feasible solution for the net social payoff maximizing problem. With this information the solution to the social payoff problem can be approximated through the introduction of new flows and thus moving away from the optimal basis for the transportation problem. The iterative procedure converges because there are a finite number of such basic flows in the transportation problem. The solution to the social payoff problem is identified by comparing the magnitudes of each of these solutions for equation 3.2. Such a procedure is quite feasible with a computerized linear programming algorithm.

VI. Some Extensions of Interest

If linear programming model based upon location arbitrage has any advantages over those proposed by Samuelson and Smith, they relate to ease of computation and flexibility. The fact that the approach is based directly on industry demand functions opens up an interesting number of extensions which appear to be productive sources of comparative statics results. The most straightforward of these alternatives which result from the role of the industry demand functions for arbitrage is the study of the effects of monopoly. For the two locality case the monopoly solution is given by minimizing transport costs subject to the condition that marginal costs are greater than marginal revenues. That is, in terms of Equation 3.4:

$$(5.1)\quad S_{ji} \geqq A_i - A_j - \frac{2F_{ji}(b_i + d_i) + (b_j + d_j)}{(b_i + d_i)(b_j + d_j)}$$

The model generalizes to an arbitrary number of localities as with the competitive situation. In the general form, problems involving mixtures of monopoly and competitive arbitrage markets can be studied. Results from the study of these problems are of interest in themselves and perhaps more importantly offer more realistic alternatives for studying applied problems.

A second option for extending the model represents an opportunity for some interesting results from alternate assumptions for the supply functions for arbitrage. In this respect, there are two alternatives. The first alternative is the introduction of transport costs which are not constant.

A more reasonable assumption in many situations is that transport costs increase with the level of the intermarket flow. If it is assumed that the transport costs increase linearly, then the resulting problem can be solved using quadratic programming methods.[15] The second immediate alternative related to the supply functions for arbitrage is the possibility of letting the supply functions depend upon more than one intermarket flow. Such a generalization would make the spatial price equilibrium model more appropriate for problems involving possibilities of transshipments. Each of the above extensions would require a substantial revision of the basic model and be subject to the restrictions mentioned in Section V but because the demand functions for arbitrage can be obtained the resulting problems are manageable both conceptually and computationally.

The approach can also be extended to alternative specifications of domestic supply and demand functions. In the event that the supply and demand functions are non-linear, the problem generalizes to a convex programming problem. A more interesting situation in the sense that it is directly relatable to the solution procedure for linear supply and demand functions occurs when the demand and supply functions are given as fixed quantities. In this situation, we know that the problem can be solved by a transportation model [7, p. 294-297]. The linear programming problem used to solve the price equilibrium problem can also be applied to the situation where demands and supplies are fixed quantities. Constraint equations are formed by relating surpluses and deficits to enter locality flows. That is,

$$(5.2) \quad 0 = A_i - A_j + \sum_{j=1}^{n} F_{ji}.$$

On rewriting the equations so that the F_{ji}'s can be taken to be non-negative, the objective function, 4.2, is minimized to give the solution to the transportation problem. The difference between the two approaches is that the transportation problem uses the stocks given in the localities and the model based on the arbitrage approach uses surpluses and deficits.

VII. Conclusion

The approach to the intermarket price equilibrium problem based on the idea of location arbitrage has, as advantages, the simplicity of the computational algorithm, the ease with which it is generalized to handle similar types of price equilibrium problems, and the opportunities for comparative statics presented by the characterization of the arbitrage industry demand functions. Major limitations of the approach and solution procedure relate to the rather peculiar nature of the arbitrage firms and the failure of the linear programming problem in directly identifying solutions to the price equilibrium problem. The nature of arbitrage firms and the simplified assumptions regarding transport costs severely limit the applicability of the model to many spatial and intertemporal problems. For applied problems which approximate closely the conditions underlying the model, it seems to compare favorably with computational procedures based on the alternative approaches to the equilibrating process.

FOOTNOTES

* This research was in part supported by NSF grant GA1100.

1. The one-way transport cost assumption rules out interesting back haul problems which have been posed in connection with such models. However even with this limitation there are a number of applied problems to which the model is applicable, e.g., problems of product storage and shipment for products which are incidental users of transport systems.

2. For an example of an application of an alternative method to an intertemporal price equilibrium problem, see Samuelson [6].

3. Recent literature on the subject begins more or less with a paper by Enke [2]. Building on the paper by Enke, Samuelson formulated what is now commonly called the spatial price equilibrium problem and showed that for linear domestic supply and demand functions a solution could be approximated by a sequency of transportation type linear programming problems [7]. The solution procedure employed was based on the maximization of the area between the excess supply and demand functions less the total transport cost--net social payoff. Subsequently, Judge and Takayama showed that the problem posed by Samuelson could be solved directly by quadratic programming techniques [5, 9]. More recently, Smith has suggested an alternative solution procedure based on the minimization of economic rent [8]. In addition to this more theoretical work on the subject, there are large numbers of applied studies based on these solution procedures. As examples of this applied work, see [3, 4].

4. These firms have only a coordinating role. Their decisions influence neither domestic demand and supply functions nor transportation costs.

5. It is important to recognize that intermarket product flows, $F_{ij} = -F_{ji}$, are treated as shifts in domestic supply functions. Additional restrictions required to guarantee the continued existence of a domestic equilibrium which is positive and unique are $c_i \leqq P_i \leqq a_i$ for all $F_{ij} \geqq 0$. The second inequality insures that $Q_i \geqq 0$. The first inequality eliminates the possibility of a discontinuity in the excess supply or demand function while prices and quantities are positive. Throughout the remainder of the paper these additional restrictions are assumed to hold.

6. $A_i = \frac{a_i - c_i}{b_i + d_i}$ and $B_i = \frac{1}{b_i + d_i}$

7. The inequality is set for the situation in which P_i is the higher domestic equilibrium price. In the event that the subtraction leaves a negative intercept for the arbitrage demand function, the inequality is reversed by multiplying the expression by minus one. It is apparent that, as with the demand functions, just one market equilibrium condition is required.

8. The programming model is deceptively simply in the two locality cases since the direction of the flow is known. In problems involving more localities we shall see that the problem of identifying the direction of flows and the competitive price equilibrium becomes somewhat more complicated.

9. The excess demand and supply functions are defined in a slightly different manner than usual. The expression 3.1 is set to zero and solved for an equilibrium price in terms of an intermarket product flow. A more appropriate name for them might have been locality price equilibrium curves. In labeling them excess demand and supply function, we are following the lead of Samuelson [7] in the price equilibrium literature.

10. The condition is $(P_2 - P_1 = T_{12})F^*_{21} = 0$. If the maximum occurs where $F_{21} > 0$, then the difference between prices is just equal to the cost of transport. If not, $F^*_{21} = 0$ and no product is transferred.

11. R^*_1 and R^*_2 are economic rents in the two markets at the isolated equilibrium price P^*_1 and P^*_2. The excess demand and supply functions plotted in Figure 1, can be expressed in terms of intermarket flows by making the appropriate change of variable in the integral.

12. This condition is also required for Samuelson's approximation procedure [7, p. 293]. It is not as restrictive as it might at first appear. With a little ingenuity in defining localities, it can be weakened considerably in applications of the model.

13. Any such combination would involve moving the product through an intermediate locality in shipment between localities. This alternative has by definition a cost at least as great as the direct transfer which can be made by using just one of the equations in the system.

14. The social payoff function is the sum of a number of quadratic functions, all of which are concave. Hence, if the optimum occurs at an interior point the condition $[P_i - P_j = T_{ij}]\ F^*_{ij} = 0$ is necessary and sufficient. The solution to the social payoff problem is obtained by changing the basis and increasing transportation costs and net social payoff. The changes in the basis continue until there exists no F_{ij} outside of the basis for which the increment in net social payoff associated with its inclusion in the basis is positive. The approximation procedure can be made efficient by first considering the inclusion of F_{ij}'s associated with constraints having the lower values in the dual of the transport problem.

15. The constraint set remains linear since the arbitrage supply functions are given now as increasing linear functions and not just constants. In the objective function the quadratic results from the fact that transport costs are functions of the F_{ij}. We have avoided situations with decreasing costs. In most cases the assumption of decreasing costs would present no problem in the transportation cost minimizing problem. It has been eliminated from the discussion here because of the detail in specification which would be required to rule out the possibility of an unstable intermarket equilibrium.

REFERENCES

[1] Berge, Claude and A. Ghouila-Houri, Programming, Games and Transportation Networks. New York: John Wiley and Sons, 1965.

[2] Enke, S., "Equilibrium Among Spatially Separated Markets: Solution by Electric Analogue," Econometrica, 19: 40-47 (January 1951).

[3] Goah, A., Efficiency in Location and Interregional Flows. Amsterdam: North Holland Publishing Company, 1965.

[4] Henderson, J. M., The Efficiency of the Coal Industry. Cambridge: Harvard University Press, 1958.

[5] Judge, G. G. and T. Takayama, "Spatial Price Equilibrium and Quadratic Programming," Journal of Farm Economics, 46: 67-93 (February 1964).

[6] Samuelson, Paul A., "Intertemporal Price Equilibrium: A Prologue to the Theory of Speculation," Weltwirtschaft Liches Archiv, 79: 181-221, 1957.

[7] Samuelson, Paul A., "Spatial Price Equilibrium and Linear Programming," American Economics Review, 42: 283-303 (June 1952).

[8] Smith, Vernon L., "Minimization of Economic Rent in Spatial Price Equilibrium," Review of Economic Studies, 30: 24-31 (February 1963).

[9] Takayama, T. and G. G. Judge, "Equilibrium Among Spatially Separated Markets: A Reformation," Econometrica, 32: 510-524 (October 1964).

INVESTMENT DECISION, UNCERTAINTY AND THE INCORPORATED ENTREPRENEUR

by

Vernon L. Smith*

This paper is about the corporate firm viewed as a limited liability entity financed by investors who make portfolio decisions that maximize their expected utility of wealth at the end of a single period of corporate real investment. All uncertainty in the model is due to uncertainty about the rate of return on corporate physical productive investment opportunities. That is, we postulate a continuum of states of nature θ, defined as the rate of return per dollar of corporate investment earned over a given period of investment. In this respect the approach is akin to that of Quirk [1] on the capital structure of firms, and Tobin [2], Arrow [3], Lintner [4], Breen [5], and others on portfolio analysis, as distinct from that of Arrow [6], Debreu [7], and others [8] who have worked with contingent commodity models of the investment decision. Some justification of this choice is in order.

I regard the contingent commodity or state preference theory of investment as the fundamental approach to investment uncertainty. Indeed, it is so fundamental in terms of its primitive data requirements that therein lies its principle disadvantage. It postulates (i) an exhaustive description of all those states of nature whose outcome can affect the payoff of economic agents, and (ii) the capacity of financial markets to issue claims (elemental securities, or "lottery tickets") to resources contingent on each state of nature. In the model of this paper such a postulate would require corporations to issue an elemental security claim for each rate of return contingency. In such models, there is no risk against which one cannot fully and ideally insure. If such a finely calibrated theory of investment decision is to be made relevant to the observed world it would be necessary to introduce explicit assumptions about the transactions costs of issuing elemental contingent claims. The theory might then show that economy, in the light of such costs, requires firms to issue only a few security types, each security representing resource claims across subsets of the set of exhaustive states of nature. Such an approach would provide an extremely fruitful extension of the contingent commodity model.

Alternatively, and this is the approach of the present paper, we begin with a direct and strong postulate that the financial sector has the capacity to issue two basic kinds of claims on a firm's real assets. This limitation is not explained by the model, but could be due to the transactions costs of finance. We simply take the resulting package constraints on state contingent claims as given.

There are three fundamental security claims in the observed world; equity or residual claims (common shares), priority claims, whether "bonded" or not (bonds, notes, preferred shares), and options (e.g. warrants, rights, puts and calls). Option certificates are perhaps not a fundamental type of security, but rather a conditional claim on basic equity claims. All other securities, such as convertible bonds, convertible preferred shares, bonds with non-detachable warrants, and so on (through the endless but very non-ideal attempts of the financial community to subdivide the states of nature), are simply specified fixed mixtures of the three basic security types. The models of this paper will deal only with common shares and debt securities.

Certain institutional and factual characteristics of observed corporations, which seem not to have been treated fully in the literature of investment theory, will be explicit throughout the discussion - limited liability, priority of claims among different security instruments, default risk on bonds, and bankruptcy. These important features I regard as of the essence of incorporated investment activity. Most of the literature abstracts from default risk, which seems curious in view of the important contribution of Quirk. Yet, in a crucial sense, default risk is what debt financing is really all about. It is quite unacceptable to argue that default is rare - even if it were (and it is not, I conjecture, if one looks at the population of all corporations), there is no theorem allowing events of small probability and large consequence to be ignored either by real decision makers or logically consistent ideal decision makers. Nor is it acceptable to argue that default risk can be ignored because major corporations never are in default; such a fact is a significant reason why we call them "major" corporations. It is precisely because default is important that its avoidance is so assiduously and so often successfully courted by corporate management.

The study of the incorporated entrepreneur is a particularly useful device for exploring the issues of debt versus equity financing under conditions which abstract from some of the complications that arise in the multiowner corporation. To this end we deal first with the problem of the equity financed incorporated entrepreneur who divides his assets between direct, limited liability, risk investment, and the holding of riskless bonds (or cash). Formally, this is just the problem of liquidity preference as treated by Arrow and others (as noted above) except for interpretation in terms of financing the firm, and the explicit treatment of limited liability and bankruptcy. A corner solution to this problem, with all wealth put into risky investment, is a necessary condition for the firm to issue debt obligations subject to default risk. We proceed thus to derive properties of the investor's indifference curves for risky investment and lending (Section 1), and for risky investment and borrowing (Section 2). The inevitable differential in default risk as between an individual's lending and borrowing activities is seen to be the basis for differential borrowing and lending rates rather than some mysterious "imperfection" in capital markets. A similar analysis is made of the potential lender to the corporation who does not have access to direct productive investment opportunities, but can divide his wealth between riskless bonds or cash, and risky corporate bonds subject to limited liability. The basis for trade between borrower and lender is developed, and the analysis reveals an important external economy in the debtor-creditor relationship: The borrower's equity in risky investment is an external economy to the lender (that is, it appears in his expected utility function), whereas the borrower experiences no external effects from the lender.

1. Equity Financing

Consider an individual incorporated entrepreneur deciding how to allocate his wealth between a risky productive investment opportunity (his corporate equity investment) and riskless bonds, such as Treasury bills or other highly secure investments. The following notation will be employed:

W_o - investor-entrepreneur's initial wealth.

W_T - investor-entrepreneur's terminal wealth at end of the investment period, T.

θ - random return per dollar invested by corporation.

$\theta+1$ - random cash flow per dollar invested by corporation.

r - known certain rate of interest on riskless bonds.

y - dollar investment in corporation (= common stock investment).

W_o-y - dollar investment in riskless bonds.

It is understood that the analysis applies to the i'th member of an economy of many independent entrepreneurs but the redundant subscript i on the above variables is omitted. Our individual is assumed to make choices consistent with a utility function $U(W_T)$ that measures the subjective value of any terminal wealth level, and an expected utility $V(y) \equiv E[U(W_T)]$ that measures the subjective value of any risky investment level, y. It will be assumed that $U' > 0$, $U'' < 0$, i.e. individuals are risk aversive.

Investor Choice Between Risky Stock and Riskless Bonds. For any distribution (y,W-y) between stocks and bonds, the corporation's cash flow at T is $(\theta+1)y$, and the investor's terminal wealth function is

W_T:	Cash Flow Contingency; Return Contingency:
$(1+r)(W_o-y)$	$(\theta+1)y \leq 0$; $\theta \leq -1$,
$(1+r)(W_o-y) + (1+\theta)y$	$(\theta+1)y > 0$; $\theta > -1$.

In the equity financed corporate institution, when cash flow is negative, accounts payable are in default, and stockholder liability is limited to the amount of their original investment. The value of the investor's portfolio at T is then simply his investment in bonds plus interest $(1+r)(W_o-y)$. Bonds represent his "buffer inventory" or insurance protection against losses on corporate account. If cash flow is positive, the entire amount is claimed by stockholders in the equity financed corporation, so that the investor's portfolio at T, has a market value $(1+r)(W_o-y) + (1+\theta)y$ or $W_o + \theta y + r(W_o-y)$, which is his initial wealth modified by the returns on stock and bond investments.

The investor is assumed to have a subjective probability density $f(\theta)$ over the rate of return on risky investment. Following Quirk [9], this assumes stochastic constant returns to scale, i.e. the density is independent of the amount invested, $f(\theta;y) = f(\theta)$, for all y.

Expected utility is then

$$(1.1) \quad V(y) = \int_{-\infty}^{-1} U\{(1+r)(W_o-y)\}f(\theta)d\theta + \int_{-1}^{\infty} U\{(1+r)(W_o-y) + (1+\theta)y\}f(\theta)d\theta$$

$$= U\{(1+r)(W_o-y)\}Pr(\theta \leq -1) + E_{-1}[U\{(1+r)(W_o-y) + (1+\theta)y\}]$$

where $E_{-1}[\cdot]$ stands for the partial expectation $E[\cdot]$, $\theta > -1$. In the development to follow we make use of the first two derivatives of (1.1):

$$(1.2)\quad V'(y) = -Pr(\theta \leq -1)U'\{(1+r)(W_o-y)\}(1+r) + E_{-1}[U'\{(1+r)(W_o-y) + (1+\theta)y\}(\theta-r)]$$

$$(1.3)\quad V''(y) = Pr(\theta \leq -1)U''\{(1+r)(W_o-y)\}(1+r)^2 + E_{-1}[U''\{(1+r)(W_o-y) + (1+\theta)y\}(\theta-r)^2]$$

Note first that risk aversion, $U'' < 0$, implies $V'' < 0$. We want to $\max_{W \geq y \geq 0} V(y)$, and there are three and only three cases [10]:

Case (i). $V'(0) \leq 0.\ y^o = 0.$

$$\begin{aligned} V'(0) &= -Pr(\theta \leq -1)U'\{W_o(1+r)\}(1+r) \\ &\quad + U'\{W_o(1+r)\}[E_{-1}(\theta) - rPr(\theta > -1)] \\ &= U'\{W_o(1+r)\}\{-Pr(\theta \leq -1)(1+r) + E_{-1}(\theta) \\ &\quad - r[1 - Pr(\theta \leq -1)]\} \leq 0 \end{aligned}$$

$$\text{or } E_{-1}(\theta) - Pr(\theta \leq -1) \leq r.$$

The expression on the left is expected return per dollar from risky investment net of bankruptcy losses, i.e. $E_{-1}(\theta)$ is expected return contingent upon a positive cash flow, and $Pr(\theta \leq -1)$ is expected bankruptcy loss per dollar invested. Hence, we have the well-known result that there will be no investment in risky stocks unless the net expected return exceeds the interest on riskless bonds. Hereafter we assume that $E_{-1}(\theta) - Pr(\theta \leq -1) > r$.

Observe also from this case that if the net expected return on risky investment exceeds r, then always some part of wealth will be so invested, i.e. $V'(0) > 0$ and $y^o > 0$.

Case (ii). $V'(0) > 0,\ V'(W_o) < 0,\ V'(y^o) = 0,\ 0 < y^o < W_o$.

In this case we have a strictly interior solution, with some positive amount of wealth being invested in both shares and riskless bonds.

Case (iii). $V'(W_o) \geq 0,\ y^o = W_o$.

(1.2') $$V'(W_o) = -Pr(\theta \leq -1)U'(0)(1+r) + E_{-1}[U'\{W_o(1+\theta)\}(\theta-r)] \geq 0.$$

In this case, all wealth is invested in shares. Note that if $\theta \geq r$, i.e. $Pr(\theta \geq r) = 1$, then $U'\{W_o(1+\theta)\}(\theta-r) \geq 0$, $Pr(\theta \leq -1) = 0$, and therefore $V'(W_o) \geq 0$. If the return on risky investment is at least as good as the interest on riskless bonds, all wealth will be invested in shares.

Formulation as a Constrained Maximum. For purposes of comparison with the traditional theory of choice, it is instructive to formulate the above choice as a constrained maximum problem. To this end, define $x' = (1+r)x = (1+r)(W_o-y)$ as the "face" or maturity value of bonds bought at the discount price $1/(1+r)$, with x being the expenditure for bonds. The expected utility function is now,

(1.4) $$\Phi(x',y) = U(x')Pr(\theta \leq -1) + E_{-1}[U\{x' + y(1+\theta)\}],$$

a function only of the asset holdings x' and y. The budget (wealth) constraint is $W_o = x'/(1+r) + y$, depending in the usual way upon prices and the choice objects (x',y).

The criterion $\Phi(x',y)$ defines indifference curves with the usual, though more special (due to the independence axiom in von Neuman-Morganstern utility theory), properties. We have,

(1.5) $$\Phi_{x'} = Pr(\theta \leq -1)U'(x') + E_{-1}[U'\{x' + y(1+\theta)\}] > 0$$

(1.6) $$\Phi_y = E_{-1}[U'\{x' + y(1+\theta)\}(1+\theta)] > 0.$$

Hence, the indifference curves have a negative slope, $(dy/dx') = -\Phi_{x'}/\Phi_y < 0$.

We can also show that the indifference curves are convex, or that

(1.7) $$(d^2y/dx'^2) = -(1/\Phi_y)(\Phi_{x'x'} - 2p\Phi_{x'y} + p^2\Phi_{yy}) > 0,$$

where $p = \Phi_y/\Phi_{x'}$.

Computing the second partial derivatives from (1.5) and (1.6), and substituting into (1.7) gives

$$(d^2y/dx'^2) = -(1/\Phi_y)(Pr(\theta \leq -1)U''\{x'\} + E_{-1}[U''\{x' + y(1+\theta)\}] - 2pE_{-1}[U''\{x' + y(1+\theta)\}(1+\theta)] + p^2E_{-1}[U''\{x' + y(1+\theta)\}(1+\theta)^2])$$

$$= -(1/\Phi_y)(\Pr(\theta \leq -1)U''\{x'\} + E_{-1}[U''\{x' + y(1+\theta)\}$$
$$\{p(1+\theta) - 1\}^2]) > 0 \quad \text{if } U'' < 0.$$

The indifference curves have a third property of interest primarily because it has provided the intuitive foundation for mean-variance or mean-"safety level" attempts to formulate the problem of decision under uncertainty: As risky investment increases along a given indifference curve the mathematical expectation of wealth cannot decrease. Consequently, an increase in risk may be associated with higher mean wealth. Of course it does not follow that variance or "safety level" can serve as acceptable means of measuring something called "risk". To establish the property, from the definition of W_T we compute

$$E(W_T) = x'\Pr(\theta \leq -1) + E_{-1}[x' + (1+\theta)y] = x' + yE_{-1}(1+\theta).$$

Holding $\Phi(x',y)$ constant,

$$dE/dy = \partial E/\partial y + (\partial E/\partial x')(dx'/dy) \tag{1.8}$$
$$= E_{-1}(1+\theta) - (\Phi_y/\Phi_{x'}).$$

But from (1.5) and (1.6), we have $(\Phi_y/\Phi_{x'})_{y=0} = E_{-1}(1+\theta)$, $(dE/dy)_{y=0} = 0$. Since $d(\Phi_y/\Phi_{x'})/dy = -d^2x'/dy^2 < 0$, it follows that $E_{-1}(1+\theta) = (\Phi_y/\Phi_{x'})_{y=0} \geq (\Phi_y/\Phi_{x'})_{y \geq 0}$, and from (1.8) we have $(dE/dy)_{y \geq 0} \geq 0$.

The decision problem is to $\max_{x' \geq 0, y \geq 0} \Phi(x',y)$ subject to the wealth constraint. In view of the properties of $\Phi(x',y)$, necessary and sufficient conditions for a maximum at (x'^o,y^o) are

(1.9) $\Phi_{x'} - \lambda/s \leq 0$, with $x'^o = 0$, if $<$ holds.

(1.10) $\Phi_y - \lambda \leq 0$, with $y^o = 0$, if $<$ holds.

(1.11) $W_o = (x'/s) + y$,

where λ is the Lagrange multiplier, interpreted as the marginal expected utility of wealth, and $s = 1+r$.

Risk Aversion and the Demand for Risky Shares. In this section we examine the effect of ceteris paribus changes in investor wealth, and the price of bonds, on the demand for shares.

By differentiating the equilibrium conditions (1.9)-(1.11) for the case of an interior solution, and solving for dy^o/dW_o in the usual way, we get

$$(1.12) \quad dy^o/dW_o = -\frac{-\Phi_{x'x'} + (1/s)\Phi_{x'y}}{(1/s)^2(-s^2\Phi_{x'x'} + 2s\Phi_{x'y} - \Phi_{yy})},$$

and the following theorem can be stated.

Theorem. For an interior solution (x'^o, y^o), $(dy^o/dW_o) > 0$ if $-U''$ is a decreasing function of wealth, i.e. the marginal utility of wealth is convex.

From (1.7), we have $D > 0$, so that sign (dy^o/dW_o) = sign A, where A is the numerator and D is the denominator in (1.12). Substituting for $\Phi_{x'x'}$, $\Phi_{x'y}$, and $x'^o = (W_o - y^o)s$, we can write,

$$sA = -Pr(\theta \leq -1)U''(x'^o)s + \int_{-1}^{r} U''\{W_o s + y^o(\theta - r)\}(\theta - r)f(\theta)d\theta$$

$$+ \int_{r}^{\infty} U''\{W_o s + y^o(\theta - r)\}(\theta - r)f(\theta)d\theta.$$

But if $-U''$ is decreasing, $-U''(x'^o) > -U''(W_o s)$, since $x'^o < W_o s$. In the first integral, since $(\theta - r) < 0$, $W_o s + y^o(\theta - r) < W_o s$, and $U''\{W_o s + y(\theta - r)\}(\theta - r) > U''(W_o s)(\theta - r)$. Similarly in the second integral, since $(\theta - r) > 0$, $W_o s + y^o(\theta - r) > W_o s$, and $U''\{W_o s + y^o(\theta - r)\}(\theta - r) > U''\{W_o s\}(\theta - r)$. Hence, $sA > U''(W_o s)[-Pr(\theta \leq -1) + E_{-1}(\theta) - r] > 0$, from the discussion of Case (i) above.

A convex marginal utility function is not a sufficiently strong condition to insure $dx'^o/dW_o > 0$. That is, $(dx'^o/dW_o = s(1 - \frac{dy^o}{dW_o}) \gtrless 0$, if $(dy^o/dW_o) > 0$. This means that although shares are a wealth superior good, it is possible for bonds (or cash, if $r = 0$) to be a wealth inferior good. Bonds are wealth superior if $(dy^o/dW_o) < 1$, i.e. a dollar of additional wealth induces less than a dollar additional expenditure on stock. The usual results from classical demand theory also follow.

For example, we can deduce

$$(1.13) \quad dx'^o/d(1/s) = -\Phi_y/D - x'^o(dx'^o/dW_o),$$

where $(1/s)$ is the price of bonds.

Consequently, if bonds are wealth superior, $(dx'^{o}/dW_{o}) > 0$, they are necessarily price superior, $dx'^{o}/d(1/s) < 0$. If bonds are price inferior, $(dx'^{o}/d(1/s) > 0$, they are necessarily wealth inferior, $(dx'^{o}/dW_{o} < 0$.

Arrow [11] and Pratt [12] discuss a strong measure of risk aversion, viz relative or proportional risk aversion,

(1.14) $$R^{*}(W_T) = -\frac{W_T U''(W_T)}{U'(W_T)} .$$

$R^{*}(W_T)$ is the elasticity of the marginal utility of wealth and is invariant with both the utility units and the wealth units. $R^{*}(W_T) = 1$ implies the Bernoulli logarithmic utility function. Arrow shows that if $R^{*}(W_T)$ is increasing, the elasticity of the demand for money is at least 1. In the context of the present model, increasing proportional risk aversion implies

(1.15) $$(Ex'^{o}/EW_{o}) \geq 1+r,$$

where (Ex'^{o}/EW_{o}) is the wealth elasticity of the demand for bonds.

It follows that bonds are definitely a wealth superior good, since

$$(dx'^{o}/dW_{o}) \geq x'^{o}(1+r)/W_{o} > 0,$$

but now it is possible (for very large equilibrium holdings of bonds) for shares to be wealth inferior

$$(dy^{o}/dW_{o}) = 1 - (1/s)(dx'^{o}/dW_{o}) \leq 1 - x'^{o}/W_{o} < 0,$$

if $x'^{o} > W$. (Remember that x' is measured in terms of maturity value, and the budget constraint and nonnegativity require <u>expenditure</u> to not exceed wealth, i.e. $x'^{o}/(1+r) \leq W_{o}$).

<u>Limited versus Unlimited Liability</u>. The essence of incorporation, as an economic institution, is the granting of limited liability to its investors. It is therefore important in elaborating a theory of the corporate firm to demonstrate explicitly the effects of limited liability.

In the absence of incorporation our investor-entrepreneur, who, faced with the same opportunities as before, ventures y on a risky investment with random return θ, stands to lose not only y, but all or a portion of his investment $W-y$ in riskless bonds. Then his wealth state, W_T, as a function of θ becomes,

W_T:	θ contingency:
0,	if $(1+r)(W_o-y) + (1+\theta)y \leq 0$, then $\theta \leq \theta' \equiv r - (1+r)W_o/y$
$(1+r)(W-y) + (1+\theta)y$,	$\theta > \theta'$.

For any return below θ', the individual must compensate for losses on risk account up to the full amount of his holdings of riskless bonds. For returns above θ', he ends the investment period with some positive level of wealth. His losses, in other words, are now limited only by personal bankruptcy protections. Figure 1 provides a comparison of wealth under limited liability with wealth under unlimited liability.

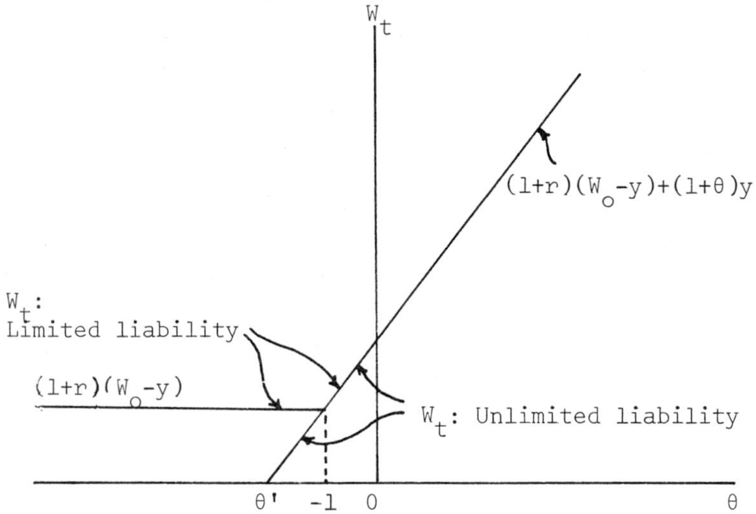

Figure 1

Expected utility is now

$$V_u(y) = E_{\theta'}[U\{(1+r)(W-y) + (1+\theta)y\}] \leq V(y)$$

where $V(y)$ is given by (1.1).

For all investment levels y, expected utility under limited liability is never dominated by expected utility under unlimited liability.

2. Debt-Equity Financing

In Case (iii) of the analysis of an entrepreneur-investor's choice between shares and riskless bonds, when $V'(W_o) \geq 0$, the investor will desire to put all his wealth into equity investment. If the inequality holds, this raises immediately the question of whether he might prefer to increase the leverage of his investment by borrowing to invest $y > W_o$ in stock. Any such preference depends upon the terms at which he can borrow. As an incorporated entrepreneur, he may choose to borrow on corporate account in which case we introduce the whole problem of corporate leverage, or debt financing, through the issuance of bonds that carry a claim prior to that of the stockholder, on the corporation's cash flow.

Investor Demand for Risky Stock and for Bond Finance. The symbols W_o, W_T, and θ are defined as in Section 1. We now let $z \geq 0$ be the level of corporate entrepreneurial borrowing or bond issuance at the beginning of the investment period. Total corporate investment is now $z + W_o = y \geq W_o$, and we let r^* be the contractual rate of interest on the risky corporate bonds. By the contractual rate is meant the rate that must be paid, if earned, before the incorporated owner is entitled to any equity claims.

Terminal wealth, W_T, for our individual will now be a function of z, θ, and r^* as follows:

W_T:	Cash Flow Contingency; Return Contingency:
0	$(\theta+1)(z+W_o) \leq (r^*+1)z$; $\theta \leq \dfrac{r^*z-W_o}{z+W_o} = \theta^*$.
$(\theta+1)(z+W_o) - (r^*+1)z = W_o + \theta(z+W_o) - r^*z$	$(\theta+1)(z+W_o) > (r^*+1)z$; $\theta > \theta^*$.

θ^* is that rate of return on total corporate investment which is just sufficient to repay the bondholder his principal plus the contractual rate on risky corporate bonds. The corporation is in default on its interest obligation to the bondholder if $-W_o/(z+W_o) \leq \theta < \theta^*$, and it is in default on both interest and principle if $\theta < -W_o/(z+W_o)$. The bondholder loses the entire investment, if $\theta < -1$, corresponding to corporate bankruptcy. For all these contingencies, our incorporated entrepreneur receives nothing because of the bondholder's legally prior claim. But if $\theta > \theta^*$, the entrepreneur receives the entire cash flow in excess of the obligation $(r^*+1)z$ to bondholders. Hence, the entrepreneur's rate of return on his own investment is

$$\rho = \frac{\theta(z+W_o) - r^*z}{W_o}.$$

The marginal rate of change of his return with respect to the total corporate return is

$$\frac{d\rho}{d\theta} = \frac{z+W_o}{W_o} = 1+z/W_o \text{ ,}$$

the leverage factor, where z/W_o is the firm's debt-equity ratio.

A comparison of terminal wealth with and without debt financing is shown in Figure 2. An increase in debt financing from none to the level z is illustrated. The entrepreneur receives reduced wealth outcomes for all $\theta < r^*$, but higher wealth levels for $\theta > r^*$.

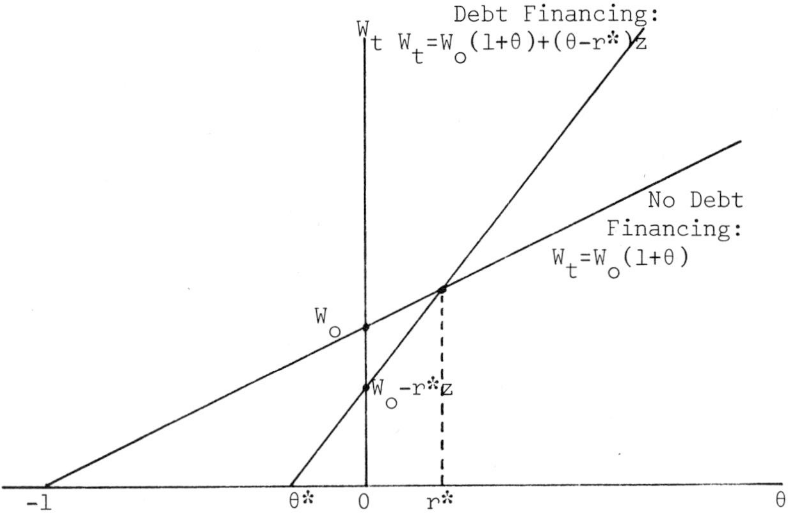

Figure 2

The entrepreneur's expected utility, setting U(0) = 0, is now

(2.1) $\quad {}^*V(z) = E[U(W_T)] = E_{\theta^*}[U\{W_o + \theta(z+W_o) - r^*z\}]$

with

(2.2) $\quad {}^*V'(z) = E_{\theta^*}[U'\{W_o + \theta(z+W_o) - r^*z\}(\theta-r^*)].$

From (2.2) observe that

$$\lim_{z\to 0} {}^*V'(z) = {}^*V'(0) = E_{-1}[U'\{W_o(1+\theta)\}(\theta-r^*)].$$

By substitution into (1.2'), we have

(2.3) $$V'(W_o) = -Pr(\theta \leq -1)U'(0)(1+r) + {}^*V'(0) + (r^*-r)E_{-1}[U'\{W_o(1+\theta)\}].$$

It is obvious (see, nevertheless, the proposition below) that no lender can be induced to hold risky corporate bonds unless $r^* > r$. Hence,

$$V'(W_o) \gtrless {}^*V'(0), \text{ according as}$$

$$(r^*-r)E_{-1}[U'\{W_o(1+\theta)\}] \gtrless Pr(\theta < -1)U'(0)(1+r).$$

At $z = 0$, or $y = W_o$, we have a discontinuity in the entrepreneur's marginal expected utility of wealth. Consequently, $V'(W_o) > 0$ is a necessary but not a sufficient condition for the issuance of corporate bonds at the rate r^*.

We identify three cases:

Case (i). $0 < V'(W_o) > {}^*V'(0) \leq 0, \; z^o = 0.$

For large enough r^*, this case will apply. The entrepreneur-owner would like to lever his risky investment, but not on the terms required by the market. This might be the situation for many small speculative corporations, who are priced out of the market for debt financing by risk aversive lenders unwilling to undertake such risky loans.

Case (ii). $V'(W_o) > {}^*V'(0) > 0, \; {}^*V'(z^o) = 0, \; z^o > 0.$

Case (iii). $0 < V'(W_o) < {}^*V'(0), \; {}^*V'(z^o) = 0, \; z^o > 0.$

In cases (ii) and (iii), we have an interior solution with corporate investment expanded beyond W_o by borrowing until marginal expected utility is zero. Notice from (2.3) that if default risk is zero, $Pr(\theta \leq -1) = 0$, then case (iii) is not possible. Figure 3 illustrates optimal debt financing for each of the three cases.

The graphs of Figure 3 assume that ${}^*V''(z) < 0$, $z \geq 0$, but $U'' < 0$ is not sufficient to guarantee this. Differentiating (2.2), gives

$$(2.4) \quad {}^*V''(z) = U'(0)f(\theta^*)W_o^2(1+r^*)^2/(z+W_o)^3$$
$$+ E_{\theta^*}\{U''[W_o + \theta(z+W_o) - r^*z](\theta-r^*)^2\},$$

in which the first term is positive, and clearly may dominate the second term (e.g. for $-U''$ a small enough constant).

If ${}^*V'(0) \geq 0$, then the demand for debt finance

$z^o = z^o(r^*)$ is given by $V'(z^o) = 0$, $z^o \geq 0$, with slope

$$dz^o/dr^* = -[\partial {}^*V'(z^o)/\partial r^*]/{}^*V''(z^o).$$

We assume ${}^*V''(z^o) < 0$ for a relative maximum. Hence, $\text{sign } dz^o/dr^* = \text{sign } \partial {}^*V'(z^o)/\partial r^*$, where

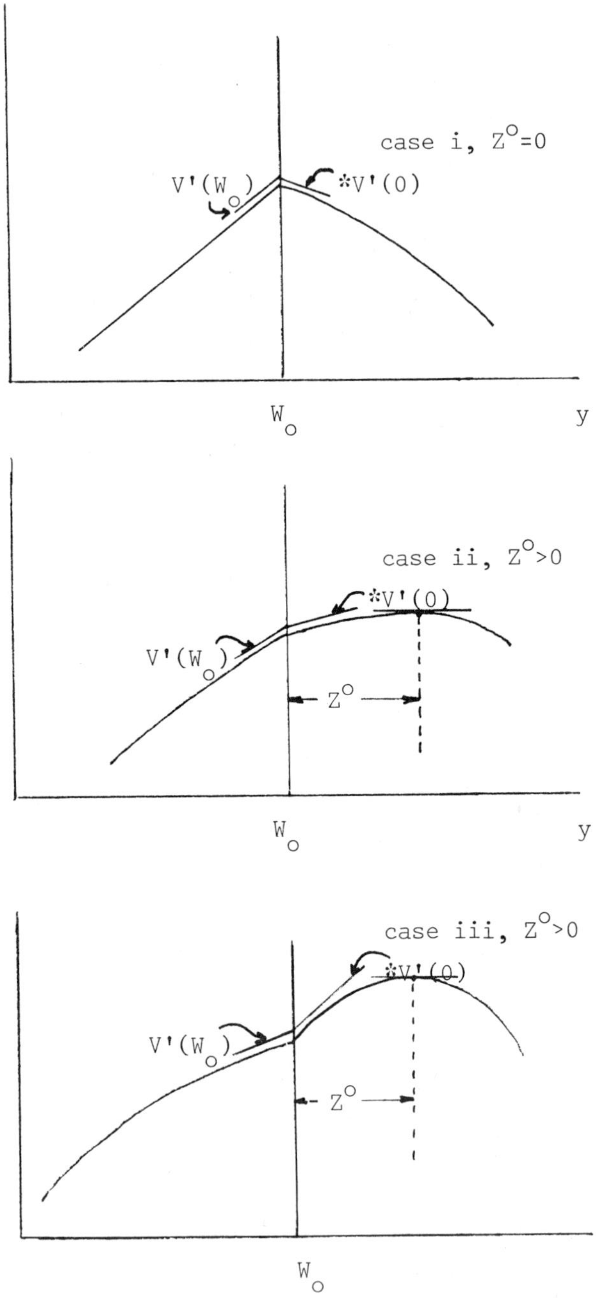
case i, $Z^{o}=0$
$V'(W_o)$
$*V'(0)$
W_o
y
case ii, $Z^{o}>0$
$*V'(0)$
$V'(W_o)$
Z^{o}
W_o
y
case iii, $Z^{o}>0$
$*V'(0)$
$V'(W_o)$
Z^{o}
W_o

Figure 3

$$(2.5)\quad \partial^* V'(z^o)/\partial r^* = U'(0)f(\theta^*)W_o(1+r^*)z^o/(z^o+W_o)^2$$
$$- z^o E_{\theta^*}\{U''[W_o + \theta(z^o + W_o) - r^* z^o](\theta - r^*)\}$$
$$- E_{\theta^*}\{U'[W_o + \theta(z^o+W_o) - r^* z^o]\}.$$

The second term in (2.5) can be shown to be positive if the entrepreneur's utility function exhibits decreasing risk aversion. But sign $\partial^* V'(z^o)/\partial r^*$ need not be negative even with decreasing risk aversion. However, since $\partial^* V'(0)/\partial r^* < 0$, for $r^* = \overline{r}^*$ such that $z^o(\overline{r}^*) = 0$, we have $dz^o/dr^* < 0$ for contractual bond rates near $\overline{r}^*$. The rate $\overline{r}^*$ is determined by the condition $^*V'(0) = 0$, which gives $\overline{r}^* = E_{-1}[U'\{W_o(1+\theta)\}\theta]/E_{-1}[U'\{W_o(1+\theta)\}]$. As r^* increases, the demand for bond finance must eventually be decreasing and become zero at $\overline{r}^*$. Thus might we have a backward bending demand curve for bond finance such as $z^o(r^*)$, as shown in Figure 4.

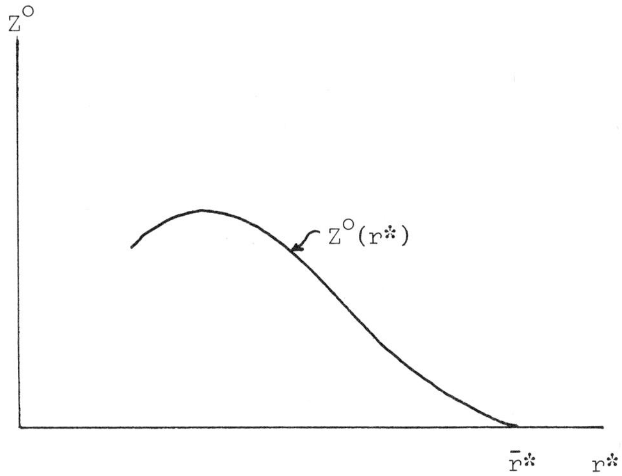

Figure 4

Indifference Curves for Levered Risky Investment. Some additional insights into the analysis of debt financing are to be obtained by examining the indifference curves for borrowing to invest in risky shares. If we let $x' = (1+r^*)(W_o - y) \leq 0$, where $-x'$ is the maturity value of corporate bonds in the absence of default risk, then terminal wealth is $W_T = x' + y(1+\theta)$, $x' \leq 0$, $y \geq W_o$. The wealth constraint on investor choice of (x',y) is $W = x'/(1+r^*) + y$. The rate of return, θ^*, below which bonds are in default can be transformed,

$$\theta^* = (r^*z - W_o)/(z+W_o) = -(x'+y)/y.$$

Hence, expected utility corresponding to (2.1) is

$$(2.6) \qquad \Psi(x',y) = \int_{-(x'+y)/y}^{\infty} U\{x' + y(1+\theta)\}f(\theta)d\theta$$

$$= E_{-(x'+y)/y}[U\{x' + y(1+\theta)\}].$$

Since,

$$(2.7) \qquad \Psi_{x'} = E_{-(x'+y)/y}[U'\{x' + y(1+\theta)\}] > 0.$$

$$(2.8) \qquad \Psi_y = E_{-(x'+y)/y}[U'\{x' + y(1+\theta)\}(1+\theta)] > 0,$$

the indifference curves have negative slope, $dy/dx' = -\Psi_{x'}/\Psi_y < 0$. Comparing (2.7) with (1.5), and (2.8) with (1.6), we have

$$\Psi_{x'}\Big|_{x'=0} = E_{-1}[U'\{y(1+\theta)\}] < \Phi_{x'}\Big|_{x'=0}$$

$$= \Pr(\theta \leq -1)U'(0) + E_{-1}[U'\{y(1+\theta)\}]$$

$$\Psi_y\Big|_{x'=0} = E_{-1}[U'\{y(1+\theta)\}(1+\theta)] = \Phi_y\Big|_{x'=0}$$

Consequently, there is a discontinuity, due to the default risk term $\Pr(\theta \leq -1)U'(0)$, in the marginal rate of substitution of bonds for shares, at $x' = 0$. That is,

$$dy/dx'\Big|_{x'=0-} = -\Psi_{x'}/\Psi_y\Big|_{x'=0} > -\Phi_{x'}/\Phi_y\Big|_{x'=0} = dy/dx'\Big|_{x=0+},$$

as shown in Figure 5.

By computing d^2y/dx'^2, we show that $U'' < 0$ is not sufficient to assure convex indifference curves:

$$(2.9) \quad d^2y/dx'^2 = -(1/\Psi_y)(E_{\theta^*}[U''\{x' + y(1+\theta)\}\{p(1+\theta)-1\}^2]$$

$$+ U'(0)f(\theta^*)\{1 - px'/y\}^2(1/y)),$$

$$\text{where } p = \Psi_{x'}/\Psi_y.$$

The first term in parentheses is negative but the second term is positive.

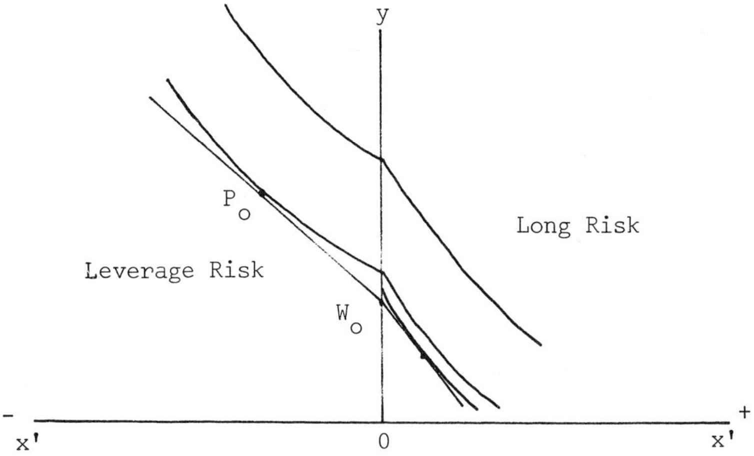

Figure 5

Figure 5 illustrates indifference curves in both the "long risk" region ($x' \geq 0$, $y \geq 0$), and the "leverage risk" region ($x' \leq 0$, $y \geq W_o$), where in the latter we assume $d^2y/dx'^2 > 0$ throughout. A portfolio expenditure opportunity line corresponding to wealth, W_o, and $r^* > r$ is also shown, with a debt financed equilibrium at P_o.

It is clear from Figure 5, and the above analysis, that the idea of equal borrowing and lending rates is not even tenable and certainly has nothing to do with a concept of perfectly competitive markets. Equality of such rates would correspond to a curious world in which investors would either diversify between holding Treasury bonds and risky shares or borrow to lever risky investment. There would be no boundary optima for an investor, with all wealth in risky investment. The discontinuity in the substitution rate at $x' = 0$, and the resulting divergence that must exist between the borrowing and lending rate is a direct consequence of the fact that borrowing and lending present asymmetrical conditions of risk. As a lender I do not normally experience the same conditions of risk as he who lends to me when I engage in borrowing. Hence, in the analysis above, the principles involved are not altered if we assume that the investor can purchase risky bonds instead of Treasury bonds. The bonds which he can purchase will not in general show the same default risk as those he can issue.

Lender's Choice Between Risky Corporate Bonds and Riskless Bonds: The Supply of Debt Finance. Turning now to the supply side of the market for corporate entrepreneurial debt financing, we postulate the existence of investors who do not have available to them, or do not have the knowledge to exploit, the direct productive investment opportunities of incorporated entrepreneurs. Such an investor in our simple world must make a portfolio choice between riskless government obligations and lending at risk of default to an incorporated entrepreneur by purchasing his bonds. For the present we consider only a single lender providing debt finance to a single entrepreneur.

Consider an individual lender with initial wealth W_o^*, who purchases z^* dollars worth of bonds at the contractual rate r^* from the entrepreneur of the previous sections, and $W_o^*-z^*$ dollars worth of riskless bonds at the assured rate r. The lender's terminal wealth contingencies are then as follows:

W_T^*:	Cash Flow Contingency; Return Contingency:
$W = (W_o^*-z^*)(1+r)$	$(\theta+1)(z^*+W_o) \leq 0$; $\theta \leq -1$.
$W' = (W_o^*-z^*)(1+r) + (z^*+W_o)(1+\theta) = W_o^* + W_o + \theta(z^*+W_o) + r(W_o^*-z^*)$	$0 < (\theta+1)(z^*+W_o) \leq (1+r^*)z^*$; $-1 < \theta \leq \dfrac{r^*z^*-W_o}{z^*+W_o} = \theta^*$
$W'' = z^*(1+r^*) + (W_o^*-z^*)(1+r) = W_o^*(1+r) + (r^*-r)z^*$	$(1+r^*)z^* < (\theta+1)(z^*+W_o) < \infty$; $\theta^* < \theta < \infty$

For all rate of return contingencies $\theta \leq -1$, the corporation is bankrupt, with both the lender and the entrepreneur owner losing their entire investment. The lender, however, is left with his buffer purchase of riskless bonds plus interest, $(W_o^*-z^*)(1+r)$. For those rate of return contingencies such that $-1 < \theta \leq \theta^*$, the corporate cash flow is positive but does not exceed the prior claim of the lender for principal plus interest on his corporate bond holdings. The entrepreneur loses his investment W_o and the bond holder receives the entire cash flow, $(\theta+1)(z^*+W_o)$, in addition to $(W_o^*-z^*)(1+r)$ from his investment in riskless bonds.

Finally, for return contingencies $\theta > \theta^*$, the lender receives principal plus the full contractual rate on corporate bonds $z^*(1+r^*)$ in addition to his investment plus interest on riskless bonds. The bondholder's terminal wealth as a function of θ is indicated by the solid line in Figure 6 (cf Figure 2 showing terminal wealth for the corporate borrower).

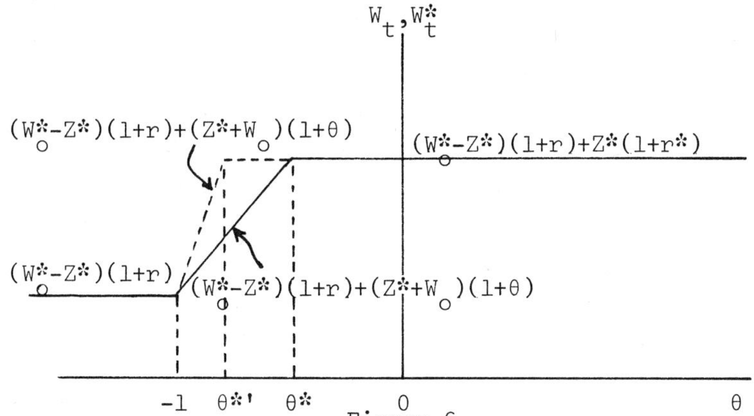

Figure 6

Expected utility for the corporate bondholder is

$$L(z^*) = U(W)\Pr(\theta \leq -1) + \int_{-1}^{\theta^*} U(W')f(\theta)d\theta + U(W'')\Pr(\theta > \theta^*), \tag{2.10}$$

with first and second derivatives,

$$L'(z^*) = -U'(W)(1+r)\Pr(\theta \leq -1) + \int_{-1}^{\theta^*} U'(W')(\theta-r)f(\theta)d\theta + U'(W'')(r^*-r)\Pr(\theta > \theta^*), \tag{2.11}$$

$$L''(z^*) = U''(W)(1+r)^2\Pr(\theta \leq -1) + \int_{-1}^{\theta^*} U''(W')(\theta-r)^2 f(\theta)d\theta + U''(W'')(r^*-r)^2\Pr(\theta > \theta^*) + U'(W'')f(\theta^*)(\theta^*-r^*)W_o(1+r)/(z^*+W_o)^2. \tag{2.12}$$

In (2.12), since $\theta^* < r^*$, $L''(z^*) < 0$ if $U'' \leq 0$.

As in the analysis of the choice between shares and riskless bonds, there are three kinds of solutions z^{*o}. If $L'(0) \leq 0$, then $z^{*o} = 0$, and we have a solution with the entire portfolio consisting of riskless bonds. This solution applies if the expected return, net of default risk, on risky corporate bonds does not exceed the return on riskless bonds. That is

$$L'(0) = U'\{W_o^*(1+r)\}[-(1+r)Pr(\theta \leq -1) + (r^*-r)Pr(\theta > -1)] \leq 0$$

if and only if $-Pr(\theta \leq -1) + r^*Pr(\theta > -1) \leq r$. This is just another application of the proposition that no part of an unfavorable gamble will be taken. If $-Pr(\theta \leq -1) + r^*Pr(\theta > -1) > r$, then some corporate debt will be purchased. Furthermore, this implies

$$r^* > \frac{r + Pr(\theta < -1)}{Pr(\theta > -1)} > r,$$

and we have the proposition: <u>No lender will hold risky corporate bonds unless the interest rate thereon exceeds that of riskless bonds</u>.

If $L'(0) \geq 0$, $L'(W_o^*) \leq 0$, then the optimal supply of debt finance $z^{*o} = z^{*o}(r^*)$ is given by $L'(z^{*o}) = 0$, $z^{*o} \geq 0$. The slope of this supply function is $dz^{*o}/dr^* = -(\partial L'(z^{*o})/\partial r^*)/L''(z^{*o})$, and sign $(dz^{*o}/dr^*) =$ sign $(\partial L'(z^{*o})/\partial r^*)$, where

$$(2.13)\quad \partial L'(z^{*o})/\partial r^* = -U'(W'')f(\theta^*)W_o(1+r^*)z^{*o}/(z^{*o}+W_o)^2 + [U''(W'')(r^*-r)z^{*o} + U'(W'')]Pr(\theta > \theta^*),\ \theta^* = \frac{r^*z^{*o}-W_o}{z^{*o}+W_o}.$$

Since the third term of (2.13) is positive, while the first two terms are negative we cannot deduce sign $(\partial L'(z^{*o})/\partial r^*)$ on the basis of qualitative considerations alone. However, if we let $r^* = \underline{r}^*$ such that $L'(0) = 0$, i.e.

$$\underline{r}^* = [r + Pr(\theta \leq -1)]/Pr(\theta > -1),$$

we have

$$(2.13')\quad \partial L'(0)/\partial r^* = U'\{W_o^*(1+r)\}Pr(\theta > -1) > 0.$$

Hence, for r^* near $\underline{r}^*$, at least, we are assured of a positively sloped supply function of debt finance. Figure 7 illustrates a supply curve suggested by the above considerations.

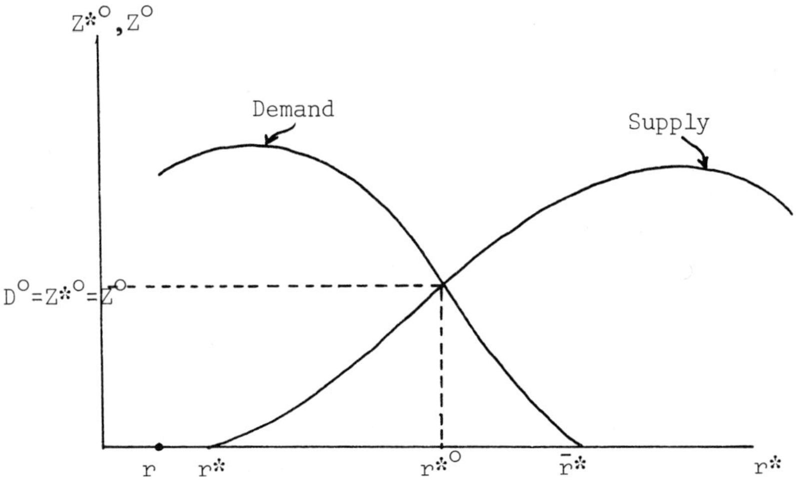

Figure 7

The Market for Corporate Bonds. In an economy of N identical corporate entrepreneurs and N identical lenders, the individual supply and demand curves for debt finance serve also to represent the market for risky corporate bonds. The equilibrium contractual rate on such bonds is r^{*o}, with each firm's total capitalization D^o+W_o of which W_o is equity and $D^o = z^{*o} = z^o$ is debt (Figure 7). Hence, under these very special conditions, the problem of optimal debt versus equity financing reduces to that of determining the rate $r^{*o} \geq 0$ on risky bonds that equalizes the supply and demand for debt finance. If $\underline{r}^* > \bar{r}^*$ in Figure 7, then $D^o = 0$ and the firms are entirely equity financed.

Interpretation of Capital Rationing by Lenders. Our analysis of the supply and demand for bond finance can be used to interpret the phenomenon of capital rationing. Capital rationing in the above model is defined as an inability of entrepreneur-borrowers to obtain additional debt finance by offering to pay a higher contractual interest rate. Quirk [14] has already demonstrated a case in which capital rationing is inevitable using a mean-variance expected utility of income model.

To get capital rationing it is only necessary to assume that the supply and demand for bond finance appears something like that shown in Figure 8. That is, (i) there exists a maximum quantity of debt finance, $\hat{z}^*$, that a lender will supply to a borrower at a contractual rate $\hat{r}^*$, and (ii) borrower demand at $\hat{r}^*$ exceeds the quantity supplied. As an example, from (2.11), for a lender maximizing the expected value of wealth ($U' \equiv 1$), the supply function of finance is defined by

$$(2.11') \qquad L'(z^{*o}) = -\Pr(\theta \leq -1) - r + r^{*}\Pr(\theta > \theta^{*}) + \int_{-1}^{\theta^*} \theta f(\theta)d\theta = 0$$

and therefore

$$dz^{*o}/dr^{*} = -\frac{z^{*o}+W_o}{W_o(1+r^*)}\left[\frac{(z^{*o}+W_o)\Pr(\theta > \theta^{*})}{(\theta^*-r^*)f(\theta^*)} + z^{*o}\right].$$

Hence, at $z^{*o} = \hat{z}^{*}$, we have $dz^{*o}/dr^{*} = 0$, where $\hat{z}^{*}$ satisfies

$$(\hat{z}^{*}+W_o)\Pr(\theta > \theta^{*}) + \hat{z}^{*}(\theta^{*}-r^{*})f(\theta^{*}) = 0,$$

$$\theta^{*} < r^{*} \text{ for all finite } z^{*}.$$

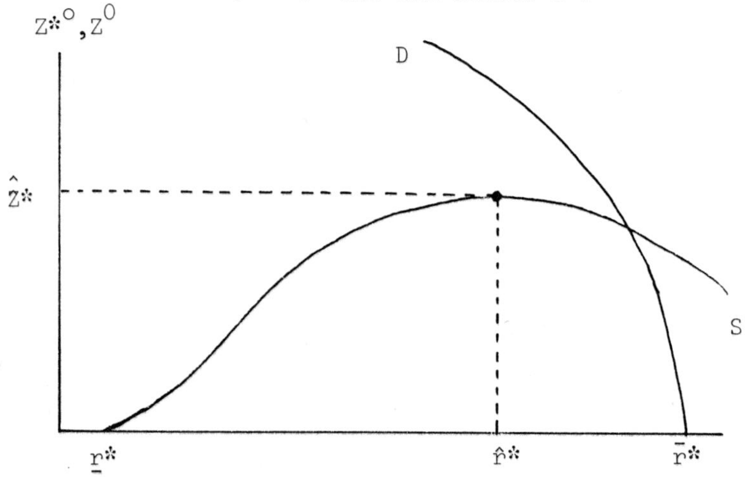

Figure 8

(Furthermore, d^2z^{*o}/dr^{*2} is strictly negative if $f'(\theta^{*}) > 0$). At $\hat{z}^{*}$ the level of debt and the risk of default are so great that no further increase in the contractual rate can induce the lender to supply more funds. In Figure 8, at $\hat{r}^{*}$, the borrower gets the largest loan possible, and at that interest rate there is an excess demand for debt finance.

Externality Inherent in the Debtor-Creditor Transaction. The expression (2.10) for lender expected utility contains an important externality parameter which is basic to understanding the nature of the debtor-creditor relationship.

The lender's expected utility, and therefore his supply of finance z^{*o}, depends on the borrower's equity (wealth, W_o) in the risky investment. In the analysis of the demand for bond finance, the borrower's expected utility (2.1) was independent of the wealth position of the lender. This asymmetry is inherent in the debtor-creditor relationship under risk.

Specifically, the borrower's equity inflicts an external economy on the lender. That is, from (2.10),

$$\partial L(z^*)/\partial W_o = \int_{-1}^{\theta^*} U'\{(W_o^*-z^*)(1+r) + (z^*+W_o)(1+\theta)\}f(\theta)d\theta > 0,$$

and the greater the borrower's stake in the risky investment activity, the greater the lender's expected utility at every level of borrowing. Furthermore, under very weak conditions the greater is this equity, the greater will be the lender's supply of finance at any given contractual rate r^*. To show this, we have

$$dz^{*o}/dW_o = -(\partial L'(z^{*o})/\partial W_o)/L''(z^{*o}),$$

so that

$$\text{sign } dz^{*o}/dW_o = \text{sign } \partial L'(z^{*o})/\partial W_o .$$

But

$$\partial L'(z^{*o})/\partial W_o = \int_{-1}^{\theta^*} U''\{(W_o^*-z^{*o})(1+r) + z^{*o}(1+r^*)\}$$

$$(\theta-r)(1+\theta)f(\theta)d\theta$$

$$- U'\{(W_o^*-z^{*o})(1+r) + z^{*o}(1+r^*)\}$$

$$f(\theta^*)(\theta^*-r^*)z^{*o}(1+r^*)/(z^{*o}+W_o)^2 > 0$$

if the integral is positive, since $\theta^* < r^*$ in the second term. A sufficient condition for the integral to be positive is $\theta^* < r$, which could be violated only for very large levels of debt financing, i.e. $z^{*o} > (1+r)W_o/(r^*-r)$.

These considerations make it clear why bankers and other lenders have such a deep interest in the personal financial affairs of borrowers, and in particular why loans such as mortgages are geared to borrower's equity. The rich get richer in part because of the external economies they provide lenders. "Discrimination" in favor of wealthier borrowers in the loan market is often judged to be evidence of "imperfections in the capital markets." In fact the reverse is true. Lenders would be irrational, and the loan market imperfect indeed, if lenders ignored the financial state of borrowers. Similarly, it is sometimes claimed that differences in the rate on different debt instruments is evidence of "imperfection". Yet two borrowers, alike in every respect except for the uses to which they will put borrowed funds, will clearly face different theoretical borrowing rates because of different default risk to lenders.

Indifference Curves and the Lender. As a consequence of the above externality problem we cannot formulate the lender's portfolio problem as a constrained maximum in which the criterion function contains only quantities of securities, and with wealth and price parameters appearing only in the budget constraint. Thus, in the spirit of the borrower's analysis, if we define $x^* = (1+r^*)z^*$ as the contractual maturity value or "face value" of corporate bonds held by the lender and, similarly, $x' = (1+r)(W_o^*-z^*)$ as his holdings of governments, then his utility function corresponding to (2.10) is

$$\begin{aligned}\chi(x',x^*|W_o,r^*) &= U(x')\Pr(\theta \leq -1) \\ &+ \int_{-1}^{\theta^*} U\{x' + x^*(1+\theta)/(1+r^*) \\ &+ W_o(1+\theta)\}f(\theta)d\theta \\ &+ U\{x' + x^*\}\Pr(\theta > \theta^*)\end{aligned}$$

where

$$\theta^* = \frac{r^*z^*-W_o}{z^*+W_o} = \frac{r^*x^* - W_o(1+r^*)}{x^* + W_o(1+r^*)} .$$

The lender's budget constraint is $W_o^* = x'/(1+r) + x^*/(1+r^*)$. Hence, the lender's indifference curves are "contaminated" by the borrower's equity, W_o, and the interest rate r^*. A change in W_o alters only the borrower's exchange opportunities, while it changes the lender's utility opportunities. r^* affects the exchange opportunities of both traders, but also affects the lender's utility opportunities. The conventional "Edgeworth Box" analysis does not apply.

FOOTNOTES

[*] I am grateful to the National Science Foundation for their support of this study.

[1] Quirk, J.P., "The Capital Structure of Firms and the Risk of Failure", International Economic Review, Vol. 2 (May, 1961).

[2] Tobin, J., "Liquidity Preference as Behavior Toward Risk", Review of Economic Studies, Vol. 25 (February, 1958).

[3] Arrow, K.J., "The Economics of Uncertainty", Lecture Notes for Economics 285, Stanford University, unpublished, and Aspects of the Theory of Risk-Bearing, (Helsinki: 1965).

[4] Lintner, J., "The Valuation of Risk Assets and the Selection of Risky Investments in Stock Portfolios and Capital Budgets", Review of Economics and Statistics, Vol. 47 (February, 1965).

[5] Breen, W., "Specific Versus General Models of Portfolio Selection", Oxford Economics Papers, Vol. 20 (November, 1968).

[6] Arrow, K.J., "The Role of Securities in the Optimal Allocation of Risk Bearing", Review of Economic Studies, Vol. 31 (April, 1964).

[7] Debreu, G., Theory of Value, (New York, 1959).

[8] See for example, J. Hirshleifer, "Investment Decision under Uncertainty", Quarterly Journal of Economics, Vol. 79 (November, 1965) and Vol. 80 (May, 1966). For a modification of the contingent commodity approach using a stock market, see P. Diamond, "The Role of a Stock Market in a General Equilibrium Model with Technological Uncertainty", American Economic Review, Vol. 57 (September, 1967).

[9] op. cit., p. 213.

[10] cf Arrow, Aspects of the Theory of Risk-Bearing, pp. 39-41 in respect to the demand for money.

[11] Arrow, op. cit.

[12] Pratt, J.W., "Risk Aversion in the Small and in the Large", Econometrica, Vol. 32 (January-April, 1964).

[13] Quirk, op. cit.

THE ABSTRACT TRANSPORTATION PROBLEM

by

Arnold M. Faden*
Iowa State University

1. Introduction

In this paper we generalize the transportation problem of linear programming to the case of a possibly infinite number of sources and sinks.

Why bother to do this? In the first place, the surface of the earth is a continua and we may always think of transportation as a re-distribution of mass from one portion of this surface to another. Many transportation problems appearing in the literature achieve their finite character by a lumping together of continua into a finite number of pieces, which are treated as points: for example, treating countries as single points in international trade models.

However, the possible realm of application of the abstract transportation model goes well beyond transportation *per se*. It is well known that a wide variety of models - of resource allocation, scheduling, etc. - can be thrown into the transportation format. Problems of the "caterer" form, for example, involve the redistribution of mass from one point in time to another. Since time is a continuum, such problems are often most naturally formulated with a continuum of origins and distinations. Again, there is an infinity of types of possible commodities or industrial processes; thus, a problem of the form, "how shall I assign my resources among various activities?", is again a problem with an infinity of sources and sinks.

Although this paper is not concerned directly with numerical applications, one possible "practical-man's" objection should be laid to rest. It is not true that the abstract transportation model must be approximated finitely - by the lumping process mentioned above - to achieve numerical results. What practice requires is that the set of possible answers be represented by a parameter space of relatively low dimension. This can be achieved by the lumping process, but can also be achieved in other ways, depending on the particular problem. This is illustrated by statistics, where continuous distributions are put to practical use by working with families of them indexed by a small number of parameters.

2. Formulating the Model

The transportation problem with m sources and n sinks is:

Find mn non-negative numbers x_{ij} $(i = 1,\ldots,m;\ j = 1,\ldots,n)$ satisfying

$$\sum_j x_{ij} \leq a_i \qquad (i = 1,\ldots,m), \tag{1}$$

$$\sum_i x_{ij} \geq b_j \qquad (j = 1,\ldots,n), \tag{2}$$

and minimizing

$$\sum_{i,j} r_{ij} x_{ij} \,. \tag{3}$$

Here a_i is the capacity of source i, b_j is the requirement at sink j, and r_{ij} is the cost incurred per unit shipped from source i to sink j.

The natural generalization of this uses measures and integrals. We now define the necessary concepts [1].

$x \in E$ signifies that x is a member of E. Set E is contained in set F, written $E \subset F$, if every member of E is a member of F. The union of sets E and F, written $E \cup F$, is the set whose members are members of E or F or both. More generally, if $\mathcal{G}$ is an arbitrary collection of sets, its union, written $\cup\mathcal{G}$, is the set whose members are members of at least one of the sets of $\mathcal{G}$. The intersection of sets E and F, written $E \cap F$, is the set whose members are members of both E and F. If $\mathcal{G}$ is an arbitrary collection of sets, its intersection, written $\cap\mathcal{G}$, is the set whose members are members of all of the $\mathcal{G}$ sets. The complement of set F in set E, written $E\backslash F$, is the set whose members are members of E but not of F. The empty set, written $\emptyset$, is the set which has no members. A set E is countable if its members can be enumerated in a finite or infinite sequence $\{e_1, e_2, \ldots\}$.

Let A be a fixed set, and Σ a collection of subsets of A; Σ is a sigma-field over A if (1) $A \in \Sigma$, and (2) if $E \in \Sigma$, then $(A\backslash E) \in \Sigma$, and (3) if $\mathcal{G}$ is any countable collection of Σ-sets, then $\cup\mathcal{G} \in \Sigma$. The pair (A,Σ) is called a measurable space, and the members of Σ are called measurable sets.

Let (A,Σ') and (B,Σ'') be two measurable spaces. The product measurable space, written $(A \times B,\ \Sigma' \times \Sigma'')$ is defined as follows. $A \times B$ is the cartesian product of A and B, the set of all ordered pairs (x,y), $(x \in A,\ y \in B)$. Any subset of $A \times B$ of the form $E \times F$, $(E \in \Sigma',\ F \in \Sigma'')$ is called a measurable rectangle. $\Sigma' \times \Sigma''$ is the class of all sets common to all sigma-fields over $A \times B$ which have all measurable rectangles as members. $\Sigma' \times \Sigma''$ itself can be shown to be a sigma-field over $A \times B$, the sigma-field generated by the measurable rectangles.

A bounded, non-negative function, μ, whose domain is a sigma-field, is a measure if $\mu(\cup\mathcal{G}) = \Sigma_{n=1}^{\infty}\mu(G_n)$ whenever $\mathcal{G}$ is a countable collection $\{G_1,G_2,G_3,\ldots\}$ of measurable sets which are disjoint ($G_m \cap G_n = \emptyset$ for all $m \neq n$) [2]. A probability on (A,Σ) is a measure μ with domain Σ for which $\mu(A) = 1$.

The notation $\{x|\ldots\}$ represents the set of all x having the property stated after the bar. For example, $\{x|f(x) > c\}$ is the set of all x for which the value of a certain function f exceeds the number c. Given a measurable space (A,Σ), a function f with domain A is said to be measurable, if the sets $\{x|f(x) > c\}$ are measurable for all real numbers c. It can be shown that the substitution of "$\geq$", "$\leq$", or "<" for ">" in this definition yields the same set of functions.

If f is a bounded measurable non-negative function, and μ a measure, both with respect to (A,Σ), the integral of f with respect to μ, written $\int_A f\, d\mu$, is defined as $\int_0^\infty \mu\{x|f(x) > t\}\, dt$, where the integral on the right is an ordinary Riemann integral of the indicated (monotone decreasing) function on the real line. If f takes on negative values, we split it into its positive and negative parts: $f(x) = \max(f(x),0) - \max(-f(x),0)$, take the integral of each part, and subtract [3].

We are now ready to formulate the abstract transportation problem: Given two triples, (A,Σ',μ') and (B,Σ'',μ''), and a real-valued function r with domain $A \times B$, where

(i) Σ' is a sigma-field over set A, and μ' is a measure on Σ'; and similarly for Σ'', B, and μ'';

(ii) r is bounded, and measurable, with respect to the product sigma-field $\Sigma' \times \Sigma''$ over $A \times B$;

find a measure $\emptyset$ on $(A \times B, \Sigma' \times \Sigma'')$ which satisfies

$$\emptyset(E \times B) \leq \mu'(E) \quad \text{for all } E \in \Sigma', \qquad (4)$$

$$\emptyset(A \times F) \geq \mu''(F) \quad \text{for all } F \in \Sigma'', \qquad (5)$$

and which minimizes $\int_{A\times B} r\, d\emptyset$ over all such measures. (6)

This bears direct comparison with the finite transportation problem (1), (2), (3). A and B are the origin and destination spaces, respectively. μ' is the capacity measure. The constraint (4), which is a direct generalization of (1), states that $\emptyset(E \times B)$, which is the total flow out of region E, cannot exceed $\mu'(E)$, the capacity of the sources in region E. μ'' is the requirement measure, and

(5), the generalization of (2), states that $\emptyset(A \times F)$, the total inflow into region F, must at least meet the requirement for that region, $\mu''(F)$. $\emptyset$ is the unknown flow from origin to destination: $\emptyset(E \times F)$ equals the total mass flowing from region E to region F. r generalizes the unit cost function.

A careful check of the definitions shows that, in the special case where A and B are finite sets, and Σ', Σ'' are the classes of all subsets of A and B, respectively, (4), (5), (6) reduce to (1), (2), (3).

Before going on to the analysis of the abstract transportation problem, let us look at some related work. Martin Beckmann has worked on some related but non-overlapping problems [4]. Beckmann makes essential use of the topology of 2-dimensional Euclidean space, using vector methods (gradients, curls, etc.). In this sense his is a special case of ours. On the other hand he deals with the entire flow field, whereas we restrict our attention just to origin-destination connections. Thus he is dealing essentially with a <u>transshipment</u>, rather than a transportation problem.

The abstract transshipment problem differs from the abstract transportation problem as follows: the spaces A and B, and the sigma-fields Σ' and Σ'', are identical; let us write them as (A,Σ). There is a <u>net requirement</u> (signed) measure, μ, on (A,Σ). This differs from an ordinary measure only in that it may take on negative values. The constraints (4) and (5) are replaced by:

$$\emptyset(A \times E) - \emptyset(E \times A) \geq \mu(E) \text{ for all } E \in \Sigma. \quad (7)$$

The transshipment problem, then, is to find a measure $\emptyset$ on $(A \times A, \Sigma \times \Sigma)$ which satisfies (7), and minimizes (6) over all such measures.

In the finite case there is a well known procedure for reducing transshipment to transportation problems [5]. This procedure breaks down when the number of sets in Σ is infinite. The transshipment problem is essentially distinct from (and more difficult than) the transportation problem in the general case. We shall concentrate our attention on the latter; it should be pointed out, however, that several of the theorems we derive have analogs for the transshipment problem.

The true <u>locus classicus</u> for the abstract transportation problem is found in the work of L.V. Kantorovich [6]. He deals with the problem of (4)-(6) except for two minor points: the constraints are taken to be equalities, and A is identified with B. (This last identification involves no real loss of generality, but can be misleading, as we shall see.) He discusses the existence of optimal solutions and their connection with "potentials" (that is, dual prices, in the terminology which developed later on) - a remarkable achievement for its time. Kantorovich's article is peculiar in several respects. It is all of three pages long, and written with extreme brevity and apparent haste. In fact, the major theorem - stating the existence of dual prices associated with an optimal flow - is false, as one can show by a simple counter example [7]. (The root of the error, by the way, lies in the fact that the constraints imposed are those of the transportation problem, while the dual prices are defined in a way appropriate to the transshipment problem. If the unit cost function r violates the triangle inequality - as it well might - one can get a counter-example, as footnote 7 illustrates). More surprising is the fact that the method of proof used appears to be insufficient to prove the corrected version of the theorem.

Our aim in the bulk of this paper is to go over the ground sketched out by Kantorovich, to derive in a rigorous fashion conditions for the existence of optimal solutions, and to give a "pseudo-constructive" method for finding dual prices from an optimal solution.

3. Feasibility

We begin the investigation of the abstract transportation problem, (4)-(6), with a simple feasibility result.

Theorem 1. There exists a feasible solution to the constraints (4), (5) iff

$$\mu'(A) \geq \mu''(B). \tag{8}$$

Proof: If $\emptyset$ is a feasible solution, then $\mu'(A) \geq \emptyset(A \times B) \geq \mu''(B)$, so the stated condition is necessary.

Conversely, let $\mu'(A) \geq \mu''(B)$; if $\mu'(A) = 0$, both μ' and μ'' are identically zero, and then the identically zero measure on $\Sigma' \times \Sigma''$ is obviously feasible. If $\mu'(A) > 0$, define the function $\emptyset$ on measurable rectangles $E \times F$ by

$$\emptyset(E \times F) = \frac{\mu'(E) \cdot \mu''(F)}{\mu'(A)}. \tag{9}$$

It is a standard measure theorem that such a "product" function can be extended to a measure over the product space $(A \times B, \Sigma' \times \Sigma'')$. One checks immediately that this measure is feasible, since

$$\emptyset(E \times B) = \frac{\mu'(E) \cdot \mu''(B)}{\mu'(A)} \leq \mu'(E), \text{ and}$$

$$\emptyset(A \times F) = \mu''(F). \qquad \text{QED}$$

This may be stated: a feasible solution exists iff total capacity of sources at least matches total requirements of sinks. This well known result for the finite case thus carries over in general.

We are also interested in the abstract transportation problem for the case where the constraints in (4) and (5) are stated as equalities:

$$\emptyset(E \times B) = \mu'(E) \quad \text{for all } E \in \Sigma' \tag{10}$$

$$\emptyset(A \times F) = \mu''(F) \quad \text{for all } F \in \Sigma'' \tag{11}$$

Theorem 2. If $\mu'(A) = \mu''(B)$, then any feasible solution to (4), (5) satisfies these constraints with equality (that is, it is in fact feasible for the stricter constraints (10), (11)).

Proof: Suppose, for example, that some constraint in (4) is satisfied with strict inequality: $\emptyset(G \times B) < \mu'(G)$ for some $G \in \Sigma'$; then $\mu''(B) \leq \emptyset(A \times B) = \emptyset(G \times B) + \emptyset((A \setminus G) \times B) < \mu'(G) + \mu'(A \setminus G) = \mu'(A)$, a contradiction. The proof for a strict (5) inequality is similar.

QED

We now have an equally simple feasibility result for the equality-constrained case:

Theorem 3. There exists a feasible solution to the constraints (10), (11), iff

$$\mu'(A) = \mu''(B). \tag{12}$$

Proof: If $\emptyset$ is feasible, then $\mu'(A) = \emptyset(A \times B) = \mu''(B)$. If $\mu'(A) = \mu''(B)$, then Theorem 1 tells us that there is a feasible solution to (4) and (5), and Theorem 2 that these constraints are satisfied as equalities. QED

4. Duality

Every finite linear program has a dual, and the dual of the transportation problem (1)-(3) is

Find non-negative numbers p_i $(i = 1,\ldots,m)$ and q_j $(j = 1,\ldots,n)$ satisfying

$$q_j - p_i \leq r_{ij} \quad (i = 1,\ldots,m;\ j = 1,\ldots,n) \tag{13}$$

and maximizing: $$\sum_j q_j b_j - \sum_i p_i a_i. \tag{14}$$

The dual of the transportation problem with equality constraints is the same as this, except that p_i and q_j are not constrained to be non-negative.

Analogously, we define the dual of the abstract transportation problem (4)-(6) to be -

Find a bounded, non-negative, function, p, with domain A, measurable with respect to Σ', and a bounded, non-negative, function, q, with domain B, measurable with respect to Σ'', satisfying

$$q(y) - p(x) \leq r(x,y) \quad \text{for all } x \in A,\ y \in B, \tag{15}$$

and maximizing: $$\int_B q\ d\mu'' - \int_A p\ d\mu'. \tag{16}$$

The dual of the abstract transportation problem with equality constraints is defined to be the same as this, except that p and q need not be non-negative.

Apart from the obvious formal similarities between these abstract duals and the finite duals, many of the standard relations between primal and dual carry over to the general case. We first define one more concept.

Given a measure $\emptyset$ on $(A \times B, \Sigma' \times \Sigma'')$, its left-marginal measure, $\emptyset'$, is the measure defined on (A, Σ') by the rule:

$$\emptyset'(E) = \emptyset(E \times B), \quad \text{all } E \in \Sigma'. \tag{17}$$

Similary, $\emptyset''$, the right-marginal measure of $\emptyset$, is defined on (B, Σ'') by the rule:

$$\emptyset''(F) = \emptyset(A \times F), \quad \text{all } F \in \Sigma''. \tag{18}$$

(If $\emptyset$ is a probability, its marginals coincide with the usual notion of marginal probabilities.) In terms of marginals, the basic transportation constraints (4) and (5) assume the simple form -

$$\emptyset' \leq \mu', \text{ and} \tag{19}$$

$$\emptyset'' \geq \mu''. \tag{20}$$

Theorem 4. If $\emptyset$ is feasible for the abstract transportation problem (4)-(5), and (p,q) is feasible for the dual, (15), then

$$\int_{A\times B} r\ d\emptyset \geq \int_B q\ d\mu'' - \int_A p\ d\mu'. \tag{21}$$

Proof: We adopt the simple convention that "p" stands both for a function with domain A, and for the function with domain $A \times B$ defined by $p(x,y) = p(x)$, all $x \in A$, $y \in B$; similarly, "q" stands for two functions, with domains B, and $A \times B$, related by $q(x,y) = q(y)$; which function we are talking about is clear from the domain of integration. Then

$$\int_{A\times B} r\,d\emptyset \geq \int_{A\times B} (q-p)\,d\emptyset = \int_{A\times B} q\,d\emptyset - \int_{A\times B} p\,d\emptyset =$$

$$\int_B q\,d\emptyset'' - \int_A p\,d\emptyset' \geq \int_B q\,d\mu'' - \int_A p\,d\mu'. \qquad (22)$$

(The first inequality follows from (15), the equalities reflect standard integration theorems, and the last inequality follows from (19) and (20), together with the fact that p and q are non-negative.) QED

Theorem 5. If $\emptyset$ is feasible for the abstract transportation problem with equality constraints, and (p,q) is feasible for the dual of this problem, then (21) is still valid.

Proof: Same as above, except that the last "$\geq$" should be replaced by "=". QED

These theorems carry over the fact that, in a pair of linear programs, the value of the maximum program never exceeds the value of the minimum program, for any pair of feasible values.

We are now interested in conditions under which the inequality (21) becomes an equality, because, in view of theorems 4 and 5, this would guarantee that $\emptyset$, and (p,q) are optimal for their respective programs.

Definition. Let $\emptyset$ be feasible for the abstract transportation problem (4)-(5), and $(p,q) \geq 0$ feasible for the dual problem (15). (p,q) is a measure potential for $\emptyset$ if the following three conditions are satisfied:

$$\emptyset\{(x,y)\,|\,q(y) - p(x) < r(x,y)\} = 0, \qquad (23)$$

$$\emptyset'\{x\,|\,p(x) > 0\} = \mu'\{x\,|\,p(x) > 0\}, \text{ and} \qquad (24)$$

$$\emptyset''\{y\,|\,q(y) > 0\} = \mu''\{y\,|\,q(y) > 0\}. \qquad (25)$$

(23) states that there is no flow on the set of source-sink pairs for which (15) is satisfied with strict inequality. (24) states that capacity is used completely on the set of sources for which $p > 0$. (25) states that requirements are just met on the set of sinks for which $q > 0$.

The same definition also serves for the pair of equality-constrained programs, except that (p,q) need not be non-negative. Note also that for equality constraints, (24) and (25) are automatically fulfilled, so that they may be omitted from the definition.

Theorem 6. For a given feasible pair, $\emptyset$ and (p,q), relation (21) is an equality iff (p,q) is a measure potential for $\emptyset$. (This applies both to the inequality and the equality-constrained programs.)

Proof: Examining the chain of relations (22), we find that the first "$\geq$" becomes an equality iff (23) is fulfilled, and the last "$\geq$" becomes an equality iff (24) and (25) are fulfilled. QED

Corollary. If $\emptyset$ and (p,q) are feasible for their respective programs, and (p,q) is a measure potential for $\emptyset$, then both are optimal for their programs.

The definition and Theorem 6 generalizes the familiar "complementary slackness" conditions of linear programming, according to which equality is attained in dual program values iff strict inequality in one program's constraints is matched by a zero value of the corresponding variable in the other. The further (and deeper) result in finite linear programming theory that "complementary slackness" is a necessary condition for optimality, does not necessarily carry over to the infinite case.

5. Existence of Optimal Solutions

Up to this point, measure-theoretic concepts have sufficed to define our concepts and prove our theorems. From here on topological concepts will also be needed. Indeed, the author does not know of any method of proving the existence of optimal solutions to the abstract transportation problem using measure-theoretic concepts alone. Also, we know of no way to construct measure potentials directly from optimal solutions. Instead we give a construction for the related notion of "topological potential", and under certain additional conditions these turn out to be measure potentials as well. The basic definitions follow.

Given a fixed set A, let $\mathfrak{J}$ be a collection of subsets of A. $\mathfrak{J}$ is a topology over A if (1) $A \in \mathfrak{J}$, and the empty set $\emptyset \in \mathfrak{J}$; (2) if $G_1 \in \mathfrak{J}$ and $G_2 \in \mathfrak{J}$, then $G_1 \cap G_2 \in \mathfrak{J}$; (3) if $\mathfrak{G}$ is any collection of $\mathfrak{J}$-sets, then $\cup\mathfrak{G} \in \mathfrak{J}$. The pair $(A,\mathfrak{J})$ is a topological space. The members of $\mathfrak{J}$ are called the open sets. A set is closed if its complement in A is open.

Let $(A,\mathfrak{J}')$ and $(B,\mathfrak{J}'')$ be two topological spaces. The product topological space, written $(A \times B, \mathfrak{J}' \times \mathfrak{J}'')$, is defined as follows. $A \times B$ is the cartesian product of A and B. Any subset of $A \times B$ of the form $G' \times G''$ ($G' \in \mathfrak{J}'$, $G'' \in \mathfrak{J}''$) is called an open rectangle. $\mathfrak{J}' \times \mathfrak{J}''$ is the class of all sets which are unions of an arbitrary number of open rectangles, together with the empty set. It can be shown that $\mathfrak{J}' \times \mathfrak{J}''$ is, indeed, a topology over $A \times B$.

A topological space $(A,\mathfrak{J})$ is separable if there is a countable set $E \subset A$ such that every non-empty open set has a member in common with E. A real-valued function f with domain A is continuous for the topology $\mathfrak{J}$ if every set of the form $\{x | a < f(x) < b\}$, where a and b are real numbers, is open.

A metric on a set, A, is a real-valued function, d, with domain $A \times A$, having the properties (1) $d(x,x) = 0$; (2) $d(x,y) > 0$ if $x \neq y$; (3) $d(x,y) = d(y,x)$; and (4) $d(x,y) + d(y,z) \geq d(x,z)$, for all $x,y,z \in A$. The pair (A,d) is a metric space. A sequence, $x_1, x_2, \ldots$, in a metric space converges to x if, for any positive number ϵ, there is an integer N, such that $d(x_n,x) < \epsilon$ for all $n > N$. A metric space is complete if, for any sequence $x_1, x_2, \ldots$ having the property that $d(x_m,x_n) < \epsilon$ whenever m and n exceed some integer N, depending on the positive number ϵ, there is an x to which the sequence converges. (Roughly, when the points of a sequence get indefinitely close to each other, they get indefinitely close to some fixed point of the space.)

Any metric on A determines a topology on A as follows: a set $E \subset A$ is open if, for every point $x \in E$ there is a positive number ϵ such that all points within distance ϵ of x are members of E. A topology which is generated by some metric in this way is said to be metrizable. If it is generated by some complete metric it is said to be topologically complete. A set K in a metrizable topological space $(A,\mathfrak{J})$ is compact if any sequence of members of K has a subsequence which converges to a member of K. If the subsequence is merely known to converge to a member of A, the set is relatively compact.

We will need certain concepts which involve both measure-theoretic and topological notions. The Borel field of a topological space is the smallest sigma-field of which every open set is a member. (More exactly, it is the sigma-field to which a set belongs iff it belongs to every sigma-field to which all open sets belong.) The members of the Borel field are called Borel sets. Let $(A,\mathfrak{J})$ be a metrizable topological space, let Σ be its Borel field, and let μ be a measure on Σ. μ is said to be tight if, for every positive number ϵ, there is a compact set K such that $\mu(A \setminus K) < \epsilon$. Let $\mathfrak{M}$ be a collection of measures on Σ. $\mathfrak{M}$ is uniformly tight if (1) there is a number M such that $\mu(A) \leq M$ for all measures $\mu \in \mathfrak{M}$, and (2) for every positive number ϵ there is a compact set K such that $\mu(A \setminus K) < \epsilon$ for all $\mu \in \mathfrak{M}$. (Note that this requires more than that each measure of $\mathfrak{M}$ be individually tight.) Let μ^* be a measure on Σ, and $\mu_1, \mu_2, \ldots$ a sequence of measures on Σ; the sequence $\mu_1, \mu_2, \ldots$ is said to converge weakly to μ^* if, for every real-valued function f with domain A which is bounded, and continuous with respect to $\mathfrak{J}$, we have

$$\lim_{n\to\infty} \int_A f \, d\mu_n = \int_A f \, d\mu^* \tag{26}$$

(in the ordinary sense of limit of a sequence of real numbers). The set of measures $\mathfrak{M}$ is <u>weakly relatively compact</u> if every sequence of measures in $\mathfrak{M}$ contains a subsequence which converges weakly to some measure (not necessarily a member of $\mathfrak{M}$).

Finally, we need one or two concepts concerning real numbers. The <u>supremum</u> (abbreviated "sup") of a set of real numbers is the smallest number not exceeded by any of the numbers in the set; the <u>infimum</u> ("inf") is the largest number which is not greater than any number of the set. (If the set has a greatest number, it is the supremum; similarly, if it has a least number, that number is the infimum.) Given a sequence of real numbers, $x_1, x_2, \ldots$, let y_k be the supremum of the subsequence beginning with the k'th term: $x_k, x_{k+1}, \ldots$; the limit of the sequence $y_1, y_2, \ldots$ formed in this way is called the <u>lim sup</u> of the original sequence. <u>Lim inf</u> of the original sequence is defined in the same way from the sequence of infima.

With these definitions taken care of, we are ready to proceed. The following two basic results from the theory of weak convergence play an essential role in our existence proofs [8].

<u>Lemma 1</u>. (Prohorov-Varadarajan) Let $\mathfrak{M}$ be a collection of measures on the Borel field of a metrizable topological space. If $\mathfrak{M}$ is uniformly tight, then $\mathfrak{M}$ is weakly relatively compact.

<u>Lemma 2</u>. (A.D. Aleksandrov) The following three conditions are equivalent.

(a) The sequence $\mu_1, \mu_2, \ldots$ of measures in $\mathfrak{M}$ converges weakly to μ^*;

(b) Lim sup $\mu_n(F) \leq \mu^*(F)$, for every closed set F. (27)

(c) Lim inf $\mu_n(G) \geq \mu^*(G)$, for every open set G. (28)

We are now ready to state our first existence theorem. For reasons which will become clear later, we treat the abstract transportation problem only for the case where total capacity equals total requirement. To assess the practical scope of this theorem, it should be noted that N-dimensional Euclidean space is separable and topologically complete; thus the following theorem and its generalizations would appear to cover almost all cases to be met with in practice.

<u>Theorem 7</u>. Let (A, Σ', μ'), (B, Σ'', μ''), and r be as in the abstract transportation problem, (4)-(6). In addition,

assume that Σ' is the Borel field of a topology $\mathfrak{T}'$ over A, which is separable and topologically complete; similarly, Σ'' is assumed to be the Borel field of a topology $\mathfrak{T}''$ over B, which is separable and topologically complete. r is also assumed to be continuous with respect to the product topology $(A \times B, \mathfrak{T}' \times \mathfrak{T}'')$. Finally, assume $\mu'(A) = \mu''(B)$.

Then there exists an optimal solution $\emptyset^*$ to the abstract transportation problem.

Proof: There exists a feasible solution, by Theorem 1. Also the set of values assumed by the objective function (6) is bounded, since r is bounded, and feasible $\emptyset$'s are bounded by constraint (4). Hence there exists a finite infimum, V, and a sequence of feasible flows $\emptyset_1, \emptyset_2, \ldots$ such that

$$\lim_{n\to\infty} \int_{A\times B} r \, d\emptyset_n = V. \tag{29}$$

We will show that $\emptyset_1, \emptyset_2, \ldots$ converges weakly to an optimal measure. It is known that, in a separable and topologically complete space, any measure on the Borel field is tight (Ulam's theorem; see Billingsley p. 5-6). Thus μ' and μ'' are tight. Hence, for all positive ϵ, there are compact sets $K' \subset A$, $K'' \subset B$, such that $\mu'(A\backslash K') < \epsilon$ ε and $\mu''(B\backslash K'') < \varepsilon$.

Now $K' \times K''$ is compact in the product topology (Tihonov's theorem), and one verifies that, for any feasible $\emptyset$,

$$\emptyset(A\times B \;\; K'\times K'') \leq \emptyset(A \times (B \;\; K'')) + \emptyset((A \;\; K') \times B) =$$
$$\mu''(B \;\; K'') + \mu'(A \;\; K') < 2\epsilon \tag{30}$$

(The equality in (30) follows from the fact that all constraints in (4) and (5) are actually equalities here - from Theorem 2 above.) Hence the set of feasible solutions is uniformly tight. We now apply Prohorov's theorem (Lemma 1) to conclude that the set of feasible solutions is weakly relatively compact. (To justify this, we note that $\mathfrak{T}' \times \mathfrak{T}''$ is metrizable since its components are, and $\Sigma' \times \Sigma''$ is the Borel field of $\mathfrak{T}' \times \mathfrak{T}''$ since $\mathfrak{T}'$ and $\mathfrak{T}''$ are separable as well.)

Thus the sequence $\emptyset_1, \emptyset_2, \ldots$ contains a subsequence which converges weakly. For simplicity we use the same notation for this subsequence. It is clear that (29) still applies to the subsequence. Letting $\emptyset^*$ be the weak limit of the subsequence, we obtain

$$V = \lim_{n\to\infty} \int_{A\times B} r \, d\emptyset_n = \int_{A\times B} r \, d\emptyset^*, \tag{31}$$

from the definition of weak convergence. Thus $\emptyset^*$ attains the infimum, and we need only show that it is feasible to prove that it is optimal.

To prove feasibility, let $\emptyset_n'$, $\emptyset_n''$, $\emptyset^{*\prime}$, and $\emptyset^{*\prime\prime}$, be the left and right marginal measures of $\emptyset_n$ and $\emptyset^*$, respectively ($n = 1,2,\ldots$). The fact that $\emptyset_1,\emptyset_2,\ldots$ converges weakly to $\emptyset^*$, implies that $\emptyset_1',\emptyset_2',\ldots$ converges weakly to $\emptyset^{*\prime}$, and similarly for the right-marginals. (Mann-Wald theorem; see Billingsley, p. 30-31.)

Now let G be any open subset of A. We obtain

$$\mu'(G) \geq \liminf \emptyset_n'(G) \geq \emptyset^{*\prime}(G). \qquad (32)$$

(The first inequality comes from the fact that each measure $\emptyset_1,\emptyset_2,\ldots$ is feasible, hence satisfies (4); the second comes from Lemma 2.)

Similarly, let F be any closed subset of B. We obtain

$$\mu''(F) \leq \limsup \emptyset_n''(F) \leq \emptyset^{*\prime\prime}(F). \qquad (33)$$

It is known that the measure of any Borel set of a metrizable topological space equals the infimum of the measures of the open sets containing it, and also equals the supremum of the measures of the closed sets contained in it. Let E be any Borel subset of A. We obtain

$$\mu'(E) = \inf\{\mu'(G) \mid G \supset E, G \text{ open}\} \geq \inf\{\emptyset^{*\prime}(G) \mid G \supset E, G \text{ open}\} = \emptyset^{*\prime}(E) \qquad (34)$$

(The inequality comes from (32).) Also, if E is any Borel subset of B, we obtain

$$\mu''(E) = \sup\{\mu''(F) \mid F \subset E, F \text{ closed}\} \leq \sup\{\emptyset^{*\prime\prime}(F) \mid F \subset E, F \text{ closed}\} = \emptyset^{*\prime\prime}(E). \qquad (35)$$

(The inequality comes from (33).)

$\emptyset^*$ satisfies the constraints (4), according to (34), and the constraints (5), according to (35). Hence it is feasible, hence optimal. QED

What happens if we allow $\mu'(A)$ to be greater than $\mu''(B)$? That is, we consider the more general case in which the capacity of sources can exceed the requirement of sinks. Surprisingly, Theorem 7 breaks down:

Theorem 8. There is an abstract transportation problem satisfying all the premises of Theorem 7, except that $\mu'(A) > \mu''(B)$, for which no optimal solution exists.

Proof: Let there be just one source, a, of capacity 1. Let there be a countable number of sinks: $B = \{b_1,b_2,\ldots\}$ with requirements identically zero. Let every subset of B be open. Let the unit transport cost function be: $r(a,b_n) = 1/n - 1$. One easily verifies that all the premises of Theorem 7 hold (except, of course, that $\mu'(A) = 1$, $\mu''(B) = 0$). Yet there is no optimal flow, since if n is the smallest integer for which $\emptyset\{a,b_n\} > 0$, shifting this flow to the sink b_{n+1} reduces costs, while the identically zero flow is the worst of all. QED

There are, however, certain conditions under which we can still assert the existence of an optimal flow in the slack capacity case.

Theorem 9. Let the premises of Theorem 7 be altered as follows.
(1) $\mu'(A) \geq \mu''(B)$ (replacing the stronger condition $\mu'(A) = \mu''(B)$)
(2) $(B,\mathfrak{J}'')$ is compact and metrizable (replacing the weaker condition that $(B,\mathfrak{J}'')$ is separable and topologically complete).

Then an optimal solution exists to the abstract transportation problem.

Proof: The place where the proof of Theorem 7 breaks down if we replace $\mu'(A) = \mu''(B)$ by an inequality is in relation (30), where we cannot assert that

$$\emptyset(A \times (B\setminus K'')) + \emptyset((A\setminus K') \times B) = \mu''(B\setminus K'') + \mu'(A\setminus K'),$$

since Theorem 2 does not apply. However, if B itself is compact, we can replace K'' by B, to obtain

$$\emptyset(A \times B\setminus K' \times B) = \emptyset((A\setminus K') \times B) \leq \mu'(A\setminus K') < \epsilon. \quad (36)$$

Hence the set of feasible solutions is again uniformly tight, and the proof proceeds exactly as in Theorem 7. QED

Theorem 10. Let the premises of Theorem 7 be altered as follows: $\mu'(A) \geq \mu''(B)$, and r is non-negative.

Then an optimal solution exists to the abstract transportation problem.

We just outline the proof, rather than carrying out the somewhat tedious details. Given the original problem, we construct a new problem by adding an extra point (z) to the destination space B. We extend the topology $\mathfrak{J}''$ by specifying that $G \cup (z)$ is to be open iff G is open in $\mathfrak{J}''$. We extend the measure by specifying that the requirement for the singleton set (z) is to be $\mu'(A) - \mu''(B)$. Finally, we extend the function r by specifying that $r(x,z) = 0$ for all $x \in A$.

This new problem satisfies all the premises of Theorem

7, including the condition that total capacity = total requirement. (Incidentally, this construction is the abstract form of the standard trick of adding an artificial sink to take up the slack in an inequality-constrained finite transportation problem.) Hence there exists an optimal flow ϕ^{**} for it. Let ϕ^* be this flow restricted to the original product space $A \times B$. We claim that ϕ^* is optimal for the original problem.

To show this, let ϕ be any feasible flow for the original problem. Using the Radon-Nikodym theorem, we can show the existence of another feasible flow, $\tilde{\phi}$, which satisfies

$$\tilde{\phi} \leq \phi, \tag{37}$$

and satisfies the destination requirements exactly:

$$\tilde{\phi}(A \times E) = \mu''(E), \quad \text{for all } E \in \Sigma''. \tag{38}$$

It follows from (38) that $\tilde{\phi}$ has an extension, $\tilde{\tilde{\phi}}$, to the extended space $A \times (B \cap (z))$ which is feasible for the modified transportation problem. Finally, putting everything together, we obtain

$$\begin{aligned} \int_{A\times B} r \, d\phi^* &= \int_{A\times(B\cup(z))} r \, d\phi^{**} \\ &\leq \int_{A\times(B\cup(z))} r \, d\tilde{\tilde{\phi}} = \int_{A\times B} r \, d\tilde{\phi} \leq \int_{A\times B} r \, d\phi, \end{aligned} \tag{39}$$

which proves that ϕ^* is optimal.
(The equalities in (39) follow from the fact that $r(x,z)= 0$; the first inequality follows from the optimality of ϕ^{**} for the modified transportation problem; the last inequality follows from $r \geq 0$ and (37).) QED

Finally, we give two results which extend the scope of Theorem 7 considerably.

Theorem 11. Let the premises of Theorem 7 be weakened to read: $(A,\mathfrak{J}')$ and $(B,\mathfrak{J}'')$ are Borel subsets of separable and topologically complete spaces. Then there still exists an optimal solution.

Proof: The only place where topological completeness is used in the proof of Theorem 7 is to imply that μ' and μ'' are tight measures. But any measure on a space satisfying the weakened premises above is necessarily tight. (See Parthasarathy, p. 29-30.) QED

In practical terms, Theorem 11 means that existence can be asserted not only when the origin-destination spaces,

A and B, are Euclidean spaces of arbitrary finite dimension, but also when they are more or less arbitrary subsets.

Theorem 12. Let the premises of Theorem 7 be satisfied. Let λ and ν be two given measures on $(A \times B, \Sigma' \times \Sigma'')$, and let feasible flows be required to satisfy not only (4) and (5), but to lie between λ and ν:

$$\lambda(E) \leq \emptyset(E) \leq \nu(E), \text{ for all } E \in \Sigma' \times \Sigma''. \qquad (40)$$

Then, if there exists a feasible flow satisfying (4), (5), and (40), there exists an optimal flow for these constraints.

Proof: The proof of Theorem 7 applies without change, except that we must explicitly assume the existence of a feasible solution to get started, since Theorem 1 is not available. Thus, we know there exists a sequence, $\emptyset_1, \emptyset_2, \ldots$ of feasible solutions which converges weakly to a measure $\emptyset^*$ satisfying (4) and (5), and which achieves the infimum of the objective function (6). It remains to show that $\emptyset^*$ satisfies (40). This can be done in exactly the same way that the satisfaction of (4) and (5) are proved; namely, we show that

$$\nu(G) \geq \emptyset^*(G) \qquad (41)$$

for any open set $G \subset A \times B$, and that

$$\lambda(F) \leq \emptyset^*(F) \qquad (42)$$

for any closed set $F \subset A \times B$, by the same arguments leading to (32) and (33). Then, since $\Sigma' \times \Sigma''$ is the Borel field of the metrizable space $(A \times B, \mathfrak{J}' \times \mathfrak{J}'')$, the inequalities (41) and (42) can be extended to all Borel sets of $A \times B$, by the arguments of (34) and (35). Thus (40) is satisfied, $\emptyset^*$ is feasible for the more restrictive problem, hence optimal for it. QED [9]

6. Existence of Potentials

We have seen that, if $\emptyset$ and (p,q) are feasible for their respective problems, and (p,q) is a measure potential for $\emptyset$, then $\emptyset$ is optimal. Here we want to tackle the converse (and much more difficult) problem. If $\emptyset$ is optimal, is there a dual-feasible pair of functions (p,q) which is a measure potential for $\emptyset$?

Actually, as we have mentioned, our results do not produce measure potentials directly, but a related property called a topological potential. We proceed to define this.

Let the quadruple $(A, \mathfrak{J}, \Sigma, \mu)$ be, respectively, a set A, a topology $\mathfrak{J}$ over A, a sigma-field Σ over A, and a measure

μ on Σ. (We do not necessarily assume that $\mathfrak{J} \subset \Sigma$, as we have been doing up to now.) Set $E \subset A$ is a neighborhood of point $x \in A$ if there is an open set G such that $x \in G$ and $G \subset E$. x is a point of support of the measure μ if every measurable neighborhood of x has positive μ-measure. The set of all points of support is called the support of μ.

Definition. Let $\emptyset$ be feasible for the abstract transportation problem (4)-(5), and $(p,q) \geq 0$ feasible for the dual problem (15). (p,q) is a topological potential for $\emptyset$ if the following three conditions are satisfied:

If $(x,y) \in A \times B$ is a point of support of $\emptyset$, then

$$q(y) - p(x) = r(x,y). \tag{43}$$

If $x \in A$ is a point of support of $(\mu' - \emptyset')$, then

$$p(x) = 0. \tag{44}$$

If $y \in B$ is a point of support of $(\emptyset'' - \mu'')$, then

$$q(y) = 0. \tag{45}$$

In (43), (x,y) being a point of support of $\emptyset$ refers, of course, to the product space, so that the quadruple used in defining the concept would be $(A \times B, \mathfrak{J}' \times \mathfrak{J}'', \Sigma' \times \Sigma'', \emptyset)$. In (44), $\emptyset'$ is the left-marginal measure of $\emptyset$, so that $(\mu' - \emptyset')$ is the measure of unused capacity of of the sources; the corresponding quadruple is $(A, \mathfrak{J}', \Sigma', \mu' - \emptyset')$. In (45), $(\emptyset'' - \mu'')$ is the measure of the oversupply above requirements arriving at the sinks; the corresponding quadruple is $(B, \mathfrak{J}'', \Sigma'', \emptyset'' - \mu'')$.

The same definition also serves for the pair of equality-constrained programs, except that (p,q) need not be non-negative. Note also that for equality constraints, (44) and (45) are automatically fulfilled, so that they may be omitted from the definition. (This follows from the fact that, for equality constraints, $(\mu' - \emptyset')$ and $(\emptyset'' - \mu'')$ are identically zero, and therefore have no points of support; (44) and (45) are thus vacuously true.)

(43)-(45) have as much claim to generalize the "complementary slackness" conditions of duality theory as do the corresponding conditions (23)-(25) for measure potentials. Indeed, all three concepts coincide for the finite case (with all subsets open and measurable). (x,y) being a point of support of $\emptyset$ generalizes the notion in the finite case that there is a positive flow from origin x to destination y. The complementary slackness condition requires in this case that the dual relation for the pair (x,y) be fulfilled with equality, and this is exactly what (43) requires.

Again, if there is unused capacity at a source, the complementary slackness condition requires that the dual variable be zero, just as relation (44) does. Relation (45) is a generalization of the analogous condition for oversupplied sinks.

It is of interest to find conditions under which a topological potential will also be a measure potential, for this, combined with the other results of the present section, will guarantee that an optimal solution of the primal problem implies an optimal solution to the dual such that the two problems have the same value. We need the following topological concept.

Definition. A topological space has the strong Lindelöf property if, for every collection of open sets $\mathcal{G}$, there is a countable subcollection $\mathcal{G}' \subset \mathcal{G}$, such that $\cup\mathcal{G} = \cup\mathcal{G}'$.

Any subset of Euclidean N-space - indeed, any separable metrizable space - has the strong Lindelöf property, so that it includes most cases of practical interest. We now have

Theorem 13. If (p,q) is a topological potential for $\emptyset$, and the product space $(A \times B, \mathfrak{J}' \times \mathfrak{J}'')$ has the strong Lindelöf property, then (p,q) is a measure potential for $\emptyset$.

Proof: First we show that (43) implies (23). A point (x,y) such that $q(y) - p(x) < r(x,y)$ is not a point of support of $\emptyset$, according to (43); hence it has a measurable neighborhood $N_{(x,y)}$ of $\emptyset$-measure zero. There is an open set $G_{(x,y)}$ such that $(x,y) \in G_{(x,y)} \subset N_{(x,y)}$. Consider the collection, $\mathcal{G}$, of all these open sets, one for each point (x,y) for which the strict inequality holds: $q(y) - p(x) < r(x,y)$. By the strong Lindelöf property, there is a countable subcollection $\{G_1, G_2, \ldots\}$ whose union equals $\cup\mathcal{G}$. Let $\{N_1, N_2, \ldots\}$ be the neighborhoods in which these G-sets are respectively contained. We then have

$$\{(x,y) \mid q(y) - p(x) < r(x,y)\} \subset (\cup\mathcal{G}) = (G_1 \cup G_2 \cup \ldots) \subset (N_1 \cup N_2 \cup \ldots). \tag{46}$$

Hence

$$\emptyset\{(x,y) \mid q(y) - p(x) < r(x,y)\} \leq \emptyset(N_1 \cup N_2 \cup \ldots) \leq \emptyset(N_1) + \emptyset(N_2) + \ldots = 0, \tag{47}$$

and this yields (23).

For the equality constrained case the proof is completed, since (24) and (25) are automatically fulfilled. For the inequality-constrained case, we have $(p,q) \geq 0$, and we now show that (44) implies (24) and (45) implies (25).

First, it is easily verified that the component spaces $(A,\mathfrak{J}')$ and $(B,\mathfrak{J}'')$ inherit the strong Lindelöf property from the product space.

From this point, the proofs copy the above reasoning exactly. We consider the set of points x in A such that $p(x) > 0$, find a neighborhood of each one of $(\mu' - \emptyset')$-measure zero, duplicate the reasoning involving open sets, and conclude that

$$(\mu' - \emptyset')\{x|p(x) > 0\} = 0, \tag{48}$$

which is the same as (24). Similarly, starting from the points y in B such that $q(y) > 0$, we find neighborhoods of $(\emptyset'' - \mu'')$-measure zero, and conclude that

$$(\emptyset'' - \mu'')\{y|q(y) > 0\} = 0, \tag{49}$$

which is the same as (25). QED

A condition for the opposite implication to hold is easier to find and to prove:

Theorem 14. If (p,q) is a measure potential for $\emptyset$, and each of the three sets: (1) $\{(x,y)|q(y) - p(x) < r(x,y)\}$; (2) $\{x|p(x) > 0\}$; (3) $\{y|q(y) > 0\}$ is open in its respective space (1) $(A \times B,\mathfrak{J}' \times \mathfrak{J}'')$, (2) $(A,\mathfrak{J}')$, (3) $(B,\mathfrak{J}'')$), then (p,q) is a topological potential for $\emptyset$. (In the equality-constrained case, it is sufficient for the first set to be open.)

Proof: We will show that, if (43), (44), (45), respectively, is false, and the first, second, third set, respectively, is open, then (23),(24),(25), respectively, is false.

Suppose (43) is false. Then there is a point of support (x^o,y^o) of $\emptyset$ for which $q(y^o) - p(x^o) < r(x^o,y^o)$. The set $\{(x,y)|q(y) - p(x) < r(x,y)\}$, being open by assumption, is a neighborhood of (x^o,y^o); it is also measurable, hence it has positive $\emptyset$-measure, which is to say that (23) is false.

This already proves the theorem for the equality-constrained case. For the inequality-constrained case, we have $(p,q) \geq 0$. The reasoning is the same: Suppose (44) is false. Then there is a point of support x^o of $(\mu' - \emptyset')$ for which $p(x^o) > 0$. The set $\{x|p(x) > 0\}$ is measurable and open, hence

$$(\mu' - \emptyset')\{x|p(x) > 0\} > 0, \text{ contrary to (24).}$$

Similarly for (45) and (25). QED

Note that neither of these theorems makes any assumptions about the relations between the topologies and sigma-fields.

We now come to the main business of this section, which is to construct a topological potential associated with a given optimal solution to the abstract transportation problem. We shall concentrate on the equality-constrained case, which is somewhat easier to deal with, and indicate later what happens when we go to inequalities. The assumptions that have to be made to carry through the construction are quite moderate; the proofs, unfortunately, are rather long. We begin by proving a basic lemma, which is then applied to the proof of the main result.

Lemma 3. Let (A,Σ',μ'), (B,Σ'',μ'') and r be as in the transportation problem, (4)-(6), where, however, we insist that all constraints be satisfied with equality: (10), (11). Let $\emptyset$ be an optimal solution for this problem. Also assume that there are topologies $\mathfrak{J}'$ over A, $\mathfrak{J}''$ over B, such that $\mathfrak{J}' \subset \Sigma'$, $\mathfrak{J}'' \subset \Sigma''$, and r is continuous with respect to $\mathfrak{J}' \times \mathfrak{J}''$. (We need not assume that $\mathfrak{J}' \times \mathfrak{J}'' \subset \Sigma' \times \Sigma''$.)

Then, if $a_1,\ldots,a_n$ are any n points of A, $b_1,\ldots,b_n$ any n points of B (not necessarily distinct in either case), such that (a_i,b_i) is in the support of $\emptyset$ for $(i = 1,\ldots,n)$, it follows that

$$a_1b_1 + a_2b_2 + \ldots + a_nb_n \leq a_1b_2 + a_2b_3 + \ldots + a_{n-1}b_n + a_nb_1, \tag{50}$$

(where we have abbreviated r(x,y) as xy, a notation we shall use throughout this section).

Proof: Choose a positive number ϵ. There are n open sets, $L_1,\ldots,L_n$ in A, and n open sets $M_1,\ldots,M_n$ in B, with the following properties:

$a_i \in L_i$, $b_i \in M_i$ $(i = 1,\ldots,n)$,

$$xy > a_ib_i - \epsilon \text{ for all } x \in L_i,\ y \in M_i \ (i = 1,\ldots,n), \tag{51}$$

$$xy < a_ib_{i+1} + \epsilon \text{ for all } x \in L_i,\ y \in M_{i+1} \ (i = 1,\ldots,n) \tag{52}$$

(where we write M_1 for M_{n+1}, b_1 for b_{n+1}).

To see this, note that, by the continuity of r, there are open sets about a_i and b_i such that (51) is satisfied, and open sets about a_i and b_{i+1} such that (52) is satisfied. This yields two open sets about each of the points $(a_1,\ldots,a_n\ b_1,\ldots,b_n)$. The intersection of these two satisfy all conditions simultaneously.

$$\text{Let } C = \frac{1}{n} \min_i [\emptyset(L_i \times M_i)]. \tag{53}$$

C is positive, since $L_i \times M_i$ is a measurable neighborhood of (a_i, b_i), a point of support of $\emptyset$.

We now alter the flow $\emptyset$ by adding to it n measures $\emptyset_i^*$ $(i = 1,\ldots,n)$ and subtracting from it another n measures $\emptyset_i^{**}$ $(i = 1,\ldots,n)$. These are defined as follows on measurable rectangles $E \times F$ $(E \in \Sigma', F \in \Sigma'')$.

$$\emptyset_i^{**}(E \times F) = \frac{C\, \emptyset\, ((E \times F) \cap (L_i \times M_i))}{\emptyset(L_i \times M_i)}, \quad (i = 1,\ldots,n) \tag{54}$$

$$\emptyset_i^{*}(E \times F) = \frac{C\, \emptyset\, ((E \cap L_i) \times M_i)\; \emptyset\, (L_{i+1} \times (F \cap M_{i+1}))}{\emptyset(L_i \times M_i)\; \emptyset\, (L_{i+1} \times M_{i+1})} \tag{55}$$

$$(i = 1,\ldots,n).$$

(1 is to be substituted for n+1 in the formula for $\emptyset_n^*$.)

It is easy to see that (54) defines a measure; it is, in fact, proportional to $\emptyset$ in the rectangle $L_i \times M_i$, and zero outside it. (55) is zero outside the rectangle $L_i \times M_{i+1}$, and is in "product-measure" form on the rectangle. A standard extension theorem assures us that it also extends to a measure on $\Sigma' \times \Sigma''$.

We claim that the altered flow, $\emptyset + \Sigma_{i=1}^{n} (\emptyset_i^* - \emptyset_i^{**})$, remains feasible for the transportation problem with equality constraints. First we note that

$$\emptyset_i^*(E \times B) = \emptyset_i^{**}(E \times B) = \frac{C\, \emptyset\, ((E \cap L_i) \times M_i)}{\emptyset(L_i \times M_i)}, \tag{56}$$

$$(i = 1,\ldots,n)$$

so that the marginal condition (10) remains satisfied. Also

$$\emptyset_{i-1}^*(A \times F) = \emptyset_i^{**}(A \times F) = \frac{C\, \emptyset\, (L_i \times (F \cap M_i))}{\emptyset(L_i \times M_i)}, \tag{57}$$

$$(i = 1,\ldots,n)$$

(n is to be substituted for zero in $\emptyset_o^*(A \times F)$).

Adding up over all changes again leads to cancellation, so that the marginal conditions (11) remain satisfied.

It remains to show only that the altered flow is non-negative everywhere. The only negative summands appear on the rectangles $L_i \times M_i$. If the measurable set E is contained in a certain number of these rectangles, the quantity

$$C\ \emptyset(E) \sum \frac{1}{\emptyset(L_i \times M_i)} \qquad (58)$$

is subtracted. (Here the summation extends over those i for which $E \subset L_i \times M_i$.) From the definition of C, this quantity cannot exceed $\emptyset(E)$, the original flow value. Hence non-negativity is preserved. This shows that the altered flow is feasible.

Since $\emptyset$ is optimal, the change in transportation costs induced by $\Sigma_{i=1}^{n} (\emptyset_i^* - \emptyset_i^{**})$ must be non-negative. Thus

$$\sum_{i=1}^{n} \int_{A\times B} r\ d\emptyset_i^* \geq \sum_{i=1}^{n} \int_{A\times B} r\ d\emptyset_i^{**}\ . \qquad (59)$$

Now $\emptyset_i^*$ is zero outside the rectangle $L_i \times M_{i+1}$; on that rectangle, the inequality (52) applies; hence

$$\int_{A\times B} [a_i b_{i+1} + \epsilon]\ d\emptyset_i^* \geq \int_{A\times B} r\ d\emptyset_i^* \ (i = 1,\ldots,n).\ (b_{n+1} \equiv b_1) \qquad (60)$$

Similarly, $\emptyset_i^{**}$ is zero outside the rectangle $L_i \times M_i$; on that rectangle, the inequality (51) applies; hence

$$\int_{A\times B} [a_i b_i - \epsilon]\ d\emptyset_i^{**} \leq \int_{A\times B} r\ d\emptyset_i^{**} \ (i = 1,\ldots,n) \qquad (61)$$

The left-hand integrands are merely constants; also $\emptyset_i^*(A \times B) = \emptyset_i^{**}(A \times B) = C$, for all $i = 1,\ldots,n$: hence, integrating out the constants, and putting (59), (60), and (61) together, we obtain

$$\begin{aligned} &C(a_1b_2 + a_2b_3 + \ldots + a_nb_1) + n\ C\ \epsilon \geq \\ &C(a_1b_1 + a_2b_2 + \ldots + a_nb_n) - n\ C\ \epsilon . \end{aligned} \qquad (62)$$

Since C is positive, and ϵ can be taken arbitrarily small, the basic inequality (50) is obtained. QED

Lemma 3 is actually a stronger result than would be obtained if we merely assumed $\emptyset$ to be optimal for the inequality-constrained problem (4)-(6). Indeed, suppose $\emptyset$ is optimal for the problem (4)-(6). Then it is necessarily also optimal for an equality-constrained subproblem, namely, the one in which its own marginals, $\emptyset'$ and $\emptyset''$, play the roles of μ' and μ'', respectively. Therefore, inequality (50) holds for this $\emptyset$.

We now come to the main result. The premises are the same as for Lemma 3. Functions (p,q) are constructed which together constitute a topological potential for $\emptyset$. That is, they are bounded and measurable, satisfy the dual feasibility condition (15), and the topological potential condition (43). Note that these are a potential for the equality-constrained problem, and as such are not guaranteed to be non-negative. (44) and (45) are automatically satisfied by the fact that $\emptyset$ is an equality-constrained optimum. p and q are "constructed" in the sense that one can write an explicit formula for them.

First we need a few concepts relating to continuity. Let $(A,\mathfrak{J})$ be a topological space, and let f be a real-valued function with domain A. f is said to be upper semi-continuous if every set of the form $\{x|f(x) < C\}$ is open (C being a real number); it is lower semi-continuous if every set of the form $\{x|f(x) > C\}$ is open. If there is a sigma-field, Σ, over A such that $\mathfrak{J} \subset \Sigma$, it follows at once from the definitions that every upper or lower semi-continuous function is measurable with respect to Σ. Let $\mathfrak{F}$ be a bounded collection of real-valued functions, all with domain A; we define inf $\mathfrak{F}$ to be that function whose value at the point $x \in A$ is the infimum of the values assumed by the members of $\mathfrak{F}$ at that point. Sup $\mathfrak{F}$ is defined analogously for the supremum. It is not hard to show that, if $\mathfrak{F}$ is a collection of continuous functions, then inf $\mathfrak{F}$ is upper semi-continuous and sup $\mathfrak{F}$ is lower semi-continuous. Let $(A \times B, \mathfrak{J}' \times \mathfrak{J}'')$ be a product space, and let r be a real-valued function with domain $A \times B$; r is equi-continuous if, for every positive number ϵ, and every $a \in A$, there is a set $G' \in \mathfrak{J}'$ such that $a \in G'$, and $|r(x,y) - r(a,y)| < \epsilon$ for all $x \in G'$, $y \in B$, and, for every $\epsilon > 0$ and every $b \in B$, there is a set $G'' \in \mathfrak{J}''$ such that $b \in G''$, and $|r(x,y) - r(x,b)| < \epsilon$ for all $x \in A$, $y \in G''$. Let (A,d) be a metric space, and let f be a function with domain A; f is uniformly continuous if, for all positive ϵ, there is a positive δ such that $d(x_1,x_2) < \delta$ implies that $|f(x_1) - f(x_2)| < \epsilon$.

Let (A,d') and (B,d") be two metric spaces, and r a function with domain $A \times B$; r is uniformly continuous if, for all positive ϵ, there is a positive δ such that $d'(x_1,x_2) < \delta$ and $d''(y_1,y_2) < \delta$ imply that $|r(x_1,y_1) - r(x_2,y_2)| < \epsilon$ ($x_1,x_2 \in A$, and $y_1,y_2 \in B$).

Theorem 15. Let (A,Σ',μ'), (B,Σ'',μ''), and r be as in the transportation problem with equality constraints, (10), (11), and (6). Let $\emptyset$ be an optimal solution for this problem. Assume that there are topologies $\mathfrak{J}'$ over A, and $\mathfrak{J}''$ over B, such that $\mathfrak{J}' \subset \Sigma'$, $\mathfrak{J}'' \subset \Sigma''$, and r is continuous with respect to $\mathfrak{J}' \times \mathfrak{J}''$. Then there exist functions, p and q (with domains A and B, respectively) such that (p,q) is a topological potential for $\emptyset$; furthermore, p is lower and q is upper semi-continuous.

Proof: For any $a \in A$, we define p(a) as follows:
(Let x stand for points of A, y for points of B, and abbreviate r(x,y) as xy).

Consider the class of all finite sequences $(x_o, y_1, x_1, \ldots, y_n, x_n)$ beginning with $a = x_o$, having the property that (x_i, y_i) is a point of support for $\emptyset$ $(i = 1, \ldots, n)$. The value of this sequence is defined to be

$$-x_o y_1 + x_1 y_1 - x_1 y_2 + x_2 y_2 - \ldots + x_n y_n. \tag{63}$$

(n is an arbitrary integer; we also allow the "sequence" consisting of x_o alone; this is assigned the value zero.) p(a) is now defined as the supremum of the value of such permissible sequences beginning with a.

Having defined p, we now define q as follows: For any $b \in B$,

$$q(b) = \inf_{x \in A} [p(x) + xb] \tag{64}$$

We claim that the pair (p,q) is a topological potential for $\emptyset$. First we show that p is bounded. Clearly $p \geq 0$, since the sequence consisting of x_o alone is permissible, and has value zero.

Let $(x_o, y_1, x_1, \ldots, y_n, x_n)$ be a permissible sequence. According to (50) of Lemma 3,

$$0 \geq x_1 y_1 - x_1 y_2 + x_2 y_2 - \ldots + x_n y_n - x_n y_1 \tag{65}$$

Adding $x_n y_1 - x_o y_1$ to both sides of (65), we get (63) on the right, so that the value of any permissible sequence is bounded above by $x_n y_1 - x_o y_1$. Let $M = \sup |xy|$ over $x \in A$, $y \in B$; since r is bounded, M is finite. We have just shown that p is bounded. In fact

$$2M \geq p \geq 0. \tag{66}$$

It follows from this that q is bounded. In fact, from (64) and (66),

$$3M \geq q \geq -M. \tag{67}$$

Next we verify (15). In fact, $q(y) - p(x) \leq xy$ follows at once from the definition of q, (64).

Next we verify (43). Let (a,b) be a point of support for $\emptyset$. For any $x \in A$, we have

$$p(x) \geq -xb + ab + p(a). \tag{68}$$

To see this, note that the right-hand side of (68) is simply the supremum over all permissible sequences beginning (x,b,a...); hence it cannot exceed p(x), which is the supremum over a wider class of permissible sequences. Hence p(x) + xb attains its infimum at x = a. Therefore

$$q(b) = p(a) + ab, \tag{69}$$

so that (43) is verified.

It remains only to show that p and q are measurable with respect to their sigma-fields, Σ' and Σ'', respectively. We do this by proving the stronger result that p is lower and q upper semi-continuous.

Holding x fixed, and considering p(x) + xy as a function of y, with domain B, we note that it is continuous with respect to $\mathfrak{J}''$, since r is continuous with respect to $\mathfrak{J}' \times \mathfrak{J}''$.

$q = \inf \mathfrak{F}$, where $\mathfrak{F}$ is the collection of these functions for all possible values of $x \in A$; hence q is upper semi-continuous.

As for p, we first note that

$$p(x) \geq \sup_{y \in B} [q(y) - xy]. \tag{70}$$

This follows at once from the definition of q, (64). Now let x be a point for which p(x) > 0. For any positive ϵ, there must be a permissible sequence, beginning $(x,y_1,x_1,\ldots)$ whose value comes within ϵ of p(x):

$$p(x) - \epsilon < -xy_1 + x_1y_1 + p(x_1) \tag{71}$$

Therefore

$$p(x) - \epsilon < q(y_1) - xy_1, \tag{72}$$

from the fact that (x_1,y_1) is a point of support of $\emptyset$, together with (69).

From (70) and (72), and the fact that ϵ is arbitrary, we obtain

$$p(x) = \sup_{y \in B} [q(y) - xy], \tag{73}$$

whenever p(x) > 0. Therefore, we have in general

$$p(x) = \max [0, \sup_{y \in B} [q(y) - xy]]. \tag{74}$$

Holding y fixed, $q(y) - xy$, considered as a function of x with domain A, is continuous. Also the identically zero function is continuous. $p = \sup \mathfrak{F}$, where $\mathfrak{F}$ is now the collection of these functions for all possible values of $y \in B$, together with the identically zero function; hence p is lower semi-continuous. QED

Theorem 16. If, in addition to the premises of Theorem 15, r is equi-continuous, then there is a topological potential with p and q continuous (in their respective spaces $(A,\mathfrak{J}')$ and $(B,\mathfrak{J}'')$, of course).

If, in addition, d' on $A \times A$, and d'' on $B \times B$ are metrics such that r is uniformly continuous, then p and q are uniformly continuous.

Proof: We use the same construction as above, and show that it has these properties. Let r be equi-continuous. We show that q, defined by (64), is such that the set $\{y | \alpha < q(y) < \beta\}$ is open for all real numbers $\alpha < \beta$. Let q(b) lie in this set, and choose ε small enough so that

$$\alpha < q(b) - \epsilon < q(b) + \epsilon < \beta \qquad (75)$$

There is an open neighborhood G'' of b such that $|xy - xb| < \epsilon$ for all $x \in A$, $y \in G''$. It follows from (64) that $|q(y) - q(b)| \leq \epsilon$ for all $y \in G''$; hence, by (75), $G'' \subset \{y | \alpha < q(y) < \beta\}$; hence the latter set is open, so that q is continuous.

Analogous reasoning applies to the function

$$\tilde{p}(x) = \sup_{y \varepsilon B} [q(y) - xy], \qquad (76)$$

which is therefore continuous; hence $p = \max(0,\tilde{p})$ is continuous.

To prove the second part, assume that r is uniformly continuous with respect to the metric spaces (A,d') and (B,d''). For any positive ϵ, there is a δ such that $d''(y_1,y_2) < \delta$ implies $|xy_1 - xy_2| < \epsilon/2$ for all $x \in A$; hence, again from (64), $|q(y_1) - q(y_2)| < \epsilon$ whenever $d''(y_1,y_2) < \delta$, so that q is uniformly continuous.

Analogous reasoning applies to (76), so that $\tilde{p}$ is uniformly continuous. Hence $p = \max(0,\tilde{p})$ is uniformly continuous. QED

Just as for Lemma 3, the conclusions of Theorems 15 and 16 apply also if $\emptyset$ is optimal for the inequality-constrained transportation problem, since it is then also optimal an equality-constrained subproblem.

What has not been shown is that, in this case, there are function p,q which are also non-negative and satisfy (44) and (45) [10].

We conclude with a theorem that wraps up several of our previous results.

Theorem 17. Let (A,Σ',μ'), (B,Σ'',μ'') and r be as in the abstract transportation problem with equality constraints. Let $\emptyset$ be optimal for the problem. In addition, suppose that one can find topologies $\mathfrak{J}'$ over A and $\mathfrak{J}''$ over B, such that (1) $\mathfrak{J}' \subset \Sigma'$ and $\mathfrak{J}'' \subset \Sigma''$; (2) $\mathfrak{J}' \times \mathfrak{J}''$ has the strong Lindelöf property; (3) r is continuous with respect to $\mathfrak{J}' \times \mathfrak{J}''$.

Then there exist function (p,q) with domains A,B, which are feasible and optimal for the dual problem, and for which the value of the dual equals the value of the primal.

Proof: (p,q) constructed in Theorem 15 is a topological potential for $\emptyset$. Hence, by the strong Lindelöf property and Theorem 13, it is a measure potential. Hence, by Theorem 6, the value of the dual equals the value of the primal, so that (p,q) is dual optimal. QED

One final comment. The fact that $\emptyset$ is optimal enters into the proof of Theorem 15 in a tenuous fashion. It is used only to prove Lemma 3, and Lemma 3 is used only to prove that p is bounded. Hence, if $\emptyset$ is any feasible flow, not known to be optimal, and we carry out the construction of Theorem 15, and it turns out to be bounded, then (p,q) is a topological potential for $\emptyset$. If, in addition, the strong Lindelöf property holds for $\mathfrak{J}' \times \mathfrak{J}''$, then the reasoning in the proof of Theorem 17 assures us that $\emptyset$ is, in fact, optimal. Thus, in these circumstances, boundedness of (p,q) constructed in Theorem 15 is both necessary and sufficient for optimality of $\emptyset$.

FOOTNOTES

* Presented at Kansas-Missouri Conference on Theoretical and Applied Economics, Ames, Iowa, May 24, 1969. Much of this material will also appear in a forthcoming book, Foundations of Spatial Economics (Baltimore: Johns Hopkins Press).

1. This paper is self-contained so far as definitions go, but standard theorems are quoted without proof.

2. The Σ in this sentence stands for summation, not for a class of sets. The distinction will be clear from the context.

3. For further reading in measure theory, the reader is referred to P.R. Halmos, Measure Theory (Princeton: Van Nostrand, 1950).

4. "A continuous model of transportation", Econometrica, 20: 643-660, October, 1952; "the partial equilibrium of a continuous space market", Weltwirtschaftliches Archiv, 71: 73-87, 1953.

5. A. Orden, "The transshipment problem", Management Science, 2: 276-285, April, 1956.

6. "On the translocation of masses", Management Science, 5: 1-4, October, 1958 (originally published in Doklady Nauk USSR, 37, #7-8, 199-201, 1942).

7. Space contains 3 points $\{x,y,z\}$; the capacity at point x equals one; the requirement at point z equals one; all other capacities and requirements equal zero; $r(x,y) = 1$, $r(y,z) = 1$, $r(x,z) = 3$; all other r's arbitrary; the only feasible, hence optimal, flow is one unit from x to z; there is no Kantorovich potential for this flow, since it must satisfy the incompatible relations: $U_z - U_x = 3$; $U_z - U_y \leq 1$; $U_y - U_x \leq 1$.

8. P. Billingsley, Convergence of Probability Measures (N.Y., Wiley, 1968), Chapter I, is a very clear exposition of the theory for the special case of probabilities. K.R. Parthasarathy, Probability Measures on Metric Spaces (N.Y.: Academic Press, 1967), is also useful.

9. Also an unlimited number of further constraints of the form $\emptyset(G_i) \leq \alpha_i$ or $\emptyset(F_i) \geq \beta_i$ may be imposed, where G_i and F_i are open and closed sets, respectively, in $A \times B$. The proof that feasibility implies optimality is exactly as in Theorem 12: just put the subscript i in lines (41) and (42).

10. Incomplete investigations make it likely that the construction in Theorem 15 (or a slight modification of it, perhaps) will in fact have these properties as well, in the inequality-constrained case. At the present moment, however, this is conjectural.

REFERENCES

M. Beckmann, "A continuous model of transportation", Econometrica, 20: 643-660, October, 1952.

M. Beckmann, "The partial equilibrium of a continuous space market", Welwirtschaftliches Archiv, 71: 73-87, 1953.

P. Billingsley, Convergence of Probability Measures, (New York: Wiley, 1968).

A. Faden, Foundations of Spatial Economics, (Baltimore: Johns Hopkins Press, forthcoming).

P.R. Halmos, Measure Theory, (Princeton: Van Nostrand, 1950).

L.V. Kantorovich, "On the translocation of masses", Management Science, 5: 1-4, October, 1958 (originally published in Doklady Nauk USSR, 37: #7-8, 199-201, 1942).

A. Orden, "The transshipment problem", Management Science, 2: 276-285, April, 1956.

K.R.Parthasarathy, Probability Measures on Metric Spaces, (New York: Academic Press, 1967).

INTERNATIONAL TRADE AND DEVELOPMENT IN A SMALL COUNTRY, II*

by

Trout Rader
Washington University

1. Introduction

This paper is a sequel to [10]. Its purpose is to determine the loss of real income due to tariffs, taxes, and monopoly. To do this, one must consider competitive production and consumer behavior. For the costs and benefits of tariffs in a competitive economy the latest analysis which I have found is Johnson [6]. He also includes several references to empirical work. I do not see how to reconcile his measure of tariff loss with that which follows. Both his point of departure and his end results seem different.

In [10], there was an arbitrariness of the consumer regime. The conclusions of section 6 would have been modified if the state were restricted to tax-subsidy tariff schemes and competitive consumer choice were required. To be specific, one could no longer appeal to remark 6 whereby "a tax tariff policy leads to a potential loss if and only if government revenues are insufficient to purchase at the international price system the goods purchased by consumers before the policy." The state could place consumers at their old position, but if the home price of a good was higher that the international price relative to other goods, consumers would try to substitute it for other goods. They would replace foreign sellers, reduce government revenues from tariffs, and thereby, undermine the basis of the original subsidy.

The appropriate modification is evident from [10]. Let $P_i(x^i)$ be the set of consumptions better than x^i for consumer i. $\sum_i P_i(x^i)$ is <u>directional dense</u> if there is a unique hyperplane bounding at $\sum x^i$.

<u>Theorem 1</u>. Let preferences be locally unsaturated[2] and let $\sum_i P_i(x^i)$ be directional dense at a Pareto optimal consumption, $\sum x^i$. A tax subsidy-tariff policy leads to no potential loss if and only if

(i) government revenues are sufficient to purchase at the international price system the goods purchased by consumers before the policy, and

(ii) the home consumer price system is a positive multiple of the international price system.

Proof:

By (i) and the proof of remark 6 of [10], the government can subsidize consumers so that they are able to purchase their old consumptions in the pre-tax-subsidy-tariff situation. By (ii), they will be willing to make the purchase, whence sufficiency. If (ii) fails, then the international value of demand is reduced and by a familiar argument, (theorem 5 in [9]) one cannot do as well for everyone.

For the price system, $\bar{p}$, the hyperplane, $H(\bar{p}) = \{\hat{x} \mid \bar{p}\hat{x} \geq \bar{p}\Sigma x^i\}$, bounds $\underset{i}{\Sigma} P_i(x^i)$. It can be shown that for any price system, p, not proportional to $\bar{p}$, the consumers can improve their position by moving somewhere else in H(p). Such a movement is compatible with the budget constraint (but not with available supplies). Therefore, they cannot be restored to their old position. If the former state were cheaper than the new one, consumers must be worse off (local unsaturation). There can be no better or equal position between which consumers are indifferent and which can attain their former state. Again, such a position cannot be compatible with competitive consumer choice under the new price system, whence necessity. Q.E.D.

Corollary. Taxes on sales of goods lead to no potential loss if and only if they bear the same proportion to price for all goods.[3]

Proof:

In terms of the international price system, sales taxes do not reduce the possible income to the state and industry. Hence, the question of no potential loss turns upon whether or not the new price system is proportional to the world system. The new price system must equal the old one plus the tax since there is the option of sales or purchases in the international market. Hence, (ii) of theorem 1 is verified if and only if between different industries the tax is equalized as a proportion of price. Q.E.D.

Since all the tax-tariff theorems in [10] are proved by using a sales tax giving the same consumer prices as the compared tax-tariff-subsidy scheme, (ii) is automatically fulfilled. Hence, the theorems are valid except that theorem 18 can be strengthened to assert that without a compensating tax-subsidy scheme for consumers, a tariff on an imported good cannot lead to a no-loss situation -- whether or not the new output is more valuable than the old one.

A loss of income which nevertheless restored prices to the international level might lead to an improved level of consumption. An example would be an increase in tariff with a non-proportional sales tax. There would be a loss in state and industry income (theorems 18 of [10]) but it could be that the international price system would be restored and consumer welfare improved. The effect of a tax from an inefficient situation is resolved only in the case of taxes on incomes from fixed factors since theorem 16 of [10] still holds true. Factor incomes can be altered without changing prices. For more information, one must consider the losses and gains to consumers.

2. Loss of Producer Real Income

The loss in producer income from a tariff is the reduction in GNP, $\Sigma \bar{p}_i y_i$, where y_i is the net output of the ith industry and $\bar{p}$ is the international price system. The total loss includes the additional decrease of consumers real income due to price changes alone. The latter effect will be considered in section 3.

The notation more or less follows that of [10]:

ξ_i = the output of the ith industry of the ith good, net in the industry but gross in the economy.[4]

x^i = the input of factors j in industry i per unit gross output of i.

$X = (x^i_j)$.

y^i_j = the output of goods j by industry i per unit of output of i ($y^i_i = 1$, $y^i_j \leq 0$, for $j \neq i$).

$Y = (y^i_j)$.

x_j = quantity of factor j.

w_j = wage of factor j.

d_i = demand for the ith good by consumers.

Hereafter, derivatives are taken of y, X(w) and w; also it is sometimes interesting to differentiate ξ. If X(w) is continuously differentiable for all w and if $X(w)^{-1}$ exists,

$$\xi = X(w)^{-1}x$$

is continuously differentiable as is $y = Y\xi$. I do not know the meaning of X(w) differentiable. Fix $w_2 = 1$ and consider any $w_1(x_1)$ continuous and monotonic decreasing but differentiable everywhere except for a finite set of points. Then

$$\frac{dx_2}{dx_1} = -w_1(x_1)$$

can be solved to give a differentiable isoquant, $x_2 = g(x_1)$, with slope decreasing in absolute value. Evidently this can be extended to the whole of factor space by defining $f(x_1 x_2) = kf(x_1/k,\ x_2/k)$ for k such that $x_2/k = g(x_1/k)$ f satisfies constant returns to scale and a strict concavity assumption and is continuously differentiable, but x(w) is not everywhere differentiable.

One case where x(w) is differentiable is that where the production function is twice continuously differentiable, there is Wicksells' law $\partial^2\xi/\partial x_i \partial x_j > 0$, $i \neq j$, and for some k there is the strong condition, $\partial^2\xi/\partial x_k \partial x_j > 0$ for all $j \neq k$. Renumber the factors so that $\partial^2\xi/\partial x_o \partial x_j > 0$, $j > 0$, and let factors be given by $(\hat{x}_o, \hat{x})$, where $\hat{x}_o$ is fixed and $\hat{x}$ represents the factor employment whenever $\hat{x}_o$ of 0th factor is used. It is known that

$$\frac{\partial(\hat{x}_o,\ \hat{x})}{\partial w} = \left.\frac{\partial(x_o,\ x)}{\partial w}\right|_{x_o}$$

exists and is continuous (Rader [8]). Also, under constant returns,

$$(x_o,\ x)\ (w) = \frac{\xi}{\xi(\hat{x}_o,\ \hat{x})}\ (x_o,\ \hat{x})$$

is the product of two continuously differentiable functions of w since ξ is continuously differentiable in $(\hat{x}_o,\ \hat{x})$.

Suppose that X(w) is continuously differentiable, then it is known that for $p = wX(w)Y^{-1}$, det $\partial p/\partial w \neq 0$ for almost all p (Cronin [12, p. 35]). Since $\frac{\partial X(w)}{\partial w_i} = 0$ by cost minimization

$$\frac{\partial p}{\partial w} = X(w)Y^{-1}$$

whereupon det X(w) det $Y^{-1} \neq 0$ for almost all p or det $X(w) \neq 0$ and X^{-1} exists for almost all p. Nothing more will be said of these matters except to list the assumption of differentiability.

<u>Theorem 2</u>. If there is a Leontief technology with X continuously differentiable in w, then a new tariff leads to a loss in income from production equal to the sum over industries of the area bounded by the two quantities of net output, below the average cost curves and above the old price.

In Figure 1, the loss of a tariff in a single industry is illustrated as the shaded area, which is Marshall's [7] producer surplus. The fact that the average cost curve is rising is a consequence of price equals average cost and that output rises continuously as p_i above increases (theorems 5 and 9 of [10], which is Mrs. Robinson's [11] rising supply price. (It is assumed that there is but one profit maximizing vector of outputs given factor endowments).

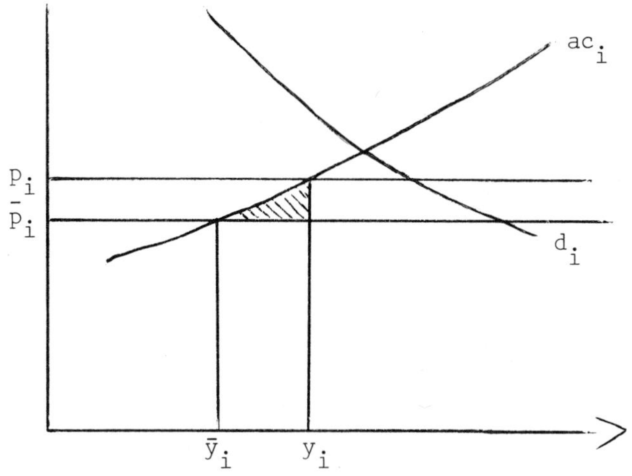

(Figure 1)

Corollary. A tariff on an intermediate product will increase the output of that good and possibly lead to a decrease in its use by other industries. Hence, its (negative) net output will decrease and the loss will be measured as above.

Proof:

Let $\bar{p}$ be the initial price system, reflecting whatever tariffs, taxes or subsidies may be in existence. Let the (ultimate) tariff be δ and gradually impose a tariff, $\varepsilon\delta$, $0 \leq \varepsilon \leq 1$. Then

$$(\bar{p} + \delta\varepsilon)Y = wX$$

is the zero profit condition for industries to operate. Differentiating with respect to ε,

$$\frac{dw}{d\varepsilon} X = \delta Y$$

(since $w\, dX/d\varepsilon = 0$ by cost minimization). Post multiplying by the industry gross outputs,

$$\frac{dwx}{d\varepsilon} = \frac{dw}{d\varepsilon} X\xi$$

$$= \delta Y\xi = \delta y. \qquad (1)$$

Total income is wx + tariff revenues = wx + $\delta\varepsilon(d-y)$ = pd. Also

$$\bar{p}d = pd - (p-\bar{p})d = pd - \delta\varepsilon d,$$

or

$$\bar{p}d = wx - \delta\varepsilon y \qquad (2)$$

Hence,

$$\frac{d\bar{p}y}{d\varepsilon} = \frac{dwx}{d\varepsilon} - \delta\varepsilon \frac{dy}{d\varepsilon} - \delta y$$

$$= - \delta\varepsilon \frac{dy}{d\varepsilon}$$

$$\Delta\bar{p}y = {}_o\int^1 \frac{d\bar{p}y}{d\varepsilon}\, d\varepsilon = - {}_o\int^1 \delta \frac{dy}{d\varepsilon}\, d\varepsilon, \text{ or}$$

$$\Delta\bar{p}y = - \Sigma\, {}_o\int^1 \delta\ \varepsilon \frac{dy_i}{d\varepsilon}\, d\varepsilon$$

$$= - \Sigma \int_{\bar{y}_i}^{y_i} \delta\ \varepsilon\ dy_i$$

$$= - \Sigma \int_{\bar{y}_i}^{y_i} (ac_i - \bar{p}_i)dy_i \qquad (3)$$

where $ac_i = - \sum_{j\neq i} y^i_j p_j + \Sigma_k x^i_k w_k$.

If the set of industries which are profitable changes, equation (1) changes. However, a collection of industries operate on a closed set of prices. Hence, the total change can be regarded as put together from the several possible combinations of industries.

To consider a function such as f = $\Delta\bar{p}y$ which is constructed piecewise from other functions, let $X_i = \{x |\ f_i(x) = f(x)\}$. A function is the integral of its almost everywhere derivative if and only if it is absolutely continuous. The theorem follows immediately from the following.

LEMMA. If the f_i are absolutely continuous and the X_i are closed, then f is absolutely continuous and

$$f(x) = f(y) + \sum_{i=1}^{n} \int_{X_i \cap (x,y) \sim \bigcup_{j<i} X_j} f_i'\, dx.$$

Proof:

Let (α_i, β_i) be disjoint intervals. Let $\alpha_i \in X_j$ and let x_j be the largest element in $X_j \cap [\alpha_i, \beta_i]$. Clearly, x_j belongs to X_k, $k \neq j$. Continuing, one obtains a chain of points for which each contiguous pair is contained in a common X_j. By appropriate numbering and rearrangement, $f(\alpha_i) - f(\beta_i) = \sum_j f(\sigma_{i,j}) - f(\delta_{i,j})$

$$= \sum_j f_j(\sigma_{i,j}) - f_j(\delta_{i,j}),\ \sigma_{i,j}, \delta_{i,j} \in (\alpha_i, \beta_i) \cap X_j$$

$$\text{or } \sum_i |f(\alpha_i) - f(\beta_i)|$$

$$\leq \sum_i \sum_j |f_j(\sigma_{i,j}) - f_j(\delta_{i,j})|$$

$$= \sum_j \left(\sum_i |f_j(\sigma_{i,j}) - f_j(\delta_{i,j})|\right)$$

If $\sum |\alpha_i - \beta_i| \to 0$,

then $\sum_i |\sigma_{i,j} - \delta_{i,j}| \to 0$ and

$\sum_i |f_j(\sigma_{i,j}) - f_j(\delta_{i,j})| \to 0$ (absolute continuity of f_j). Therefore,

$$\sum_j |f(\alpha_i) - f(\beta_i)| \to 0$$

and f is absolutely continuous. Hence, it is the integral of its almost everywhere derivative which must be f_i' for almost all x in X_i. Q.E.D.

Incidentally, if X^{-1} exists

$$\frac{d\xi}{d\varepsilon} = \Sigma \frac{\partial X^{-1}}{\partial w_i} x \frac{dw_i}{d\varepsilon} = -\Sigma X^{-1} \frac{\partial X}{\partial w_i} X^{-1} x \frac{dw_i}{d\varepsilon}, \tag{4}$$

$$\frac{dy}{d\varepsilon} = Y \frac{d\xi}{d\varepsilon} = -\Sigma X^{-1} \frac{\partial X}{\partial w_i} \xi \frac{dw_i}{d\varepsilon}$$

$$= -Y \Sigma X^{-1} \frac{\partial X}{\partial w_i} \xi \frac{dw_i}{d\varepsilon}, \tag{5}$$

and

$$\frac{dw}{d\varepsilon} = \delta YX^{-1},$$

which are terms not easy to evaluate.

Theorem 3. If there is a Leontief technology with X(w) continuously differentiable, then the establishment of monopolies or oligopolies leads to a loss of income in terms of the former prices equal to the sum over industries of the area between the demand and average costs curves bounded by the new and old gross outputs minus the area below the demand curve, above the old price and between the old and new outputs. If the goods monopolized are final products only, the loss is equal to the summed areas above the average cost curve, below the old price, and between the old and new outputs.

In Figure 2, there is an example of the loss from a monopoly in an industry producing for final consumption only. First, there is a tariff sufficient to drive foreign competition out. Then the monopoly takes effect. The total shaded areas is the sum of the monopoly loss and tariff loss. Although the same average cost is drawn for the two events, one should be cautioned that this is necessary only if there are no differences in the rest of the economy.

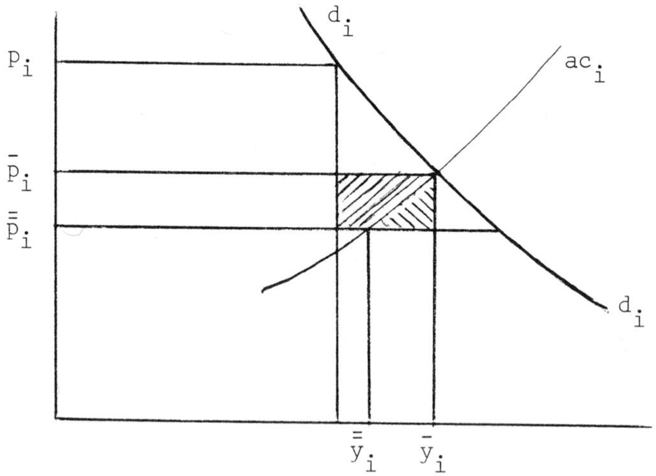

(Figure 2)

Proof:

For a monopoly or oligopoly, let final profits be δ per unit of gross output. Consider per unit profits of $\varepsilon\delta$, $0 \leq \varepsilon \leq 1$. Then the division of income is according to the law:

$$pY = wX + \delta\varepsilon$$

which gives

$$\frac{dp}{d\varepsilon} Y - \delta = \frac{dw}{d\varepsilon} X$$

(since $w\frac{dX}{d\varepsilon} = 0$ by cost minimization). Also

$$\frac{dwx}{d\varepsilon} = \frac{dw}{d\varepsilon} X\delta = \frac{dp}{d\varepsilon} Y\xi - \delta\xi$$

$$= \frac{dp}{d\varepsilon} y - \delta\xi.$$

Total income is

$$py = wx + \delta\varepsilon\xi$$

and

$$\bar{p}y = py - (p-\bar{p})y$$

$$= wx + \delta\varepsilon\xi - (p-\bar{p})y.$$

Therefore

$$\frac{d\bar{p}y}{d\varepsilon} = \frac{dp}{d\varepsilon} y - \delta\xi + \frac{d}{d\varepsilon}\delta\varepsilon\xi$$

$$- \frac{d(p-\bar{p})}{d\varepsilon} y - (p-\bar{p}) \frac{dy}{d\varepsilon}$$

$$= \delta\varepsilon \frac{d\xi}{d\varepsilon} - (p-\bar{p}) \frac{dy}{d\varepsilon},$$

or

$$\Delta py = \sum_i \int_{\bar{\xi}_i}^{\xi_i} \delta_i \, \varepsilon \, d\xi_i - \sum_i \int_{\bar{y}_i}^{y_i} (p_i - \bar{p}_i) dy_i. \quad (6)$$

If $\xi_i = y_i$, for all i,

$$\Delta\bar{p}y = \sum_i \int_{\bar{y}_i}^{y_i} (\bar{p}_i - ac_i) dy_i. \qquad \text{Q.E.D.}$$

Theorems 2 and 3 give the rules for computing the loss of real income in the case where the relative consumer prices are adjusted to the relative world prices by sales tax-subsidy schemes. In cases where consumer prices differ from world prices, a more complicated formulation is appropriate.

Changes in costs change monopoly profit per unit gross output unless the elasticity of demand is constant. Hence, tariffs which increase a monopolist's profits have an additional influence on monopoly not accounted in theorem 2. However, the tariff is easily reconciled with the case in theorem 3. Since tariffs have no effect on monopolized goods, the set of monopolized goods and goods with tariffs are disjoint. It is easy to construct the proof for the case whereby one uses the measure in theorem 2 for the tariff industries and the measure in theorem 3 for the monopolies.

3. Consumer Real Income

The measurement of changes in consumer real income is illustrated in Figure 3. In moving from d to $\bar{d}$, real income in world prices, $\bar{p}$, changes from the level of e to that of $\bar{e}$.

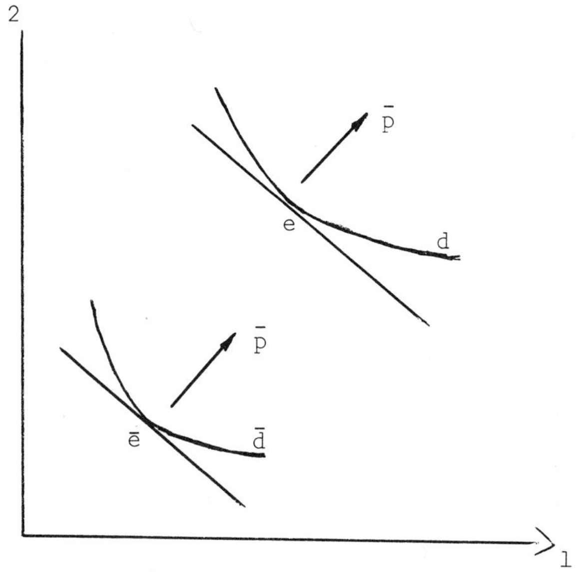

(Figure 3)

There are great difficulties in finding the change in real income whenever relative prices change. In Figure 4, there is illustrated a consumer facing a change in relative prices with fixed real income in world prices. Even if it is assumed that the preferences are fully known in the locale of experience with regard to both domestic and world prices, there is ambiguity in consumer real income -- the dotted lines are acceptable indifference curves and they yield a much greater loss in income than the indifference curves illustrated. Possibly $\bar{e}^1$ or $\bar{e}^2$ are equivalent of $\bar{d}$ or possibly some other point is. The same ambiguity is illustrated in Figure 4b with a change in prices and nominal income fixed.

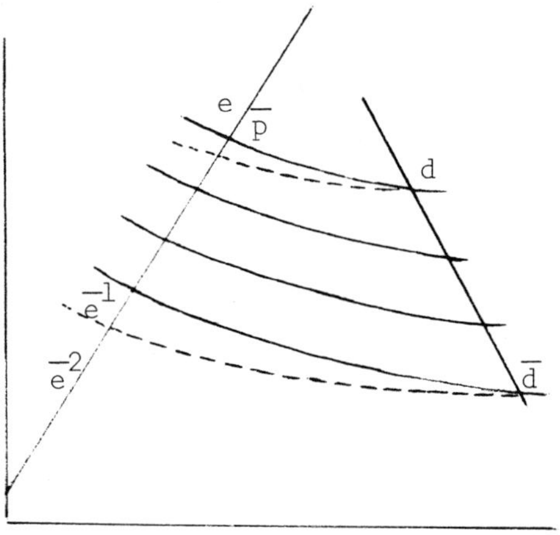

(Figure 4a)

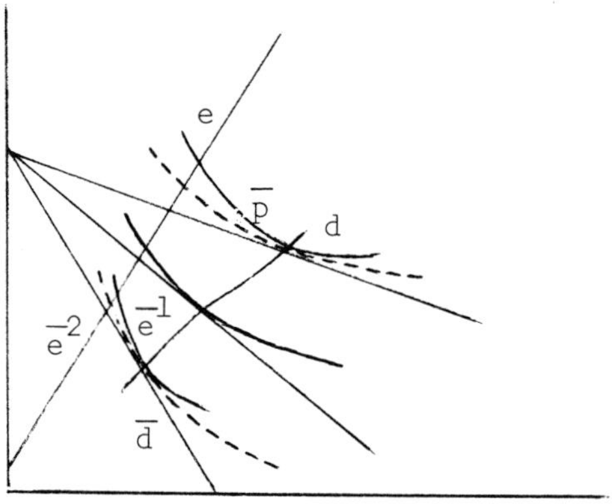

(Figure 4b)

Evidently, any holes of ignorance between the locus of demands with world prices and the locus of demands with home prices leads to great ambiguity about changes in consumer real income. Only "global" knowledge of consumers preference field can provide the correct answer. For example, Marshallian consumer surplus is a measure dependent upon the behavior of the consumer at home prices. Evidently, it may greatly overestimate the loss in real income or it may greatly underestimate that loss. Only the case of homothetic preferences is "nice" because knowing one indifference curve, one can generate all the rest.[6]

Remark 1. If home prices ratios remain fixed and if the consumer is homothetic, losses in real producer income, home prices fixed, lead to equi-proportional relative losses in real consumer income. Hence, if real producer income falls by 10%, so does real consumer income. Note that in such a state of affairs, once the change in relative prices has taken place, any further losses in real producer income lead to smaller losses in real consumer income. Income in world prices is less valuable both in gain and loss whenever home prices ratios are different from the international ones.

In the general case, only for small changes in prices can the loss in real consumer income be derived from "observed" consumer behavior. Hicks [4, ch. XVIII] has set forth a diagrammatic presentation. Here there is a mathematical one to cover cases of fixing income in both world prices and home prices. The former corresponds to the situation where the consumer is compensated for the real producer income losses and the latter where he is not. Subsequently, there appears a global theory for the homothetic case.

Define

$$(\bar{d}_o, \bar{d}) = (g^o, g)(p_o, \bar{p}_o, d_o, d)$$

to be the consumption giving the same preference level as (d_o, d) but a choice at the price system $(p_o, \bar{p})$. Throughout the analysis, p_o will be fixed. The matricies of partial derivatives of $(g^o, {}^og)$ are

$$\frac{\partial g^o}{\partial \bar{p}} = g_2^o ,$$

$$\frac{\partial g}{\partial \bar{p}} = g_2 ,$$

$$\frac{\partial g^o}{\partial d_o} = g_3^o ,$$

$$\frac{\partial g}{\partial d_o} = g_3 ,$$

$$\frac{\partial g^o}{\partial d} = g_4^o , \text{ and}$$

$$\frac{\partial g}{\partial d} = g_4 .$$

Consumer real income is defined as

$$r(d_o, d) = (p_o, \bar{p})\,(g^o, g)\,(p_o, \bar{p}_o, d_o, d))$$

$$= \sum_i \bar{p}_i\, g^i(p_o, \bar{p}_o, d_o, d).$$

Evidently, g_2^o and g_2 are the Marshall-Slutsky substitution effects. Also let

$$(p_o, p) = p_o(1, \frac{p}{p_o}),$$

$$= p_o(1, m(d_o, d))$$

where $m(d_o, d)$ is the vector of marginal rates of substitution of other goods to good zero.

Let $\partial m/\partial d_o = m_{d_o}$ and $\partial m/\partial d = m_d$

The homothetic case is of special interest.

Remark 2. If preferences are homothetic, and $p = p_o m(d)$,

$$\frac{\Sigma p_i g^i(p_o,p,e_o,e)}{\Sigma p_i d_i} = \frac{\Sigma \bar{p}_i g^i(p_o,\bar{p},e_o,e)}{\Sigma \bar{p}_i g^i(p_o,\bar{p},d_o,d)}$$

Hence, if

$$\Sigma p_i d_i = \theta,$$

$$r(y) = \frac{r(x)}{\theta}\, \Sigma p_i g^i(p_o,p,e_o,e).$$

Proof:

By homotheticity,

$$(g_o,g)\,(p_o,p,e_o,e) = k(d_o,d).$$

Therefore

$$(g_o,g)(p_o,\bar{p},e_o,e) = k(g_o,g)(p_o,\bar{p},d_o,d).$$

Premultiplying by (p_o,p) and $(p_o,\bar{p})$ respectively gives the remark. Q.E.D.

According to remark 2, changes in r can be analyzed by knowledge of the locale of d. Evaluating $\frac{dr}{d\varepsilon}$ at e = d,

$$\frac{dr}{d\varepsilon} = \frac{r(x)}{\theta}\, \Sigma p_i \frac{d}{d\varepsilon} g^i(p_o,p,e_o,e).$$

First, there is a mathematical relationship.

LEMMA 1.

$$\frac{\partial(g^o,g)}{\partial(d^o,d)} \equiv \begin{bmatrix} g_3^o & g_4^o \\ g_3 & g_4 \end{bmatrix} = I - p_o \begin{bmatrix} g_2^o \\ g_2 \end{bmatrix} \Bigg| \begin{matrix} (m_{d_o}, m_d) \\ p = m(d) \end{matrix}$$

at $g^i(p^o, p, d^o, d) = d^i$.

Proof:

In the special case $(\bar{d}_o, \bar{d}) = (d_o, d)$,

$$(d_o, d) = (g^o, g)\,(p_o, p_o m(d_o, d), d_o, d)$$

which gives

$$I = p_o \begin{bmatrix} g_2^o \\ g_2 \end{bmatrix} (m_{d_o}, m_d) + \frac{\partial(g^o, g)}{\partial(d^o, d)}.$$

Q.E.D.

Let $\bar{\theta} = (p_o, \bar{p})(d_o, d) = \Sigma \bar{p}_i d_i$ be income in world prices.

In measuring the change in a consumers real income, it is convenient to think of two steps. First, there is the change in the consumers' income in world prices, $\Delta(p_o, \bar{p})(d^o, d)$, and second, there is the change in the worth of income in consumers terms:

$$\frac{dr}{d\varepsilon} = \frac{\partial r}{\partial \bar{\theta}}\bigg|_p \frac{d\theta}{d\varepsilon} + \frac{\partial r}{\partial p}\bigg|_\theta \frac{dp}{d\varepsilon} \tag{10}$$

LEMMA 2.

At $g^i(d_o, d, p_o, p) = d_i$

$$\frac{\partial r}{\partial \bar{\theta}}\bigg|_p \quad 1 - \frac{(p_o, \bar{p})}{\bar{\theta}} \begin{bmatrix} g_2^o \\ g_2 \end{bmatrix} \frac{dp}{dk}$$

where $(d_o, d) = k(d_o, d)$. For homothetic preferences where dp/dk,

$$\frac{\partial r}{\partial \bar{\theta}}\bigg|_p = 1$$

and in general $\bar{p} \neq m(d_o, d)$ for

$$\left.\frac{\partial r}{\partial \bar{\theta}}\right|_p = \frac{r}{\bar{\theta}} .$$

Proof:

$$\left.\frac{\partial r}{\partial \bar{\theta}}\right|_p = \frac{d}{dk} \{\Sigma \bar{p}_i g^i(p_o, \bar{p}, kd_o, kd)\} \frac{dk}{d\theta}$$

$$\bar{\theta} = \Sigma \bar{p}_i d_i = k\Sigma \bar{p}_i d_i .$$

Evidently,

$$\frac{dk}{d\bar{\theta}} = \frac{1}{\Sigma \bar{p}_i d_i}$$

and evaluating at $k = 1$,

$$\left.\frac{\partial r}{\partial \bar{\theta}}\right|_p = \frac{\Sigma(\bar{p}_i)}{\Sigma \bar{p}_i d_i} \frac{\partial g^i}{\partial(d_o, d)} \frac{d(kd_o, kd)}{dk}$$

$$= \frac{1}{\bar{\theta}} (p_o, \bar{p}) \left(I - p_o \begin{bmatrix} g_2^o \\ g_2 \end{bmatrix} (m_{d_o}, m_d) \begin{bmatrix} d_o \\ d \end{bmatrix}\right.$$

$$= 1 - \frac{(p_o, \bar{p})}{\bar{\theta}} \begin{bmatrix} g_2^o \\ g_2 \end{bmatrix} \frac{dp}{dk} .$$

Apply Euler's theorem to obtain

$$\frac{\partial(g^o, g)}{\partial(d_o, d)} (d_o, d) = (g_o, g)(p_o, p, d_o, d);$$

then apply remark 2. Q.E.D.

Consider a change in p which changes x. The exact nature of the x as a function of p is left unspecified. Let $\bar{\theta} = \Sigma p_i d_i$.

LEMMA 3.

At $g^i(d_o, d, p_o, p) = x_i$,

$$\frac{\partial r}{\partial p} = (p_o, p) \begin{bmatrix} \frac{\partial d}{\partial p} - g_2^o \\ \frac{\partial d}{\partial p} - g_2 \end{bmatrix}$$

Proof:

$$\frac{\partial (g^o, g)}{\partial p} = \begin{bmatrix} g_3^o & g_4^o \\ g_3 & g_4 \end{bmatrix}_{p = m(d)} (m_{d_o}, m_d) \begin{bmatrix} \frac{\partial d_o}{\partial p} \\ \frac{\partial d}{\partial p} \end{bmatrix}$$

$$= \begin{bmatrix} \frac{\partial d^o}{\partial p} - g_2^o p_o m(d_o, d) \frac{\partial (d_o, d)}{\partial p} \\ \frac{\partial d}{\partial p} - g_2 p_o m(d_o, d) \frac{\partial (d_o, d)}{\partial p} \end{bmatrix}$$

$$= \begin{bmatrix} \frac{\partial d_o}{\partial p} - g_2^o \frac{\partial p}{\partial p} \\ \frac{\partial d}{\partial p} - g_2 \frac{\partial p}{\partial p} \end{bmatrix} = \begin{bmatrix} \frac{\partial d^o}{\partial p} - g_2^o \\ \frac{\partial d}{\partial p} - g_2 \end{bmatrix}$$

$$\frac{\partial r}{\partial p} = (p_o, p) \begin{bmatrix} \frac{\partial d^o}{\partial p} - g_2^o \\ \frac{\partial d}{\partial p} - g_2 \end{bmatrix}$$

Q.E.D.

<u>Theorem 4</u>. For the case $\theta = \Sigma p_i d_i$ fixed and $g^i(d_o, d, p_o, p) = d_i$,

$$\frac{\partial r}{\partial p} = -d.$$

If the consumer is homothetic, for $p_o m(x) \neq \bar{p}$.

$$\frac{\partial r}{\partial p} = -(\frac{r}{\theta})\ d.$$

The theorem is illustrated in Figure 5. The loss is simply the consumers surplus. To repeat in the general case the measure is meaningful only near the world price system.

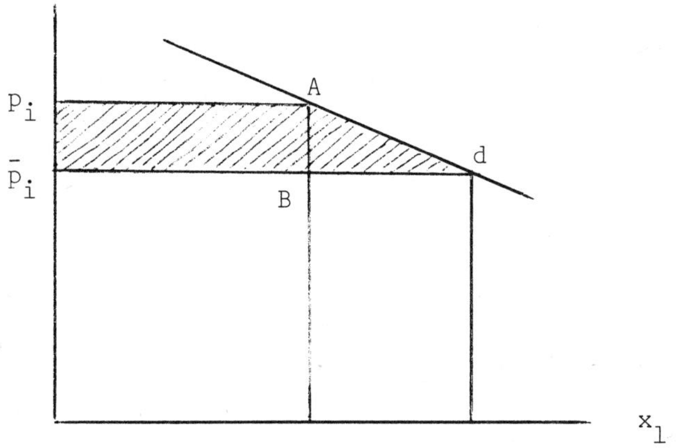

(Figure 5)

Proof:

In the case of $\Sigma p_i d_i$ constant, the Slutsky equation applied to lemma 3 gives

$$\frac{\partial r}{\partial p} = (p_o, p)\,\frac{\partial (g^o, g)}{\partial p} = \begin{bmatrix} -\dfrac{\partial d_o}{\partial \theta}\, g' \\ -\dfrac{\partial d}{\partial \theta}\, g' \end{bmatrix}$$

$$= -(\sum_j \bar{p}_j \frac{\partial d_j}{\partial \theta})\, d_i .$$

Since

$$\Sigma p_j d_j = \theta$$

$$\Sigma \bar{p}_j \frac{\partial d_j}{\partial \theta} = \Sigma p_j \frac{\partial d_j}{\partial \theta} = 1$$

or

$$\frac{\partial r}{\partial p_i} = -d_i . \qquad \text{Q.E.D.}$$

Theorem 5. If $\Sigma \bar{p}_i d_i$ is fixed and $g^i(p_o, p, d_o, d) = d_i$, then

$$\frac{\partial r}{\partial p} = 0.$$

For homothetic preferences, $\Sigma\bar{p}_i d_i$ fixed, the loss in real consumer income is the sum of the area between the demand curve and the old prices and between the quantities before and after the change in prices, weighted by r/θ in integration.

Theorem 5 covers the case of a tax where the revenues are returned as fixed subsidy. The traditional approach (Marshall [7, pp. 467-470]) identifies the triangle ABC in Figure 5 as the loss. This overstates the loss and theorems 4 and 5 give rules more in keeping with the graphical, generalized consumer surplus theory of Hicks [4, Ch. XVIII]. Such a theory depends crucially on the homotheticity of preferences.

Proof:

Let $\theta = \Sigma\hat{p}_i d_i$, $\Sigma\bar{p}_i d_i = \bar{\theta}$ fixed, $\bar{p}_i - \hat{p}_i = \Delta p_i$. Then

$$\frac{\partial\theta}{\partial p} = d + (p_o,p)\,\frac{\partial(d_o,d)}{\partial p}$$

$$= d + (p_o,\hat{p})\,\frac{\partial(d_o,d)}{\partial p} + \Delta(p_o,p)\,\frac{\partial(d_o,d)}{\partial p}$$

$$= d + \Delta(p_o,p)\,\frac{\partial(d_o,d)}{\partial p}$$

The Slutsky equation applies:

$$\frac{\partial(d_o,d)}{\partial p} = \left.\frac{\partial(d_o,d)}{\partial p}\right|_p + \left.\frac{\partial(d_o,d)}{\partial p}\right|_p \frac{\partial\theta}{\partial p}$$

$$= \left.\frac{\partial(d_o,d)}{\partial p}\right|_p + \left.\frac{\partial(d_o,d)}{\partial\theta}\right|_p \left(d + \left[\frac{\partial(d_o,d)}{\partial p}\right]' \Delta(p_o,p)'\right)$$

$$= \begin{bmatrix} g_2^o \\ g_2 \end{bmatrix} + \left.\frac{\partial(d_o,d)}{\partial\theta}\right|_p \left[\frac{\partial(d_o,d)}{\partial p}\right]' \Delta(p_o,p)'.$$

Applying lemma 3 to $p = p_o m(d)$,

$$\frac{\partial r}{\partial p} = (p_o,\bar{p}) \begin{bmatrix} g_3^o & g_4^o \\ g_3 & g_4 \end{bmatrix} \frac{\partial(d_o,d)}{\partial p}$$

$$= (p_o,\hat{p})\,\left(I - p_o \begin{bmatrix} g_2^o \\ g_2 \end{bmatrix} (m_{d_o},m_d)\right) \frac{\partial(d_o,d)}{\partial p}$$

$$= (p_o,p) \left(\begin{bmatrix} g_2^o \\ g_2 \end{bmatrix} + \frac{\partial(d_o,d)}{\partial\theta} \left[\frac{\partial(d_o,d)}{\partial p} \right]' \Delta(p_o,p)' \right.$$

$$\left. - \begin{bmatrix} g_2^o \\ g_2 \end{bmatrix} \frac{\partial p}{\partial p} \right)$$

$$= (p_o,\bar{p}) \frac{\partial(d_o,d)}{\partial\theta} \left[\frac{\partial(d_o,d)}{\partial p} \right]' \Delta(p_o,p).$$

Since,

$$(p_o,\bar{p}) \frac{\partial(d_o,d)}{\partial\theta} = \Sigma\bar{p}_j \frac{\partial d_j}{\partial\theta} = 1,$$

$$\frac{\partial r}{\partial p} = \sum_j \Delta p_j \frac{\partial d_j}{\partial p} .$$

For $\hat{p} = \bar{p}$, $\Delta p_i = 0$ and $\frac{\partial r}{\partial p} = 0$. For homothetic preferences,

$$\frac{\partial r}{\partial p} = \frac{r}{\theta} \left[\Sigma \, \Delta p_j \frac{\partial d_j}{\partial p} \right]$$

or

$$r = \sum_j \int \frac{r}{\theta} \Delta p_j \frac{\partial d_j}{\partial p} dp_j \qquad (11)$$

$$= \sum_j \int \frac{r}{\theta} \Delta p_j dd_j . \qquad \text{Q.E.D.}$$

<u>Theorem 5</u>. If the consumer k is homothetic,

$$\frac{dr^k}{d\varepsilon} = \frac{r^k}{\theta^k} \left[\frac{d\bar{\theta}^k}{d\varepsilon} + \left[\Sigma\Delta p_j \frac{\partial d_j^k}{\partial p} \right] \frac{dp}{d\varepsilon} \right]$$

where

$$\theta^k = \Sigma p_j d_j^k, \ \Delta p_j = p_j - \bar{p}_j .$$

If $\frac{r^k}{\theta^k}$ is the same for all k,

$$\frac{dr}{d\varepsilon} = \frac{r}{\theta} \left[\frac{d\bar{\theta}}{d\varepsilon} + \left[\Sigma\Delta p_j \frac{\partial d_j}{\partial p} \right] \frac{dp}{d\varepsilon} \right]$$

where

$$r = \Sigma r^k, \ \theta = \Sigma\theta^k = \text{nominal GNP},$$

$\bar{\theta} = \Sigma\bar{\theta}^k$ = real producer income

$d_j = \sum_k d^k$, is demand for j.

If $\frac{r^k}{\theta^k}$ is the same for different k, we say that the <u>burden is distributed uniformly</u>. Theorem 5 gives rules for evaluating the change in real income whenever a tariff or monopoly is imposed and the burden is distributed uniformly.

<u>Corollary 1</u>. If consumers are homothetic and the burden is distributed uniformly, the loss in real income due to a tariff is the sum over industries of

(i) areas bounded by the average costs curve as a function of net output, the net outputs before and after and the old price

(ii) plus the area between the goods demand curve and the old price

weighted in integration by the ratio of real consumer income to nominal consumer income. The rather lengthy statement of the corollary is illustrated in Figure 6a for the single industry. In Figure 6b the loss weighted by $\frac{r}{\theta}$. Note that imports are equal to $d_i - y_i$.

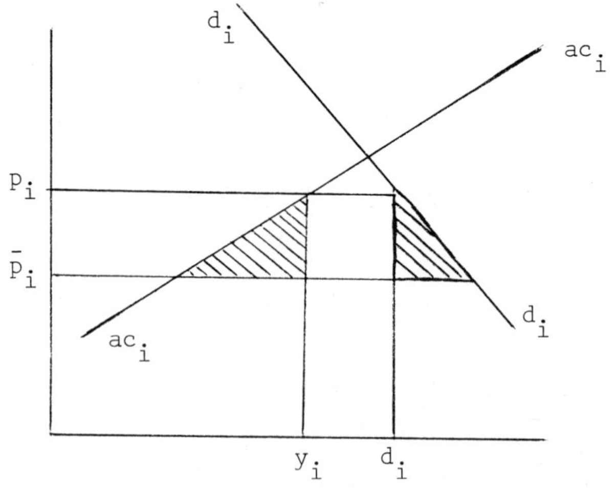

(Figure 6a)

(Figure 6b)

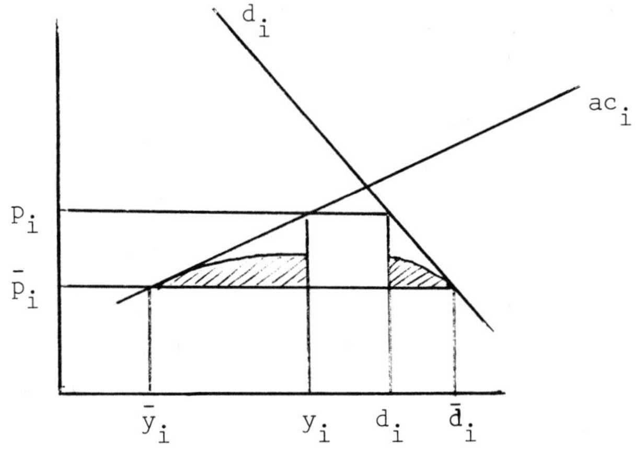

Corollary 2. If consumers are homothetic and the burden is distributed uniformly, the loss in real income due to a new monopoly is the sum (weighted by the ratio of consumer real income to consumer nominal income) over industries of

(i) the area between the demand and average cost curves and between the old and new gross outputs,

(ii) minus the area below the demand curve, above the old prices and between the old and new net outputs,

(iii) plus the area between the goods' demand and curve and the old price.

The total loss is illustrated in Figure 7, with monopoly in final goods only (slanted lines) and a tariff high enough to allow the monopoly to operate (cross hatched). Even though there is no direct consumer loss in an industry whose output is in raw materials only, the loss in producer income must still be weighted by r/θ. To measure the loss in the industry reduce the shaded area in Figure 2 by the appropriate area.

(Figure 7)

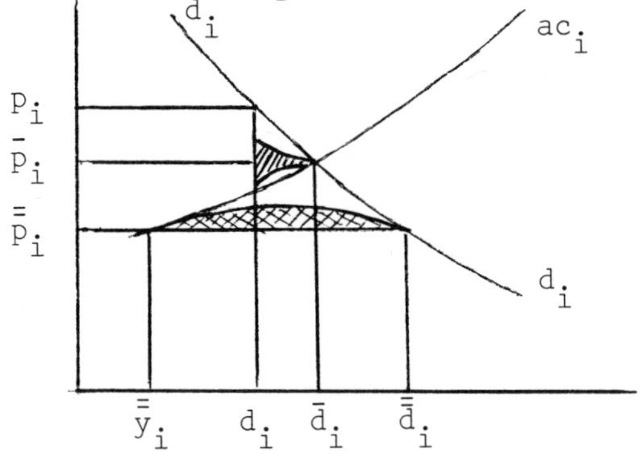

Of course should that industry be monopolized, there are price changes elsewhere which bear direct losses to consumer.

Without listing the conditions again, it is possible to account for losses due to a combination of tariffs and monopoly simply by separating out the monopoly and tariff industries. Apply the relevant measures of real consumer income to the industries separately but to the consumer price system as a whole.

As a note, Harburger's [2] estimates of monopoly loss would be sensible only in the case of homothetic consumers with a uniform distribution of loss. The aim is to use Hotelling's [5] measure. In order to ascertain the cost of capital, Harburger computes a normal rate of return for 1924-28. It is too high since it is an average rate of return whereas rents to monopoly are not returns to capital and should not be included in the average; instead of 10.4%, I think the 6% return on corporate bonds would be a better indicator of the competitive rate faced by firms in manufacturing. It is then assumed that the elasticity of demand is -1. (How marginal revenues can be zero in monopolized industries is not explained). Let $q_i = py^i$. Hence, a decrease from q_i to $\bar{q}_i$ gives an equal percentage decrease in quantity. The loss is equal to

$$\frac{1}{2}(q_i - \bar{q}_i)(\bar{d}_i - d_i) \text{ (linear demand)}$$

$$= \frac{1}{2}(q_i - \bar{q}_i)d_i \frac{(\bar{d}_i - d_i)}{d_i}$$

$$= \frac{1}{2}(q_i - \bar{q}_i)d_i \frac{(q_i - \bar{q}_i)}{q_i}$$

$$= \frac{1}{2} \frac{\left((q_i - \bar{q})d_i\right)^2}{q_i d_i} .$$

Harburger takes $(q_i - \bar{q}_i)d_i$ as equal to monopoly profit, and computes the figure $\frac{1}{10}$% of GNP as monopoly loss. Evidently, Harburger overstates the direct loss to consumers (by not weighting by $\frac{r}{\theta}$) plus the direct loss to producer by assuming constant costs. For example, doubling the elasticity and doubling that loss would increase the total loss by two. A different rate of return would give a loss from $\frac{3}{10}$% of GNP to as high as $\frac{5}{10}$% of GNP, which might be something of an overstatement but is small. Finally, the assumption of fixed international prices presumes that the U. S. is not an empirically significant factor in the overall world market.

4. A Quasi-Small Country.

A quasi-small country is defined to be one which has a world monopoly in one or more goods.

$$p = f(y-d),$$

but which faces no retaliation to its tax or tariff policies.

Were its industries organized in a competitive fashion, a quasi-small country might be able to exercize its monopoly power only indirectly. By raising the prices of other goods, the state can shift resources out of the industries with potential monopoly power. This increases their world prices, and in many instances, the country is better off.

Theorem 7. If preferences are locally unsaturated, $\Sigma P_{\dot{i}}(x^{\dot{i}})$ is convex and directional dense at $\Sigma d^{\dot{i}}$ and f is continuously differentiable, then Pareto optimality requires that consumer prices be proportional to marginal revenues.

$$\frac{\partial(y-d)f}{\partial(y-d)} = f + (y-d)\frac{\partial f}{\partial(y-d)}$$

Also, if the production set is closed, convex, and directional dense with some degree of free disposal, Pareto optimality requires that producer prices be proportional to marginal revenues and that revenues be maximized given import prices and home consumption of exported goods. There is a tax tariff-subsidy scheme which will accomplish the equality of home prices with world marginal revenues. In the case of a monopoly in one good only, a proportional increase in tariffs on other goods or subsidies for goods not imported is the desired tax-subsidy policy.

Proof:

By the continuous differentiability of f, there is but one price system defining a hyperplane tangent at the consumption, $\Sigma d^{\dot{i}}$, to the space.

$$F = \{d | f(y-d)(y-d) = f(y-\Sigma d^{\dot{i}})(y-\Sigma d^{\dot{i}})\}.$$

By local unsaturation, $\Sigma d^{\dot{i}}$ is in the boundary of $\underset{i}{\Sigma} P(d_{\dot{i}})$. By Pareto optimality, there is separation of F from $\Sigma P_{\dot{i}}(d_{\dot{i}})$ and by a directional density $\Sigma P_{\dot{i}}(d^{\dot{i}})$ has a tangent hyperplane

$$H = \{d | \hat{p}d = \hat{p}\Sigma d^{\dot{i}}\},$$

where $\hat{p}$ is normal to F. Evidently,

$$\hat{p} = \frac{\partial(y-d)f}{\partial(y-d)}$$

and it is the price system by which competitive choice is made. (By competitive choice, $\Sigma P_i(x^i)$ is to one side of H, e.g., [9, proof of theorem 5]).

For the <u>output set</u>

$$Z(x) = \{y | (x,y) \in Z\},$$

Z the production set,

$$\Sigma P_i(d^i) \cap Z(x) = \phi.$$

(Pareto optimality). For Z(x) convex, Z(x) is to one side of H (directional density of z(x)) and $\hat{p}$ is the producer price system. To see that Z(x) is directional dense, note that for $\hat{p}$ and x, there are outputs and wages, denoted $\hat{y}$ maximizes $\hat{p}y$ in Z(x) as does y. Hence, $py = \hat{p}\hat{y}$ and $py - wx = \hat{p}\hat{y} - wx$. Therefore, $\hat{p}$ is a possible price system associated with w. By the directional density of Z, $\hat{p} = p$.

If with fixed import prices, more money could be earned abroad, clearly consumption could be improved and one would not have been in a Pareto optimal position. For tariff import subsidies, or taxes and subsidies on goods not imported, δ, let

$$p = \bar{p} + \delta = kp, \quad k > 0. \qquad \text{Q.E.D.}$$

<u>Corollary</u>. If $\Sigma P_i(d^i)$ is convex and directional dense at Σd^i, Z is convex, technology is Leontief with a strict concavity assumption on continuously differentiable production functions, and all industries profitable, then Pareto optimality requires that the producer prices are proportional to marginal revenues.

Proof:

Z is directional dense [10, theorem 8]. The free disposal results from operating convex combinations of processes without taking advantage of the economies due to the strict convexity property or by keeping factors idle. Q.E.D.

For quantitative calculations, one needs to account for "real" producer income gain in taking advantage of a monopoly position and for the losses and gains to consumers from the changes in relative prices. Here a satisfactory theory is possible only if consumers are homothetic and the burden (or benefit) is distributed uniformly. The analysis of changes in producer income must be reformulated to account for changes in world prices.

<u>Theorem 8</u>. Let there be a Leontief technology with X(w)

continuously differentiable in a quasi-small country. The gain in real producer income due to a tariff is equal to the change in world value of after tariff exports minus the sum over different industries of the area between the average cost curve and the old price but bounded by the old and new net outputs. This is illustrated in Figure 8a for losses in an industry producing an imported good and in Figure 8b for gains in an industry producing an exported good (losses are shaded and gains are cross-hatched). In Figure 8b, the average cost curve corresponds to world demand plus home demand. (The change in the world value of exports is not illustrated.)

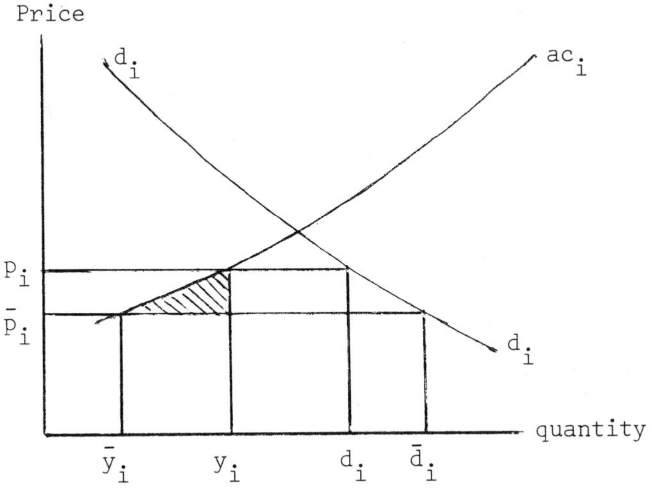

(Figure 8a)

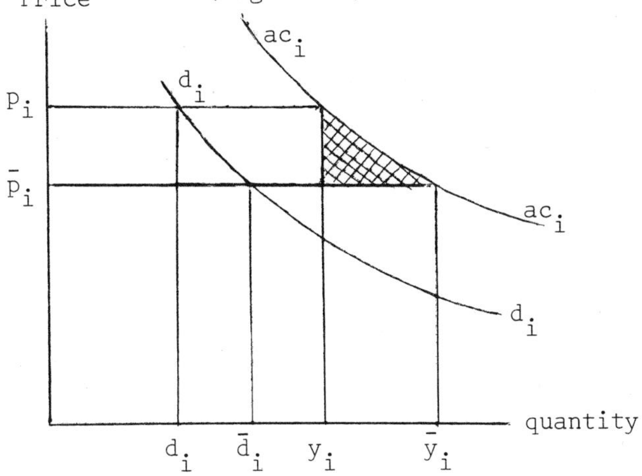

(Figure 8b)

Proof:

$(\hat{p} + \delta\varepsilon)Y = wX$ where δ is the tariff and $\hat{p}$ is world price (plus whatever old tariffs or subsidies may have been in effect). (For $\varepsilon = 0$, $\hat{p} = \bar{p}$.)

$$\frac{dw}{d\varepsilon} X = \delta Y + \frac{d\hat{p}}{d\varepsilon} Y$$

and post multiplying by ξ,

$$\frac{dpy}{d\varepsilon} = \frac{dwx}{d\varepsilon} = \delta y + \frac{d\hat{p}}{d\varepsilon} y.$$

Also, pd = total income = wx + tariff revenues

$$= wx + \delta\varepsilon(d - y),$$

and

$$\begin{aligned}\bar{p}d &= pd - (p - \bar{p})d \\ &= wx + \delta\varepsilon(d - y) - (\delta\varepsilon + \hat{p} - \bar{p})d \\ &= py - \delta\varepsilon y - (\hat{p} - \bar{p})d \\ &= (p - \delta\varepsilon)y - (\hat{p} - \bar{p})d \\ &= \hat{p}y - (\hat{p} - \bar{p})d \\ &= (\hat{p} - \bar{p})(y - d) + \bar{p}y.\end{aligned}$$

To evaluate $\bar{p}y$,

$$\begin{aligned}\frac{d\bar{p}y}{d\varepsilon} &= \frac{dpy}{d\varepsilon} - \frac{d}{d\varepsilon}\{(p - \bar{p})y\} \\ &= \frac{dwx}{d\varepsilon} - \frac{d}{d\varepsilon}\{(p - \bar{p})\} \\ &= \left[\delta + \frac{d\hat{p}}{d\varepsilon}\right]y - \left[\delta + \frac{d\hat{p}}{d\varepsilon}\right]y \\ &\quad - (p - \bar{p})\frac{dy}{d\varepsilon}.\end{aligned}$$

Therefore,

$$\Delta\bar{p}d = \Delta(\hat{p} - \bar{p})(y - d) - \int_{\varepsilon=o}^{1} (p - \bar{p})\frac{dy}{d\varepsilon}\, d\varepsilon \text{ or}$$

$$\Delta\bar{p}d = \Delta(\hat{p} - \bar{p})(y - d) - \sum_i \int_{\bar{y}_i}^{y_i} (p_i - \bar{p}_i)dy_i \qquad (8)$$

Q.E.D.

Corollary. If consumers are homothetic and the burden or gain is distributed uniformly, the gain in real consumer income due to a new tariff is

(i) the change in world value of after tariff exports,

(ii) minus the sum over different industries of the area above the old price, below the average cost curve, but between the old and new net outputs,

(iii) minus the area between the goods' home demand curve and the old price, but between the old and new demands

weighted in the process of integration by the ratio of real consumer income to nominal consumer income. In particular, for (i) there appears the term

$$- \sum_i \int_0^{\hat{p}_i - \bar{p}_i} \frac{r(d)}{\theta(d)}\, d(\hat{p}_i - \bar{p}_i).$$

The losses are illustrated in Figure 9 which reproduces the cases in Figure 8.

(Figure 9a)

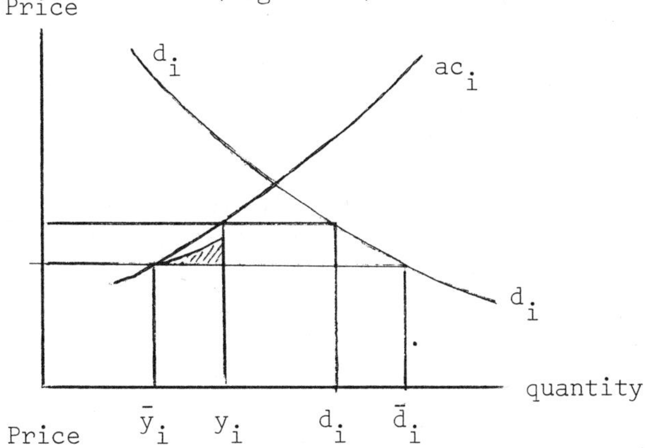

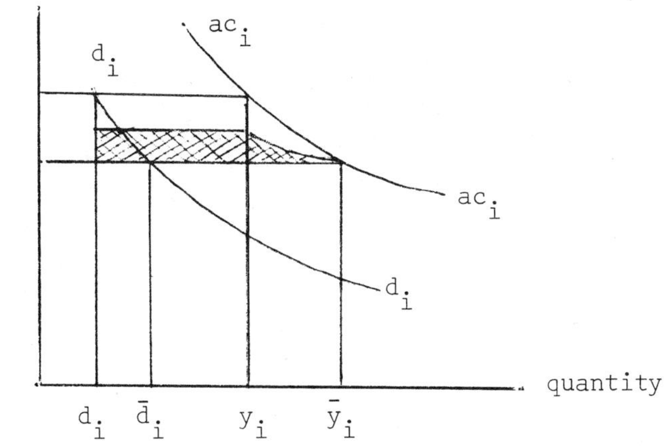

(Figure 9b)

As in the case of a small country, the untaxed goods do not fall in price. An exception would occur if the distribution effect on home demand of shifting income from the factor intensely used in the untaxed industries altered world prices. Also, as the net value added decreases in industries using protected raw materials, there is a reduction of wages of factors used relatively intensely in such industries. This causes other protected industries to buy more of the given factors and expand their output. Travis [14] has offered the above argument as an explanation of the Leontief paradox. High tariffs on labor intensive goods have caused the U. S. to export them instead of capital intensive goods. However, Basevi [1] has shown that the direct protection to labor intensive industry is more or less offset by the indirect penalty of paying higher prices for intermediate products. (The Travis argument would break down altogether for two factors. Once the price of the labor intensive good reached the point of no U. S. imports, any further tariffs would have no affect on world prices. The capital intensive good would not be exported and the country would be in a state of autarchy. Hence, tariffs could not change the factor intensity of exports unless the factor intensities were reversed between different industries.)

Recall that with fixed international prices, taxes on sales do not change outputs but only change consumer prices. For variable world prices, higher consumer prices reduce home demands and increase exports, decreasing the prices of goods of industries having world monopolies. The increase in price abroad will reduce exports and cause prices at home to rise as well.

Theorem 9. If there is a Leontief technology with $X(w)$ continuously differentiable, the loss in real producer income of a sales tax in a quasi-small country is the sum over industries of

(i) the area between the old and new prices minus tax and to the left of the average cost curve (but in net output space)

(ii) minus the change in value not counting tax of the new demand.

The loss is illustrated in Figure 10 for a single industry. In effect, demand is shifted back due to the loss in the home market.

(Figure 10)

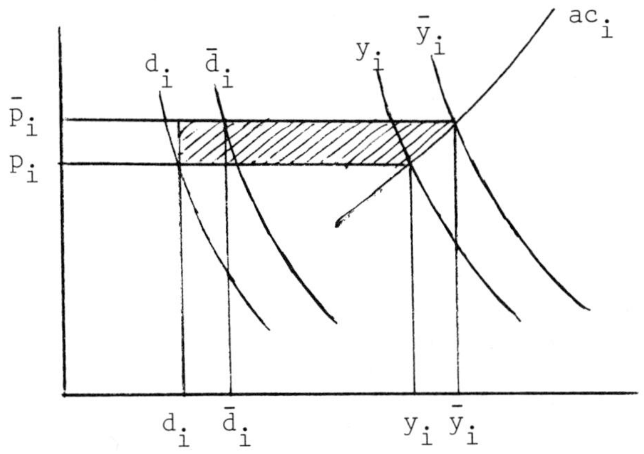

Proof:

$$pd = wx + \text{tax revenues}$$
$$= \hat{p}y + \delta\varepsilon d, \text{ and}$$
$$\bar{p}d = pd - (p - \bar{p})d$$
$$= wx + \delta\varepsilon d - (p - \bar{p})d$$
$$= wx + (\bar{p} - p)d.$$

Also,

$$\frac{dw}{d\varepsilon} X = \frac{d\hat{p}}{d\varepsilon} Y,$$

or post multiplying by ξ,

$$\frac{dwx}{d\varepsilon} = \frac{d\hat{p}}{d\varepsilon} y.$$

Hence,

$$\bar{p}d = (\bar{p} - p)d + \int_{\varepsilon=o}^{1} \frac{d\hat{p}}{d\varepsilon} y \, d\varepsilon$$

or

$$\bar{p}d = (\bar{p} - p)d - \sum_i \int_{\bar{p}_i}^{\hat{p}_i} y_i d\hat{p}_i . \qquad \text{Q.E.D.} \qquad (9)$$

Corollary. If also consumers are homothetic and the burden is distributed uniformly, the loss in consumer real income is

(i) the area between the old and new prices minus tax and to the left of the average cost curve (but in net output space),

(ii) minus the change in value not counting tax of the new demand,

(iii) minus the area between the goods' home demand curve and the old and new demands,

weighted in the process of integration by the ratios of real consumer income to nominal consumer income. In particular, for (ii), there is the term

$$- \sum_i \int_o^{\hat{p}_i - \bar{p}_i} \frac{r}{\theta} \, d\,(\hat{p}_i - \bar{p}_i).$$

For example, a corporation income tax exempting income from foreign sales is exactly like a tax on sales of those industries which for technical reasons must operate at a large scale and therefore with limited liability. A sales tax with the same tax take will leave the same residual equal to the international price. Therefore, in a small country, the tax is shifted entirely to the consumers through higher prices. Within the context of a quasi-small country, the consequent reduction of home demand increases exports and may reduce the international price.

If the income tax is also levied on earnings from foreign sales then the tax has the additional feature of an export tax. Essentially, the foreign demand curve is shifted back. Hence, the computations do not differ from that in theorem 9; it is only that $\frac{d\hat{p}}{d\varepsilon}$ is of a larger magnitude and perhaps $\frac{dy_i}{d\varepsilon}$ is also larger.

Remark 3. Theorem 9 and its corollary hold equally well for a corporation income tax except that there is added gain equal to the tax from sales for export $(\delta(y - d))$.

Remark 4. Theorem 9 and its corollary hold for an export tax except that there are two added losses, the tax from sales for export and the tax rate applied to home demand, and also consumer prices do not include the tax markup.

Remark 5. The loss of real producer income under monopoly in a quasi-small country is evaluated by the same means as in theorem 3 and corollary 2 of theorem 6. The main difference is that for the quasi-small country average costs may be rising as net output falls so that changes in net output formerly leading to losses in real producer income now lead to gains. The proofs of the remarks are left to the reader.

5. A Caveat on Development

In a developing country, high returns to capital have several desirable effects. First, a high return encourages saving. Second, there is a widespread psychological tendency for capitalists to save more than others. Perhaps, they are in the best position to appreciate its high return. Third, with wealth comes power, and states dominated by capitalists are possibly more committed to rational economic decision making than states dominated by such as land owners or laborers. Hence, moves which increase the rate of return to capital are often desirable in their long run influence on the capital stock.

In [10], there is mentioned the possibility of protecting machine intensive and/or skilled labor intensive industries in order to preserve a high return on machine and/or human capital. In the same way, tariffs which instead protect land intensive or unskilled labor intensive industries may be deleterious by reducing the real return to capital.

A possible exception occurs whenever a country has a world monopoly in a good not capital intensive. By encouraging other industries, the return to capital increases but then so does the return to the factors in the industry with a world monopoly. (Normally capital returns increase relatively to others.) Any tariff gains to capital may be wholly offset by taxes on capital imposed by the other factor owners to preserve their dominance. Even though the first two advantages to high capital returns are attained, the third may be lost. The state may follow irrational economic policies such as tariff concessions to foreign monopolies ([10, section 7]) or overly elaborate tariff systems. It should be emphasized that although the reduction of any one factor ordinarily reduces the returns to others, the myopia of taxing factors fixed in the short run only to stunt their growth in the long run is by no means unknown. For labor, this may not be so serious, but for capital it can be a social disaster. An instance is the corporation income tax, which reduces the income to factors which corporations use intensely. In many cases, it is capital, both machine and human, which suffers most (Harburger [3]). Corporation taxes are among the favorite taxes of labor owners, even though they may ultimately reduce capital, and the return to labor used complementary with capital will be lower than otherwise.

FOOTNOTES

* The research for this paper was financed by the National Science Foundation, GS 1981. Credit is due to John Chipman of the University of Minnesota whose comments originally aroused the author's interest in the theory of international trade and whose subsequent correspondence was quite helpful.

[1] $\Sigma P_i(x^i) = \{y | y = \Sigma y^i,\ y^i \in P_i(x^i)\}$

[2] Preferences are locally unsaturated if there are arbitrarily small changes in consumption which will improve the consumers' welfare.

[3] Even without directional dense ΣP_i, the tariff reduces the international value of a industrial output.

[4] This is slightly different from the case in [10]. The choice of definition for industry intensity is arbitrary and does not affect the theory.

[5] Preferences are homothetic if under competitive choice increases in income do not change the relative amounts of goods consumed. It is also said that consumers are homothetic.

[6] A proof appears in Rader, Theory of Micro Economics, forthcoming, Academic Press, chapter 5.

REFERENCES

[1] Basevi, G., "The U. S. Tariff Structure: Estimates of Effective Rates of Protection of U. S. Industries and Industrial Labor," Review of Economic Statistics, 1966, 48, 147-60.

[2] Harberger, A. C., "Monopoly and Resource Allocation," American Economic Review, XLIV, 1954, May Supplement, 77-87.

[3] Harberger, A. C., "The Incidence of the Corporation Income Tax," Journal of Political Economy, LXX, 1962, 215-40.

[4] Hicks, J. R., A Revision of the Theory of Demand, Oxford University Press, 1956, New York.

[5] Hotelling, H., "The General Welfare in Relation to

Problems of Taxation and of Railway and Utility Rates," Econometrica, July, 1938.

[6] Johnson, H. G., "The Cost of Protection and the Scientific Tariff," Journal of Political Economy, 1960, 68, 327-45.

[7] Marshall, A., Principle of Economics, 1890, Macmillan.

[8] Rader, T., "Normally Factor Demands are Never Gross Substitution," Journal of Political Economy, 1968, 76, 38-43.

[9] Rader, T., "Pairwise Optimality and Non-Competitive Behavior," in Quirk and Saposnik, eds., Papers in Quantitative Economics, I,1968, University of Kansas Press.

[10] Rader, T., "International Trade and Development in a Small Country," in Quirk and Saposnik, eds., Papers in Quantitative Economics, I, 1968, University of Kansas Press.

[11] Robinson, J., "Rising Supply Price," Economica, N. S. VII, 1941, 1-8.

[12] Travis, The Theory of Trade and Protection, Harvard University Press, Cambridge, Mass., 1964.

[13] Cronin, Jane, Fixed Points and Topological Degree in Non-Linear Analysis, American Mathematical Society, Providence, R. I., 1964.